MICROSOFT® OFFICE OUTLOOK® 2010
QuickSteps

CAROLE MATTHEWS

MARTY MATTHEWS

BOBBI SANDBERG

New York Chicago San Francisco
Lisbon London Madrid Mexico City
Milan New Delhi San Juan
Seoul Singapore Sydney Toronto

9063000002086

The McGraw·Hill Companies

Library of Congress Cataloging-in-Publication Data

Matthews, Carole Boggs.
  Microsoft Office Outlook 2010 quicksteps / Carole Matthews, Marty
Matthews, Bobbi Sandberg.
    p. cm.
  Includes bibliographical references and index.
  ISBN 978-0-07-163496-0 (alk. paper)
  1. Microsoft Outlook. 2. Business—Computer programs. 3. Time
management. 4. Personal information management—Computer
programs. 5. Electronic mail systems--Computer programs.
I. Matthews, Martin S. II. Sandberg, Bobbi. III. Title.
  HF5548.4.M525M385 2010
  005.5′7—dc22
                                                        2010015776

McGraw-Hill books are available at special quantity discounts to
use as premiums and sales promotions, or for use in corporate
training programs. To contact a representative, please e-mail us at
bulksales@mcgraw-hill.com.

All trademarks or copyrights mentioned herein are the
possession of their respective owners and McGraw-Hill makes
no claim of ownership by the mention of products that contain
these marks.

Information has been obtained by McGraw-Hill from sources
believed to be reliable. However, because of the possibility of
human or mechanical error by our sources, McGraw-Hill, or
others, McGraw-Hill does not guarantee the accuracy, adequacy,
or completeness of any information and is not responsible for any
errors or omissions or the results obtained from the use of such
information.

MICROSOFT® OFFICE OUTLOOK® 2010 QUICKSTEPS

1234567890   WDQ WDQ   109876543210

ISBN   978-0-07-163496-0
MHID   0-07-163496-7

SPONSORING EDITOR / Roger Stewart

EDITORIAL SUPERVISOR / Janet Walden

PROJECT MANAGER / Harleen Chopra, Glyph Inte

ACQUISITIONS COORDINATOR / Joya Anthony

COPY EDITOR / Lisa McCoy

PROOFREADER / Madhu Prasher

INDEXER / Valerie Perry

PRODUCTION SUPERVISOR / Jean Bodeaux

COMPOSITION / Glyph International

ILLUSTRATION / Glyph International

ART DIRECTOR, COVER / Jeff Weeks

COVER DESIGNER / Pattie Lee

SERIES CREATORS / Marty and Carole Matthews

SERIES DESIGN / Bailey Cunningham

Contents at a Glance

Contents

10

About the Authors

Carole and **Marty Matthews** have been connected to computers for over 35 years. During that time, they have been on all sides of software products: as programmers and systems analysts, and as managers and founders and co-owners of a software company. They have authored or co-authored more than 70 books. Titles include *Windows 7 QuickSteps, Microsoft Office Word 2010 QuickSteps, Dynamic Web Programming: A Beginner's Guide, Photoshop CS4 QuickSteps*, and *Microsoft Office PowerPoint 2010 QuickSteps*.

Carole and Marty live on an island in Puget Sound in Washington State with a very old cat. They have one son, Michael.

Bobbi Sandberg has been involved with computers and accounting for five decades. Her extensive background combined with her ability to explain complex concepts in plain language has made her a popular instructor, speaker, and consultant. Bobbi has been a CPA and was a geek long before it was popular. She is the co-author of *Quicken 2007 Personal Finance Software QuickSteps*. Currently semi-retired, she lives on an island surrounded by deer, chipmunks, and trees—and has at last count, 23 computers in various stages of operation.

Acknowledgments

This book is a team effort of truly talented people. Among them are:

Roger Stewart, sponsoring editor, believed in us enough to sell the series and continues to stand behind us as we go through the third edition. Thanks, Roger!

Joya Anthony, acquisitions coordinator, always a friendly and positive voice from McGraw-Hill, has made sure that the manuscript and art are intact and people have what they need. Joya is often the silent hand that makes things happen. Thanks, Joya!

Janet Walden, editorial supervisor, and **Harleen Chopra**, project manager, greased the wheels and straightened the track to make a very smooth production process. Thanks, Janet and Harleen!

Lisa McCoy, copy editor, added greatly to the readability and understandability of the book while always being a joy to work with. Thanks, Lisa!

Madhu Prasher, proofreader, has carefully gone through each page, catching errors no one else could see, always keeping the integrity of the book intact. Thank you, Madhu!

Valerie Perry, indexer, who adds so much to the usability of the book, and does so quickly and at the last moment. Thanks, Valerie!

Introduction

QuickSteps books are recipe books for computer users. They answer the question, "How do I..." by providing a quick set of steps to accomplish the most common tasks with a particular operating system or application.

The sets of steps are the central focus of the book. QuickSteps sidebars show how to quickly perform many small functions or tasks that support the primary functions. QuickFacts sidebars supply information that you need to know about a subject. Notes, Tips, and Cautions augment the steps; they are presented in a separate column so as not to interrupt the flow of the steps. The introductions are minimal rather than narrative, and numerous illustrations and figures, many with callouts, support the steps.

QuickSteps books are organized by function and the tasks needed to perform that function. Each function is a chapter. Each task, or "How To," contains the steps needed for accomplishing the function, along with the relevant Notes, Tips, Cautions, and screenshots. You can easily find the tasks you need through:

- The table of contents, which lists the functional areas (chapters) and tasks in the order they are presented

- A How To list of tasks on the opening page of each chapter

- The index, which provides an alphabetical list of the terms that are used to describe the functions and tasks

- Color-coded tabs for each chapter, or functional area, with an index to the tabs in the Contents at a Glance section (just before the table of contents)

Conventions Used in this Book

Microsoft Office Outlook 2010 QuickSteps uses several conventions designed to make the book easier for you to follow:

- A 🔍 or a ✎ in the table of contents and in the How To list in each chapter references a QuickSteps or QuickFacts sidebar in a chapter.

- **Bold type** is used for words or objects on the screen that you are to do something with—for example, "click the **File** button, and click **Print**."

- *Italic type* is used for a word or phrase that is being defined or otherwise deserves special emphasis.

- Underlined type is used for text that you are to type from the keyboard.

- SMALL CAPITAL LETTERS are used for keys on the keyboard, such as **ENTER** and **SHIFT**.

- When you are expected to enter a command, you are told to press the key(s). If you are to enter text or numbers, you are told to type them.

Chapter 1
Stepping into Outlook

When someone mentions Outlook, the first thought is generally the sending and receiving of e-mail. Outlook does handle e-mail quite competently, but it also does a lot more, including managing contacts, scheduling activities, tracking tasks, keeping a journal, and using notes. Outlook also provides the means to collaborate with others, it can be used with and from other applications, and can link to and synch up with both a team Web site using Windows SharePoint Services, and with a smart cell phone or PDA (personal digital assistant).

In this chapter you will familiarize yourself with Outlook; see how to start and leave it; use the windows, panes, ribbons, toolbars, and menus in Outlook; learn how to get help; and find out how to customize Outlook.

STARTING OUTLOOK IN OTHER WAYS

In addition to using All Programs on the Start menu, there are several other ways to start Outlook.

USE THE START MENU

After you have used Outlook once or twice, you should see it on the Start menu. The more you use it, the higher up on the menu it will be; but if you don't use it for a while, it will disappear. To combat this, you can permanently "pin" Outlook to the Start menu.

Click **Start**, right-click the **Outlook** option on the Start menu, and click **Pin To Start Menu**.

The Outlook option will move up near the top of the Start menu with other applications that are pinned there.

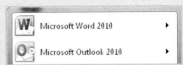

If you don't see Outlook on the Start menu, click **All Programs**, scroll down and click **Microsoft Office**, right-click **Microsoft Outlook 2010**, and click **Pin To Start Menu**. Once the Outlook icon is on Start menu, you need only to open the Start menu and click the Outlook icon to start it.

Continued . . .

Start Outlook

How you start Outlook depends on how it was installed and what has happened to it since its installation. In this section you'll see a way to start Outlook and some alternatives; you'll see how to use the Startup Wizard and how to upgrade from several other e-mail packages. You'll also see how to exit Outlook.

Use the Start Menu to Start Outlook

If there are no other icons for or shortcuts to Outlook available on your desktop, you can always start Outlook using the Start menu.

1. Start your computer if it is not already running, and log on to Windows if necessary.

2. Click **Start** . Click **All Programs**, scroll down and click **Microsoft Office**, and click **Microsoft Outlook 2010**, as shown in Figure 1-1.

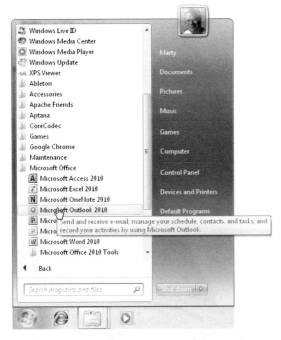

Figure 1-1: The foolproof way to start Outlook is through the Start menu.

QUICKSTEPS

CREATE A SHORTCUT TO START OUTLOOK

An easy way to start Outlook is to create a shortcut icon on the desktop, and then double-click it to start the program.

Click **Start**, click **All Programs**, click **Microsoft Office**, right-click **Microsoft Outlook 2010**, click **Send To**, and click **Desktop (Create Shortcut)**.

USE THE TASKBAR

Depending on the version of Windows that you have, you can place an Outlook shortcut on the taskbar at the bottom of your screen in two different ways. In Windows XP and Vista, you can place the Outlook shortcut in the Quick Launch toolbar, or in Windows 7 you can pin the shortcut to the taskbar itself.

USE THE QUICK LAUNCH TOOLBAR

In Windows XP and Vista, the Quick Launch toolbar is a small area on the taskbar next to the Start button. You can add an Outlook icon on the Quick Launch toolbar and use it to start Outlook. If your Quick Launch toolbar is not visible, open it and add an Outlook icon there.

1. If you don't see a Quick Launch toolbar, right-click a blank area of the taskbar, click **Toolbars**, and click **Quick Launch**. The Quick Launch toolbar is displayed.

2. **Click Start**, click **All Programs**, click **Microsoft Office**, and drag the **Microsoft Office Outlook 2010** icon to where you want it on the Quick Launch toolbar.

To start Outlook, click the icon on the Quick Launch toolbar.

Continued . . .

Use the Startup Wizard

The first time you start Outlook on either a new computer with Office 2010 or a new installation of Office 2010, the Outlook 2010 Startup Wizard will open with the Outlook 2010 Startup screen.

1. Click **Next**. Accept the default response of **Yes** to configure an e-mail account, and click **Next.**

2. Type your name, e-mail address, and password. Then retype the password. Click **Next**.

3. E-mail configuring will take several minutes. Click **Next** for both an encrypted account and one that is unencrypted. If necessary, click **Manually Configure Server Settings**, click **Next**, click **Internet E-mail**, click **Next**, enter the information provided by your Internet mail provider, and click **Next**.

4. When the configuration has finished, you will see a dialog box showing the steps that were taken and the results, as shown in Figure 1-2. Click **Finish**. The wizard will close and Outlook will open. See "Explore Outlook" later in this chapter.

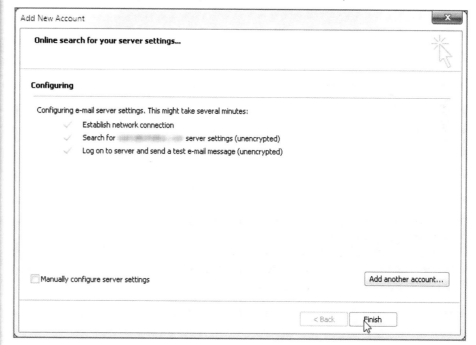

Figure 1-2: *You will see this message when your e-mail setup has successfully completed.*

In Windows 7, you can pin an Outlook icon to the taskbar where it will remain to be restarted after you have shut the program down. You may have noticed in pinning Outlook to the Start menu that you could also choose to pin it to the taskbar. Another way to accomplish this is after you have started Outlook.

1. Start Outlook in any of the ways already described. Once Outlook is running, its icon will appear on the taskbar.

2. Right-click the Outlook icon on the taskbar, and click **Pin This Program To Taskbar**.

   | Microsoft Outlook
   | Pin this program to taskbar
   | Close window

Outlook is started by clicking the icon on the taskbar.

NOTE

If you have been running another e-mail program such as Outlook Express, Windows Mail, or Windows Live Mail, and then install Outlook, you may see a message when you run the Outlook 2010 Startup Wizard asking if you want to upgrade from your other e-mail program and if you want to import your messages and addresses. See "Upgrade to Outlook."

TIP

You can save the Import Summary report by clicking **Save In Inbox.**

5. If you have been using another e-mail program, you'll be asked if you want to make Outlook 2010 your default e-mail program. If you do (this is recommended), click **Yes.**

6. If you are asked if you want to add an Outlook Connector account and you have a Web-based e-mail account on Google mail, Hotmail, or Yahoo!, click **Next**; enter your e-mail address, password, and name you want to use; and click **OK**.

Upgrade to Outlook

If you have been using Outlook 2003 or 2007, Outlook 2010 should automatically locate your previous message and contact files and move them over to it. You cannot have two versions of Outlook on your computer, so Outlook 2010 will uninstall your previous version and pick up your old files.

If you have been using Outlook Express, Windows Mail, or Windows Live Mail and you install Office 2010, you may be asked if you want to upgrade from your previous program. If you choose to upgrade, you will be asked if you want to import your e-mail messages and addresses. Click **Yes**, and you will see the progress as the files are being imported and a summary upon completion.

If you have been using one of these programs and were not asked by the Outlook 2010 Startup Wizard if you want to upgrade, you can still import your e-mail files into Outlook.

1. Start Outlook in one of the ways described earlier in this chapter.

2. Click the **File** tab, click **Open**, and click **Import**. The Import And Export Wizard will open.

3. Click **Import Internet Mail And Addresses**, and click **Next**.

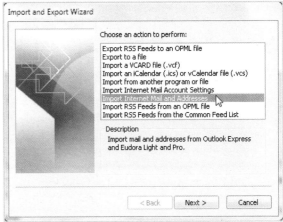

If you want to import Outlook Express, Windows Mail, or Windows Live Mail files from another computer, locate the files by starting the program on the other computer, click the **Tools** menu (if you don't see the Tools menu, press **ALT**), choose **Options**, click the **Advanced** tab (the Maintenance tab in Outlook Express), click the **Maintenance** button (skip this in Outlook Express), and click **Store Folder**. Drag across the entire address line, press **CTRL+C**, and click **OK** to close the Store Location dialog box. Then click **Start**, click **Computer**, click the computer icon at the left end of the address bar, press **CTRL+V** to copy the contents into the address bar, and click the **Go To** button or press **ENTER**. This will show you the e-mail files. Copy these e-mail files to the new computer, import them into your previous e-mail program on that computer, and then use the instructions under "Upgrade to Outlook" to import the files into Outlook.

If you are still having problems importing from Outlook Express, Windows Mail, or Windows Live Mail after reviewing all the previous steps or the Note in this section, start your other e-mail program, click **File**, click **Export**, click **Messages**, click **Microsoft Exchange**, click **Next**, and click **OK**. Select **All Folders** and click **OK**. You will see a message that your messages are being exported and their progress. When it is done, click **Finished**. In Outlook, click **File**, click **Open**, click **Import**, select **Import From Another Program Or File**, and click **Next**. Select **Outlook Express 4.x, 5.x, 6.x Or Windows Mail**, and click **Next**. Your imported messages will be placed in a folder by the name \Storage Folders\Imported Folder\.

4. Click **Outlook Express** (which includes Windows Mail), and make sure that the **Import Mail** and **Import Address Book** check boxes are selected.

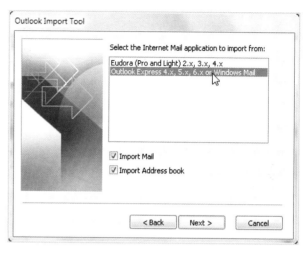

5. Click **Next**, choose how you want to handle duplicates, and then click **Finish**.

You will be told the progress as the files are being imported and will see a summary upon completion.

Exit Outlook

When you are done using Outlook, you can exit the program.

- Click the **File** tab, and click **Exit**.

  –Or–

- Click **Close** on the right of the title bar.

  –Or–

- Press **ALT+F4**.

REVIEWING VERSIONS OF OFFICE 2010

Office 2010 has a newly expanded set of versions and platforms upon which Office will run. Office is now available on three separate platforms:

- **Office 2010** is a resident program running on the user's desktop or laptop computer, as available for many years, generally referred to as the "desktop platform," although it also runs on laptops

- **Office Web Apps** accessed through a Web browser such as Internet Explorer or Firefox, which is a newly available platform with Office 2010

- **Office Mobile** accessed through a mobile device, such as a smart phone, is another newly available platform

Office 2010 on the desktop platform is available in four versions:

- **Office Starter 2010** is available preinstalled on a new computer, includes Word and Excel, has reduced functionally, and is paid for with advertising. It can be directly upgraded to one of the following full versions of Office 2010 through a product key card purchased from a retail outlet.

- **Office Home & Student 2010** is available to be installed from a DVD or via Click-To-Run over the Internet, and contains the full versions of Word, Excel, PowerPoint, and OneNote.

- **Office Home & Business 2010** is available to be installed from a DVD or via Click-To-Run over the Internet, and contains Word, Excel, PowerPoint, OneNote, and Outlook.

Continued . . .

Explore Outlook

Outlook uses a wide assortment of windows, ribbons, toolbars, menus, and special features to accomplish its functions. Much of this book explores how to find and use all of those items. In this section you'll see the most common features of the default Outlook window, including the parts of the window, the buttons on the principal toolbars, and the major menus. Also, you'll see how to use the Navigation pane and Outlook Today.

Explore the Outlook Window

The Outlook window takes on a different appearance depending on the function you want Outlook to perform. The initial view when you first start Outlook is for handling mail, as shown in Figure 1-3. However, this view changes as soon as you start to do anything else, even create e-mail, as you'll see in this chapter. Other functions are described in their corresponding chapters. The principal features of the Outlook window are described in Table 1-1.

OUTLOOK FEATURES	DESCRIPTION
Ribbon	Contains the primary controls for Outlook.
File tab	Opens the File menu and File views for opening, saving, and printing documents, and setting the options for Outlook itself.
Control menu	Contains controls for the window itself.
Quick Access toolbar	Contains the tools you most often use.
Tabs on the ribbon	Provide access to the sets of tools and features shown on the ribbon.
Reading pane	Displays the contents of the selected message in the open folder.
Title bar	Name of the open folder; contains the Control menu for the window.
Ribbon groups	Collections of tools relating to a common function.

Table 1-1: Principal Features of the Outlook Window

REVIEWING VERSIONS OF OFFICE 2010 *(Continued)*

- **Office Professional 2010** is available to be installed from a DVD or via Click-To-Run over the Internet, and contains Word, Excel, PowerPoint, OneNote, Outlook, Access, and Publisher.

There are also two enterprise editions and one academic edition available through a volume (multicopy) license. Office Standard 2010 adds Publisher to Office Home & Business, and Office Professional Plus 2010 adds SharePoint Workspace, InfoPath, and Communicator to Office Professional. Office Professional Academic 2010 is the same as Office Professional.

This book, which covers the full version of Outlook 2010, is applicable to all the editions with a full version of Outlook.

OUTLOOK FEATURES	DESCRIPTION
Minimize button	Minimizes the window to an icon on the taskbar.
Maximize button	Maximizes the window to fill the screen. When maximized, this becomes the Restore button; clicking it returns the window to its previous size.
Close	Exits Outlook and closes the window.
Help icon	Opens the Help window with information on using Outlook.
Minimize ribbon	Reduces the size of the ribbon so only the tabs show.
Minimize To-Do bar	Reduces the size of the To-Do bar to a half-inch wide summary.
Dialog Box Launcher	Opens a dialog box related to the group it is in.
Scroll arrow	Moves the contents of the pane in the direction of the arrow.
Scroll button	Moves the contents of the pane in the direction it is dragged.
Scroll bar	Moves the contents of the pane in the direction it is clicked.
To-Do bar	Contains the current month's calendar, appointments, and tasks.
Zoom buttons	Controls the magnification of the reading pane.
View buttons	Closes and opens the To-Do bar.
People pane	Displays social media and other information about the sender or receiver of e-mail, including their recent messages.
Folder pane	Displays the contents of the selected folder.
Navigation pane	Contains the means for selecting what you want to do and look at.
Status bar	Displays information about what is selected.
Button bar	Additional Outlook components not in Outlook views.
Outlook views	Allows selection of the major Outlook components or views.
Folder List	Contains the folders within the selected view.
Collapse/Expand buttons	Minimizes or expands the current list, whatever it might contain.
Minimize Navigation pane	Reduces the size of the Navigation pane to a half-inch wide summary.

*Table 1-1: **Principal Features of the Outlook Window (Continued)***

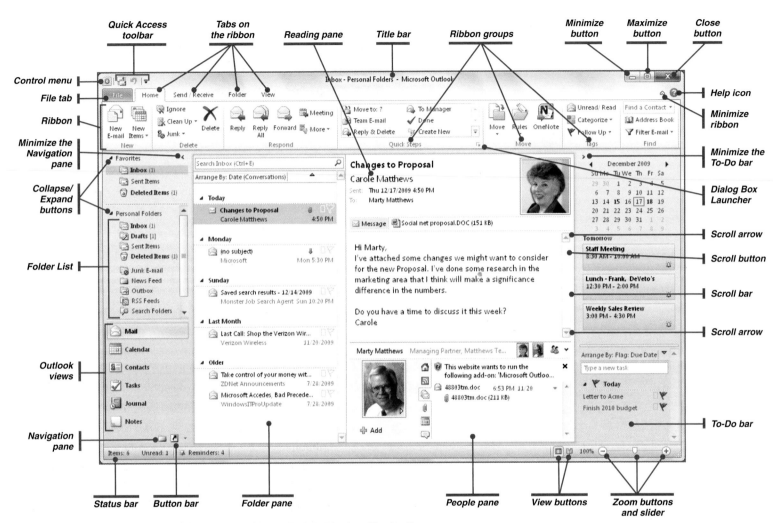

Figure 1-3: *The default Outlook window is used for handling mail.*

Become Familiar with the Ribbon

The familiar toolbars and menus from versions of Outlook prior to 2010 are gone. The original menu structure used in earlier Office products (File, Edit, View, Tools, Help, and others) was designed to accommodate fewer tasks and features. That menu structure has simply outgrown its usefulness. Microsoft's solution to the increased number of features is the *ribbon*, the container now at the top of all Office program windows that holds the tools and features you are most likely to use (see Figure 1-3). The ribbon collects tools for a given function into *groups*—for example, the Respond group provides the options for responding to a message. Groups are then organized into tabs for working on likely tasks. For example, the Send/Receive tab contains groups for various sending and receiving tasks. Each Office program has a default set of tabs, with additional *contextual* tabs that appear as the context of your work changes. For instance, when you select a picture, a Format tab containing shapes and drawing tools that you can use with the particular graphic object appears beneath the defining tools tab; when the object is unselected, the Format tab disappears.

The ribbon contains labeled buttons you can click to use a given command or tool. Depending on the tool, you are then presented with additional options in the form of a list of commands, a dialog box, or galleries of choices that reflect what you'll see in your work. Groups that contain several more tools than can be displayed in the ribbon include a Dialog Box Launcher icon that takes you directly to these other choices. The ribbon also takes advantage of Office features, including a live preview of many potential changes (for example, you can select text and see it change color as you point to various colors in the Font Color gallery without finalizing the color selection).

At the left end of the ribbon is the File tab, and above the left end of the ribbon is the Quick Access toolbar. The File tab provides access to the File menu and File view, which lets you work *with* your document (such as saving it), as

TIP

The ribbon adapts to the size of your Outlook window and your screen resolution, changing the size and shape of buttons and labels. You can see the difference yourself by increasing or decreasing the size of the window. For instance, if your Outlook window is initially not maximized, maximize it and notice how the ribbon appears, and then click the Restore button on the title bar and again notice the ribbon. Drag the right border of the Outlook window toward the left, and see how the items on the ribbon adapt to reflect their decreasing real estate.

opposed to the ribbon, which centers on working *in* your document (such as editing and formatting). The Quick Access toolbar provides an always-available location for your favorite tools. It starts out with a small default set of tools, but you can add to it. See the accompanying sections and figures for more information on the ribbon and the other elements of the Outlook window.

Use Tabs and Menus

Command tabs are displayed at the top of the ribbon or in a dialog box. Menus are displayed when you click a down arrow on a button on the ribbon, a dialog box, or a toolbar. You can use tabs and menus in the following ways:

- To open a tab or menu with the mouse, click the tab or menu.
- To open a tab or menu with the keyboard, press **ALT** and the letter that appears in a small box for the object, tab, or menu name. For example, press **ALT+F** to open the File view.
- To select a command on a tab or menu, click the tab or menu to open it, and then click the command.
- The ribbon command may have a small arrow on the icon indicating that a menu exists for that option. That menu's options may contain their own submenus as well. To open them, simply move the mouse pointer over the options you want and the submenus will open with their own options.

Change Views

The view you will have on the main Outlook window can be changed, depending on what you want to see. Typically, as shown earlier in Figure 1-3, you will see the Navigation pane, Folder pane, Reading pane, and To-Do bar, with the middle two related to the mail component. You may change these by clicking another Outlook view. For example, clicking Calendar view in the lower part of the Navigation pane will replace the Folder pane, Reading pane, and To-Do bar with the current day's calendar. Alternatively, in Mail view, clicking the Reading view button on the right of the status bar closes the Navigation pane and the To-Do bar to provide a lot more room to read an e-mail message.

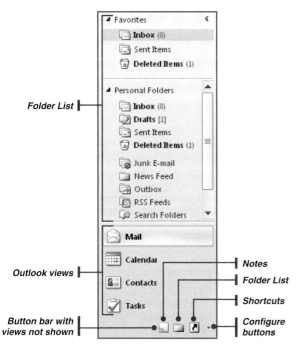

Folder List |

Outlook views |

Button bar with
views not shown |

| Notes

| Folder List

| Shortcuts

| Configure
buttons

Figure 1-4: The Navigation
pane provides the primary
control over which area
and which folder you are
working with.

Use the Navigation Pane

There are three main areas of the Navigation pane, as shown in Figure 1-4:

- **Folder List**, at the top, is where you can select the folder you want to open.
- **Outlook views**, in the middle, are where you can select the view in which to work.
- **Button bar**, at the bottom, lets you access views not available in the Outlook views.

SELECT A VIEW

The Outlook view determines which area of Outlook you will work in—for example, Mail, Calendar, or Contacts. To select a view:

- Click the appropriate Outlook view.

  –Or–

- Click the appropriate button in the button bar (see Figure 1-4).

OPEN A FOLDER

The folder that is open determines which specific documents you will work on, for example, incoming messages in the Inbox folder or notes in the Notes folder. To open a folder:

- Click the appropriate folder in the Folder List.

  –Or–

- Click the related Outlook view or button in the button bar.

DISPLAY OUTLOOK VIEWS

The number of Outlook views displayed depends on the size of the Outlook window and the size of the pane dedicated to these views. To change the number of views displayed:

- Drag the bottom window border up or down.

  –Or–

- Drag the handle between the top view and the bottom of the Folder List.

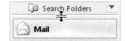

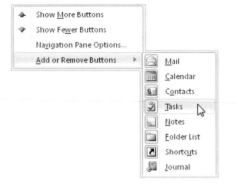

DISPLAY BUTTONS

The buttons in the button bar are just an extension of Outlook views. When you reduce the number of view bars, the options become buttons on the button bar. To change the buttons on the button bar, in addition to changing the number of Outlook views that are displayed:

1. Click the **Configure** button on the right of the button bar.
2. Click **Add Or Remove Buttons**, and then click the button you want to add or remove.

REORDER NAVIGATION PANE BUTTONS

To change the buttons or the order of the button in the Navigation pane:

1. Click the **View** tab, click **Navigation Pane**, and click **Options**. The Navigation Pane Options dialog box will appear.
2. Check the buttons you want on the Navigation pane.
3. Highlight a button, and click **Move Up** or **Move Down** to reorder the list. Click **OK** twice.

MINIMIZE THE NAVIGATION PANE

If you need more room to display a folder and its contents, you can close the Navigation pane.

- Click the **Minimize** button at the top of the Navigation pane to reduce its size. Click it again (now the Expand button) to restore the Navigation pane to its regular size.

–Or–

- Click the **View** tab, click **Navigation Pane**, and click **Minimize**. To restore the Navigation pane, repeat the process, clicking **Normal** so that a check mark is in the check box.

Customize the To-Do Bar

To customize the To-Do bar and determine what is displayed in it:

1. Click the **View** tab, click **To-Do Bar**, and click **Options**.

    –Or–

    Right-click the **To-Do Bar**, and click **Options** in the context menu.
2. Click the check boxes next to the options you want, and click **OK**.

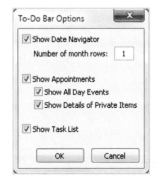

MINIMIZE THE TO-DO BAR

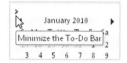

If you need additional room for the Reading pane, you can minimize the To-Do bar.

● Click the Minimize button at the top left of the To-Do bar. Click it again (now the Expand button) to restore the To-Do bar to its regular size.

–Or–

● Click the **View** tab, click **To-Do Bar**, and click **Minimized**. To restore the Navigation pane, repeat the process, clicking **Normal** so that a check mark is in the check box.

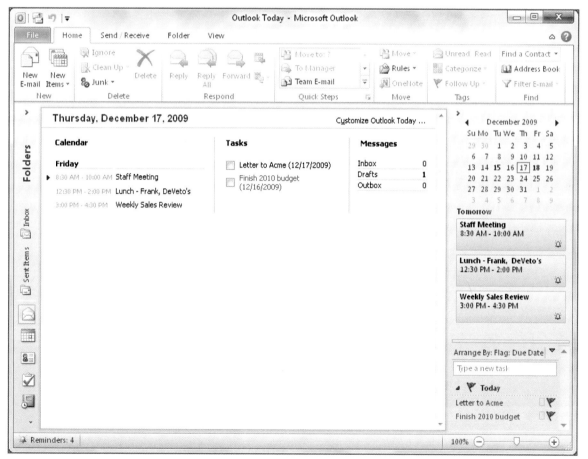

Use Outlook Today

Outlook Today gives you a summary of the information in Outlook for the current day. You can see a summary of your messages, your appointments and meetings, and the tasks you are slated to do, as shown in Figure 1-5.

OPEN OUTLOOK TODAY

If the Navigation pane is open, click **Personal Folders** at the top of the Folders List ("Personal Folders" might also be called "Outlook Data File"). If the Navigation pane is not open, click the **View** tab, click **Navigation Pane**, and click **Normal**.

Figure 1-5: Outlook Today provides a summary of information for the current day, such as appointments and tasks.

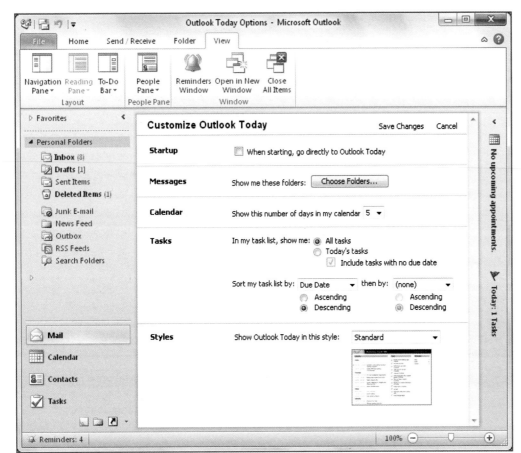

CHANGE OUTLOOK TODAY

Click **Customize Outlook Today** in the upper-right corner of the Outlook Today folder. Customize Outlook Today will open, as shown in Figure 1-6.

Customize Outlook Today ...

MAKE OUTLOOK TODAY YOUR DEFAULT PAGE

To display Outlook Today by default when you open Outlook:

1. In the Customize Outlook Today pane, opposite Startup, click **When Starting, Go Directly To Outlook Today**.

2. Click **Save Changes**.

Personalize and Customize Outlook

You can personalize Outlook, or make it your own, by changing the settings Outlook has for options such as the layout and contents of the ribbon, the tools available on the Quick Access toolbar, or your user name and initials. You can customize Outlook by changing the general default settings with regard to editing, proofing, display, and other options. Many of these options are discussed in the other chapters. Here, we will look at customizing the ribbon, the Quick Access toolbar, the display, and other options. We'll begin by looking at Office 2010's new File view.

Figure 1-6: You can tailor Outlook Today to contain only the information you want.

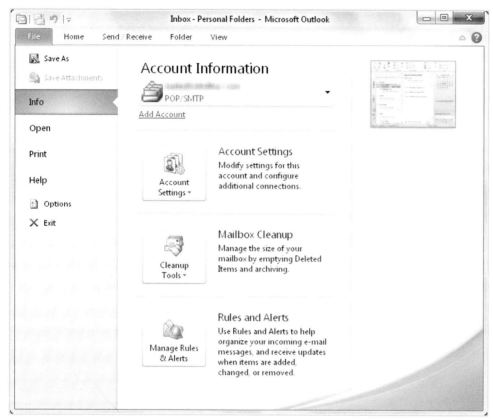

Figure 1-7: *File view provides information about the document and handles many file-related tasks.*

Work with File View

Outlook 2010 shares with the other Office 2010 programs an improved way that you can easily do many of the customization tasks, as well as access tasks that affect a total document, such as opening, closing, printing, and saving from one screen, thus avoiding the need to open several dialog boxes. This all-encompassing view is called the File view (also sometimes called the "Backstage view") since it handles many file-related tasks like saving or opening a file, an example of which is shown in Figure 1-7.

To display the File view:

1. Open Outlook using one of the methods described in "Start Outlook" and "Exit Outlook" earlier in this chapter.

2. Click the **File** tab, and then click one of the areas of interest on the left of the window. For example, clicking **Print** provides a document preview and options for printing your work.

3. When finished, click the **File** tab again (or any other tab) to return to the Outlook window.

Customize the Ribbon

The default ribbon consists of five tabs, including File (see Figure 1-3), each tab containing several groups and subgroups that contain related tasks. While Outlook strives to provide a logical hierarchy to all the tasks available to you, it also recognizes that not everyone finds Microsoft's way of thinking to be the most convenient and offers you the ability to change how things are organized.

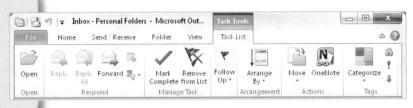

NOTE

You'll see two types of tabs on the ribbon. The Main tabs appear when you open a document and contain a generalized set of tools. Contextual Tool tabs appear when you are working with certain Outlook features, such as tasks, and contain specific tools for working with these features.

Figure 1-8: *You can easily modify the tabs and groups on the ribbon and assign tools where you want them.*

You can remove groups from the existing Main tabs, create new tabs and groups, and populate your new groups from a plethora of available commands and tasks.

To customize the ribbon:

1. Click the **File** tab, and in the left pane, click **Options**. In the Outlook Options dialog box, also in the left pane, click **Customize Ribbon**.

   –Or–

   Right-click any tool on the ribbon, and click **Customize The Ribbon**.

2. In either case, click the **Choose Commands From** drop-down arrow, and click **All Commands**. The Customize The Ribbon view, shown in Figure 1-8, displays the list of available commands, tasks, and tools on the left and a hierarchy of tabs and groups on the right.

REARRANGE TABS AND GROUPS

You can easily change the order in which your tabs and groups appear on the ribbon.

1. On the Customize The Ribbon view, click the **Customize The Ribbon** down arrow on the right, and select the type of tabs (Main or Tool) that contain the groups you want to work with.

2. To rearrange tabs, select the tab whose position on the ribbon you want to change, and click the **Move Up** and **Move Down** arrows on the right side of the tabs list to reposition the tab. (The topmost items in the list appear as the leftmost on the ribbon.)

3. To rearrange groups, click the plus sign next to the tab name to display its groups. Select the group to be moved, and then click the **Move Up** and **Move Down** arrows to the side of the tabs list to reposition the group.

4. When finished, click **OK** to close the Outlook Options dialog box.

CREATE NEW TABS AND GROUPS

You can create new tabs and groups to collect your most often used tools.

To add a new tab from within the Outlook Options dialog box, Customize Ribbon option:

1. Click **New Tab** at the bottom of the tabs list. A new custom tab and group is added to the list.

2. Select the new tab, and move it where you want it (click the up and down arrows on the right as described in the previous section "Rearrange Tabs and Groups").

3. Rename the new tab and new group by selecting the item and clicking **Rename** at the bottom of the tabs list.

   –Or–

   Right-click the tab or group, and click **Rename**.

4. In either case, type a new name, and click **OK**.

To add a new group:

1. Select the tab where you want to add a new group, and then click **New Group** at the bottom of the tabs list. The list of all groups in that tab appears with a new custom group at its bottom.

2. Rename and rearrange the group within the tab as previously described (with Rename Group, you can also select an icon to represent the group).

3. When finished, click **OK** to close the Outlook Options dialog box.

TIP

Don't be afraid to experiment with your ribbon by adding tabs and groups. You can always revert back to the default Outlook ribbon layout by clicking **Reset** under the tabs list and then choosing to either restore a selected tab or all tabs.

ADD OR REMOVE COMMANDS AND TOOLS

Once you have the tabs and groups created, named, and organized, you can add the tools you want to your custom groups. You can't add tools to an existing group.

1. On the Customize The Ribbon view, click the **Choose Commands From** down arrow. You will see a menu of categories of commands and tabs, such as Commands Not In The Ribbon or Tool Tabs. Choose a category of commands or tabs, or choose **All Commands** to see the full list. Select (highlight the tool by clicking it) the first tool you want to add to a custom group.

2. In the tabs list on the right, select the custom group to which you want to add the tool.

3. Click **Add** between the lists of commands and tabs. The command or tool is added under your group.

4. Repeat steps 1 through 3 to populate your groups with all the tools you want.

5. If you make a mistake, remove a tool from a custom group by selecting the tool and clicking **Remove**.

6. Use the **Move Up** and **Move Down** arrows to the right of the tabs list to organize the added tools within your groups, and click **OK** when finished.

Customize the Quick Access Toolbar

The Quick Access toolbar can become a "best friend" if you modify it so that it fits your personal way of working.

ADD TO THE QUICK ACCESS TOOLBAR

The Quick Access toolbar should contain the commands you most commonly use. The default tools are Send/Receive and Undo. You can add commands to it if you want.

1. Click the down arrow to the right of the Quick Access toolbar, and select one of the commands on the drop-down menu to add it to the toolbar.

   –Or–

   Click the Quick Access toolbar down arrow, and click **More Commands** to view a more expansive list of Outlook tools.

   –Or–

   Click the **File** tab, click **Options**, and click **Quick Access Toolbar**.

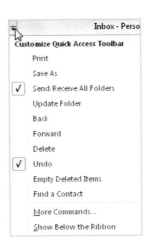

TIP

You can create a file that captures your customizations to the ribbon and the Quick Access toolbar so that you can use them on other computers running Outlook 2010. In the Outlook Options dialog box, click either **Customize Ribbon** or **Quick Access Toolbar**, click **Import/Export** in either view, and then click **Export All Customizations**. To use a previously created customization file, click **Import/Export** and then click **Import Customization File**. Depending on whether you're exporting or importing a customization file, a File Save or File Open dialog box appears that allows you to store a new file or find an existing one, respectively.

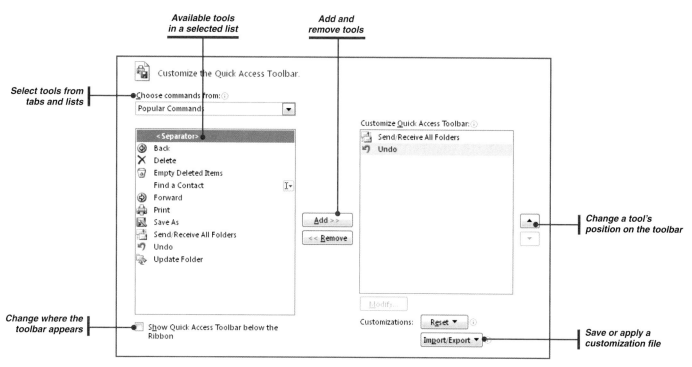

Available tools in a selected list

Add and remove tools

Select tools from tabs and lists

Change a tool's position on the toolbar

Change where the toolbar appears

Save or apply a customization file

Figure 1-9: You can customize the Quick Access toolbar by adding to and removing from it commands for easy and quick access.

NOTE

You can add a command to the Quick Access toolbar from the ribbon by right-clicking the button and choosing **Add To Quick Access Toolbar**.

In either of the last two cases, the Outlook Options dialog box appears with the Quick Access toolbar customization options, as displayed in Figure 1-9.

2. Open the **Choose Commands From** drop-down list, and select the source of the commands you want from the available options.

3. In the leftmost list box, find and click the command you want to add to the toolbar, and then click **Add** to move its name to the list box on the right. Repeat this for all the commands you want in the toolbar.

4. Click **OK** when you are finished.

Figure 1-10: The Outlook Help window provides links to several avenues of online and offline assistance.

MOVE THE QUICK ACCESS TOOLBAR

You can display the Quick Access toolbar at its default position (above the ribbon) or directly below the ribbon using one of the following methods:

- Right-click a tool on the Quick Access toolbar or on the ribbon, and click **Show Quick Access Toolbar Below The Ribbon** (once located below the ribbon, you can move it above the ribbon in the same manner).

  –Or–

- Right-click a tool in the Quick Access toolbar, and click **Customize Quick Access Toolbar** to open the Customize The Ribbon pane. Click the **Show Quick Access Toolbar Below The Ribbon** check box in the lower-left area, and click **OK** (to return the toolbar above the ribbon, open the pane and clear the check box).

REARRANGE TOOLS ON THE QUICK ACCESS TOOLBAR

You can change the order in which tools appear on the Quick Access toolbar.

1. In the Customize The Quick Access Toolbar pane, select from the list on the right the tool whose position you want to change.

2. Click the **Move Up** or **Move Down** arrows to the right of the list to move the tool. Moving the tool up moves it to the left in the on-screen toolbar; moving it down the list moves it to the right in the on-screen toolbar.

3. Click **OK** when finished.

Get Help

Microsoft provides substantial assistance to Outlook users. Outlook tailors much of the assistance offered, depending on whether you are working online or offline. If you are offline, you will get quick but more limited help. If you are or can be online, it will be slower but more comprehensive.

Obtain Help

You can obtain help in Outlook using one of the following techniques.

DISPLAY OUTLOOK HELP

The Outlook Help window, shown in Figure 1-10, provides links to several assistance tools and forums, including a table of contents, access to downloads, contact information, and late-breaking news on Outlook. To display the Outlook Help window:

- Click the **Microsoft Office Outlook Help** icon 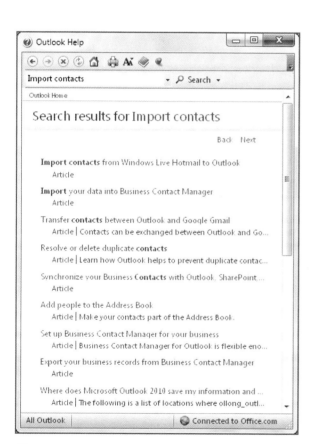 on the tab bar.

  –Or–

- Press **F1**.

Either of these commands will open the Help window shown in Figure 1-10. You can also click **File** and click **Help** for a different Help window (see "Access Other Help Options" below). There, if you click **Microsoft Office Help**, you will see the window shown in Figure 1-10.

ASK A QUESTION

You can quickly ask a question about Outlook using the Outlook Help window.

1. Type your question in the text box at the top of the Help window.
2. Press **ENTER** or click **Search**. The Outlook Help dialog box will appear, as you can see in Figure 1-11. Click one of the search results, and Microsoft Office Outlook Help will open and display the requested information.

ACCESS OTHER HELP OPTIONS

Click the **File** tab, and click **Help**. The Support window will open, as you can see in Figure 1-12, with these options:

- **Microsoft Office Help**, is the same as clicking the Help icon, described previously.
- **Getting Started** connects to the Microsoft Web site and provides information on what's new in Outlook 2010, along with tips on the basics of Outlook.
- **Contact Us** connects to the Microsoft Web site and provides suggestions on how you can contact solution centers and computer manufacturers.
- **Options** opens Outlook Options discussed in several places in this chapter.
- **Check For Updates** allows you to check for and download updates for Microsoft Windows and Outlook, as described in "Update Outlook" at the end of this chapter.

Find a Message

No matter how many messages your e-mail folders contain, Outlook can help you find a specific one. You can perform instant searches for large files, related

Figure 1-11: From the Outlook Help dialog box, you can search both online and offline Help, as well as other sources.

Figure 1-12: The Help option of the File view provides support for Outlook and Office.

messages, or messages from a particular sender. You can further qualify the search by having Outlook search only certain folders, or by specifying content for which you're searching.

PERFORM INSTANT SEARCHES

Click in the search text box in the Inbox Folder pane (or whichever folder you want to search in), and type the text for which you want to search. The search

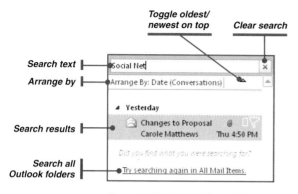

Search text

Arrange by

Search results

Search all
Outlook folders

Toggle oldest/
newest on top

Clear search

Figure 1-13: Instant Search is immediate and highly versatile for finding specific e-mail.

will immediately display beneath the search text box the found messages (see Figure 1-13).

You have these options:

- Click **Clear Search** to clear the text box and restore the previous contents. You can enter a new search.
- Click **Arrange By** to change the order for search results from the context menu.
- Click **Oldest/Youngest On Top** to toggle the date ascending/descending sequence.
- Click **Try Searching Again In All Mail Items** to expand the search to additional folders.

REFINE SEARCHES

In addition to the instant search found on the Folder pane, you can use the Search Tools Search contextual tab to refine your searches.

1. Perform an Instant Search as described previously. When you complete the search, the Search Tools Search contextual tab will open with the following tab groups that can be used to refine a search:

- **Scope** lets you choose the folders you want to include in the search.
- **Refine** lets you choose the elements you want to search on. The More drop-down list provides many more elements you can search on.
- **Options** lets you repeat previous searches and open one of several dialog boxes for more sophisticated searching:
  - **Indexing Status** displays a message box telling you the extent to which Outlook messages have been indexed.
  - **Locations To Search** lets you choose which of your accounts you want to search.

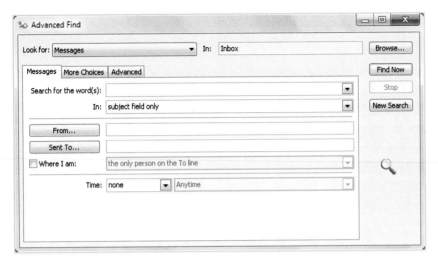

- **Advanced Find** displays the Advanced Find dialog box, where you define a search on multiple criteria with considerable detail.
- **Search Options** opens Outlook Options with the Search option selected. See the following section.

2. Click your choice and type the information needed. Click **OK** if needed. (If your choice of option does not require a dialog box, you will not need to click OK.)

CHANGE SEARCH OPTIONS

You can change some of the search defaults used with Instant Search in the Outlook Options Search options shown in Figure 1-14.

1. Display the Search options, either as described in the previous section or by clicking the **File** tab, clicking **Options**, and clicking **Search.**

NOTE

Reference tools provided with Outlook, such as a thesaurus, are available with Outlook message windows but not from the main Outlook window.

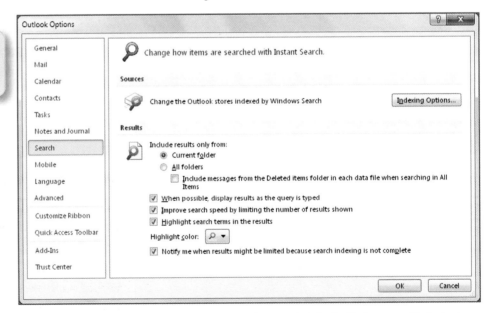

Figure 1-14: *In Search options, you can change the search defaults that are used in Instant Search.*

2. Click **Indexing Options** and then click **Modify** to select the drives and folders to be indexed so that searches can be faster. Click **OK** and then **Close** to close both Indexing dialog boxes.

3. Choose, as a default, whether to search just the currently selected folder or all folders.

4. Determine whether you want to change the defaults to display results as you type the search text, to limit the number of results so that the searches are faster, or to highlight the search text in results and change the highlight color.

5. If you choose, deselect the default to display a message if the indexing is incomplete for a selected file. If this message is displayed, it tells you that the indexing is still in process and that results will be incomplete.

6. Click **OK**.

Customize Outlook

Outlook provides a number of ways to customize both how it looks and how it operates in addition to the ribbon, Quick Access toolbar, and search customization described previously in this chapter. In this section, you'll see how to set general preferences, create a user profile, and update Outlook. Other ways to customize Outlook will be discussed in later chapters.

Set Preferences

Setting preferences allows you to adapt Outlook to your needs and work style. The Outlook Options window provides access to these settings.

Click the **File** tab, and click **Options** to open the Options dialog box.

SET GENERAL OPTIONS

The General options are displayed when you first open the Outlook Options window, as shown in Figure 1-15.

1. Select the user interface options that are correct for you. You will see more how these items are used in Chapter 2, so you might want to leave the defaults at this point.

2. Enter the user name and initials that you want to use with Outlook.

NOTE

Ways of setting preferences in each of the major areas—Mail, Calendar, Tasks, Contacts, and Notes—are discussed in the chapters that pertain to those subjects. Here, you'll see how to set general and security preferences.

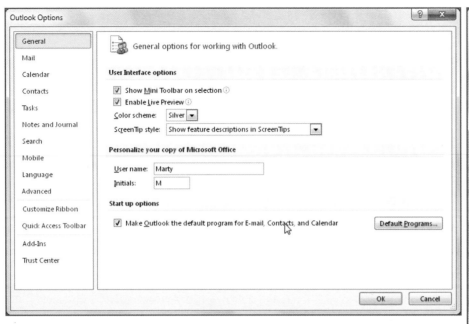

Figure 1-15: *The Outlook Options window provides a number of general preference settings.*

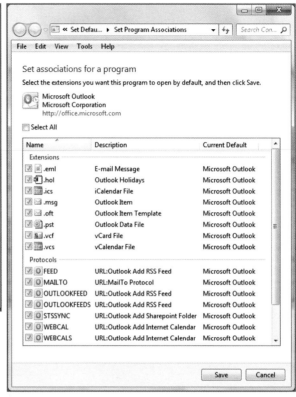

Figure 1-16: *File extensions help identify which program you are using and what kind of a file it is.*

3. Keep the **Make Outlook The Default Program For E-mail, Contacts, And Calendar** check box selected, if that is what you want.

4. Click **Default Programs**. The Set Associations For A Program dialog box will appear as you see in Figure 1-16. The default is for all associations to be selected, meaning that all files with the listed file extensions and all protocols will use Outlook. Make any desired changes, and click **Save**.

SET ADVANCED OPTIONS

1. With the Outlook Options window open, click **Advanced** on the left. The Options For Working With Outlook window will open (see Figure 1-17).

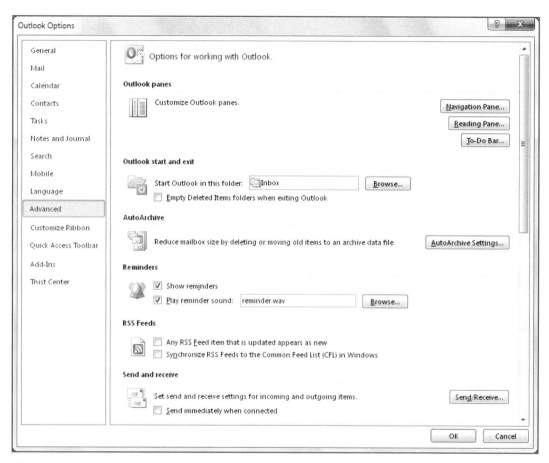

Figure 1-17: *Many of the fundamental Outlook preferences are set in the Advanced Options window.*

2. Click **Reading Pane** to open its dialog box (Navigation pane and To-Do bar options are discussed earlier in this chapter). Select under what circumstances you want items marked as read. Choose whether to keep the default of using the SPACEBAR to iterate through messages.

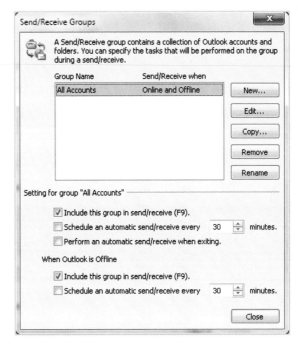

3. Click **Browse** next to Start Outlook In This Folder to open the Select Folder dialog box. Click the folder you want displayed when you open Outlook.

4. Under Send And Receive, click **Send/Receive**. Create or edit your e-mail accounts, and then choose how you want to perform your sending and receiving of e-mail. Click **Close** when you are ready.

5. Review the other options, and make any changes you want.

6. Click **OK** to close the Outlook Options window.

ADD A NEW E-MAIL ACCOUNT

1. Click the **File** tab. In the File view, Info should already be selected with your account information displayed, as shown in Figure 1-18.

2. Click **Add Account** near the top. The Add New Account dialog box appears.

   a. Type your name, e-mail address, and password twice.

   b. Choose if you want to use text messaging or manually configure your server settings, and then click **Next**.

NOTE

Setting up multiple users in Windows is different from setting up multiple Outlook user accounts. Each Windows user has a unique Outlook user profile with his or her folders and files. The multiple Outlook user accounts discussed in this chapter are for a single Windows user.

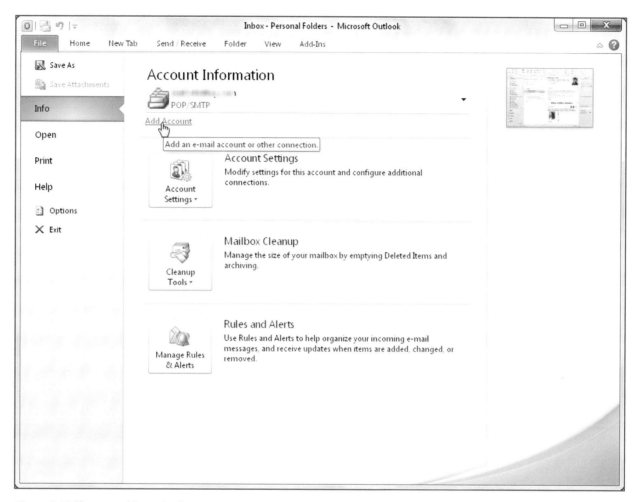

Figure 1-18: *You can add, repair, change, or remove new e-mail accounts and change the folder where e-mail messages are stored.*

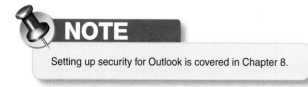

NOTE

Setting up security for Outlook is covered in Chapter 8.

c. An online search will be made to verify your settings with your server. Click **Next**. Outlook will initially test for an encrypted mail server. If one is not found, click **Next** to test for an unencrypted mail server.

3. When the settings have been confirmed, click **Finish**.

Update Outlook

Periodically, Microsoft comes out with updates for Office and Outlook (these are almost always problem fixes and not enhancements). You can check for available updates and download and install them from the Microsoft Web site.

1. Click the **File** tab, and click **Help**.

2. On the Support page, click **Check For Updates**. Your Web browser may open and connect to the Microsoft Online Web site. Then the Windows Control Panel will open to Windows Update, as shown in Figure 1-19. This will update both Windows and Office.

3. Click **Check For Updates**. Your system will be checked for any necessary updates, and you will be given the opportunity to download and install them if you choose. When you have downloaded the updates you want, close your Web browser.

TIP

To empty your Deleted Items folder and reduce the storage required for old items, right-click the folder, click **Empty Folder**, and click **Yes** to confirm the action. Your folder will be emptied.

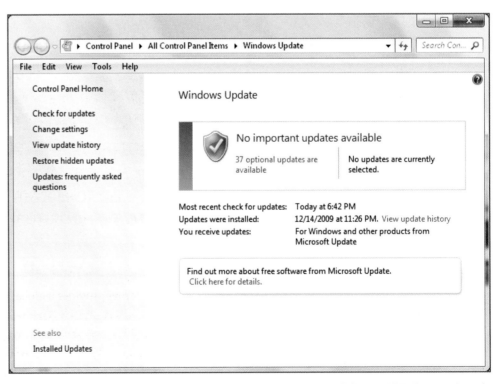

*Figure 1-19: **One of the primary reasons to check for and download Office and Windows updates is to get needed security patches.***

Chapter 2

Receiving and Handling E-mail

Most people get Outlook so that they can send and receive e-mail. For anyone who has Internet access, e-mail has essentially replaced letter writing. As great as e-mail is, however, it's possible to get overwhelmed by the amount of mail that arrives—much of it *spam*, or anonymously mass-mailed junk. In this chapter, you'll learn how to create e-mail accounts, receive e-mail, and deal with the messages that come in.

Set Up E-mail

The Internet provides a global pipeline through which e-mail flows; therefore, you need a connection that lets you tap into that pipeline. Both local and national Internet service providers (ISPs) offer e-mail with their Internet connections. At your work or business, you may have an e-mail account over a local area network (LAN) that also connects to the Internet. You can also obtain e-mail accounts on the Internet that are independent of the connection. You can access these Internet accounts (Gmail by Google, for example) from anywhere

2

1
3
4
5
6
7
8
9
10

UICKSTEPS

GETTING A GMAIL ACCOUNT

Gmail by Google, one of many Internet-based HTTP services, is free, and you can access it from any Internet connection in the world, so you don't even need to own a computer. You can see the Gmail opening window in Figure 2-1. To set up a Gmail account:

1. In Windows XP and Vista, click **Start** and click **Internet**. In Windows 7, click the **Internet Explorer** icon on the taskbar.

2. In your browser's address bar, type www.gmail.com, and press **ENTER**.

3. Click **Create An Account**.

4. Fill in all the applicable fields on the registration form. Enter the login name you want for the account, leaving out the "@gmail.com" part, and then click **Check Availability** to check whether the login name you want is available. Read the Google Terms of Service agreement, and click **I Accept.**

5. Read the introductory information, and click **Show Me My Account** to look at your Gmail account on a browser, as shown in Figure 2-2.

6. When you are ready, reopen Outlook, click the **File** tab, and in Info view click **Add Account**. Enter your name, your new Gmail e-mail address (someone@gmail.com), and your Gmail password (twice); and click **Next.**

7. When you are told that your new account has been found and set up, click **Finish**. Back in Outlook, your Gmail messages will appear, as shown in Figure 2-3.

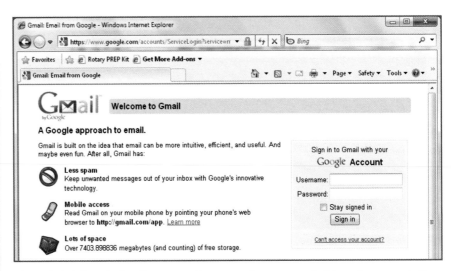

Figure 2-1: A Google Gmail account gives you a large amount of free storage and allows the sending and receiving of large files.

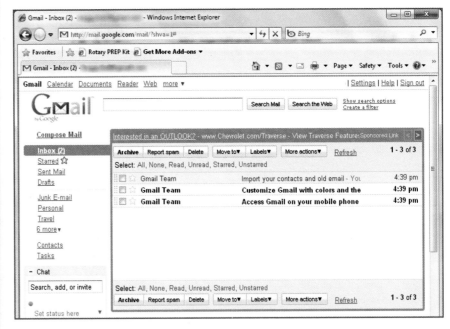

Figure 2-2: Gmail's browser mail application allows you to work with your mail anywhere, with any computer.

NOTE

To get a Gmail account, you must already have an Internet browser and a connection to the Internet. The instructions here assume you do.

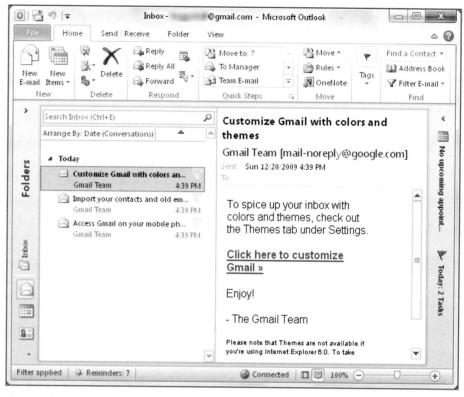

Figure 2-3: In addition to seeing your Gmail in a browser window, you can see it in Outlook.

in the world. These three ways of accessing Internet e-mail—ISPs, corporate connections, and Internet e-mail—use different types of e-mail systems:

- **POP3** (Post Office Protocol 3), used by ISPs, retrieves e-mail from a dedicated mail server, and is usually combined with SMTP (Simple Mail Transfer Protocol) to send e-mail from a separate server.

- **MAPI** (Messaging Application Programming Interface) lets businesses handle e-mail on Microsoft Exchange Servers and LANs.

- **HTTP** (HyperText Transfer Protocol) transfers information from servers on the World Wide Web to browsers (that's why your browser's address line starts with "http://") and is used with Hotmail and other Internet mail accounts.

TIP

To find out where your e-mail data files are located, click the **File** tab, in the Info view that opens by default, click the **Account Settings** down arrow, and select **Account Settings** from the drop-down menu. Click the account you want to locate, and in the lower part of the Account Settings dialog box opposite Change Folder, you'll see the path and file name of the Personal Folders.

Selected account delivers new messages to the following location:

Change Folder   **Personal Folders\Inbox**
    in data file O:\Users\Marty\AppData\Local\Microsoft\Outlook\Outlook.pst

TIP

To remove an e-mail account, click the **File** tab, in Info view click the **Account Settings** down arrow, and then click **Account Settings** again to open the Account Settings dialog box. Click the account to select it, and then click **Remove**. Click **Yes** to confirm the removal of the account, and click **Close**.

TIP

If you like where the old Preview pane was located in earlier versions of Outlook, you can place the Reading pane beneath the Folder pane: Click the **View** tab, click **Reading Pane**, and click **Bottom**. (You can also turn it off and open its Options dialog box.)

Get Online

Whether you choose dial-up or a high-speed service like DSL (digital subscriber line) or cable Internet, getting online requires hardware, software, and some system configuration. It's possible that everything you need is already installed or that your computer came with extra disks for getting online. First, find an ISP:

- **Get a recommendation** from satisfied friends.
- **Look in the yellow pages** under "Internet Service Providers" or "Internet Access Providers."
- **Look on your computer**. Many computer manufacturers include software from nationwide Internet providers, such as AOL, EarthLink, and others.

If you find what you want in an Internet provider already on your computer, double-click the provider's icon, or click the link and follow the instructions. If you have a disk that came with your computer or from an ISP, pop it in and follow the instructions. If you use a local provider, their tech support people will usually walk you through the entire setup process on the phone.

Receive E-mail

With at least one e-mail account installed in Outlook, you're ready to receive mail. Everything is done in Outlook's Mail view, shown in Figure 2-4, and opened by clicking **Mail** in Outlook views in the lower-left area of the Outlook window.

Check for E-mail

Once you are set up, it's easy to download mail.

1. Make sure you're connected to the Internet or can be automatically connected and that **Mail** is selected in the Outlook views of the Navigation pane.

2. Click **Send/Receive** on the Quick Access toolbar.

   –Or–

   Press **F9**.

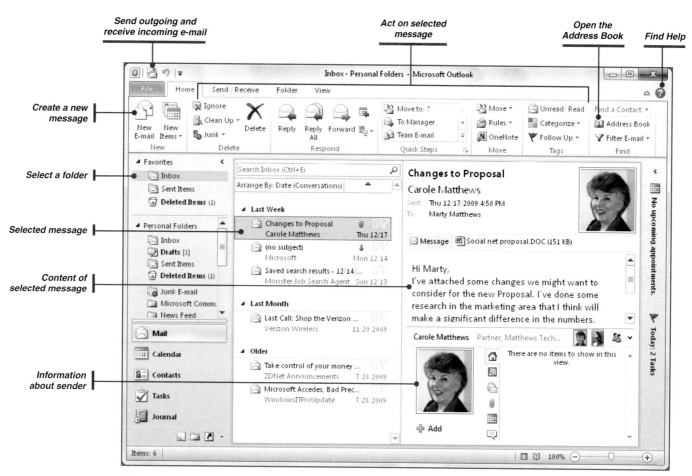

Send outgoing and receive incoming e-mail

Act on selected message

Open the Address Book

Find Help

Create a new message

Select a folder

Selected message

Content of selected message

Information about sender

Figure 2-4: *The Mail view provides one-click access to the most common operations.*

3. If it is not already open, click the **Inbox** icon in the Navigation pane, and watch the mail come in. If you have several e-mail accounts, you can select the Inbox icon from among the several that you have. You may need to scroll through the Folder List and first click the account to see the Inbox.

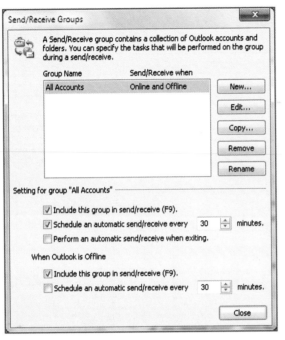

Figure 2-5: *The Options dialog box is where you can customize many Outlook processes.*

Not only can Outlook periodically check your e-mail provider for you, but it can also do it automatically. Desktop alerts are subtle, given the way they quietly fade in and out.

1. Click the **File** tab, click **Options**, and click **Advanced**.

2. Under Send And Receive, click **Send/Receive**. The Send/Receive Groups dialog box appears, as you can see in Figure 2-5.

3. Under the Setting For Group "All Accounts" section, click **Schedule An Automatic Send/Receive Every**, type or click the spinner to enter the number of minutes to elapse between checking, and click **Close**.

Read E-mail

Besides being easy to obtain, e-mail messages are effortless to open and read. There are two ways to view the body of the message:

- Double-click the message and read it in the window that opens, as shown in Figure 2-6.

  –Or–

- Click the message and read it in the Reading pane, scrolling as needed.

Of course, you can also control which accounts you check, what kinds of e-mail you let in, and how it is presented to you.

Download Sender and Subject Information Only

If you are inundated with e-mail, or if messages contain really large files (like lots of photos), you might want to choose among your messages for specific ones to download to Outlook. You can save time downloading e-mail, especially with large files—which you may want to download at a later time. This only works on your POP server e-mail (not on HTTP server e-mail, such as Gmail). First, you instruct Outlook to download only the headers, and then you mark the headers for which you want to download the messages.

Alternatives for responding to this message

Create a meeting from this message

Forward this message as an attachment

Move this message to various folders

Flag, categorize, or mark this message as unread

Find text in this message

Move this and future messages in this conversation to the Deleted Items folder

Mark this and future items from this sender and domain as junk

Message header information

Attachment to message

Content of the message

Find related messages

Select text or object

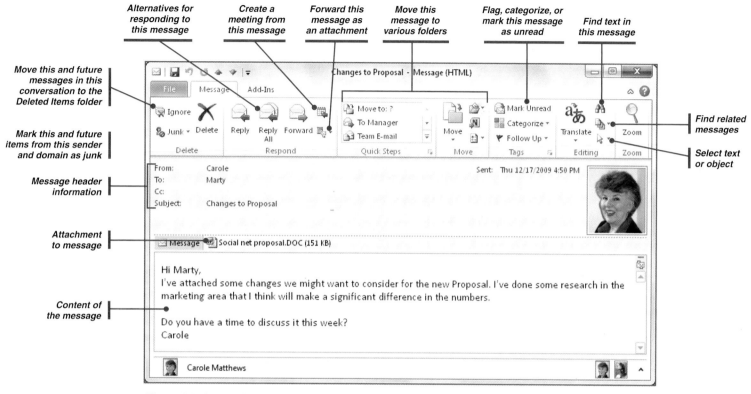

Figure 2-6: An e-mail message window contains all the information and tools you need to respond.

Download Headers

Download all mail headers in this folder.

A mail header contains some message fields such as the e-mail address of the sender, subject and date.

RECEIVE HEADERS MANUALLY

1. Click **Inbox** (or whatever folder you want to download).

2. Click the **Send/Receive** tab, and click **Download Headers**.

The headers, assuming you have e-mail waiting to be downloaded, will be downloaded to your selected folder. There will be an identifying icon like this:

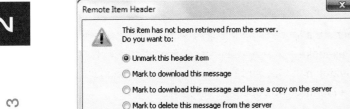

MARK HEADERS TO DOWNLOAD, COPY, OR DELETE

1. Double-click a header-only message in the Inbox folder to open the Remote Item Header dialog box, which allows you to unmark the header or mark its message to be downloaded, copied on the server, or deleted.

   –Or–

   Right-click a header-only message in the folder to open the context menu, which also allows you to mark the header message to be downloaded or deleted, as well as many of the moving and categorizing actions on a message's Home tab.

2. Repeat the process for all headers, and then click **Send/Receive** to perform the actions selected.

RECEIVE HEADERS AUTOMATICALLY

If you want to download only headers from your POP server accounts every time, you can set up Outlook to do so.

1. Click the **File** tab, click **Options**, and click **Advanced**.

2. Under Send And Receive, click **Send/Receive**. The Send/Receive Groups dialog box will appear.

3. Make sure **All Accounts** is selected, and click **Edit**. All your e-mail accounts are listed on the left.

4. Click the desired POP account.

5. Under Folder Options, click **Download Headers Only**, as shown in Figure 2-7, click **OK**, click **Close**, and click **OK** once more to return to Outlook.

PROCESS HEADERS

When your headers have been marked, you can download them.

1. Click the **Send/Receive** tab.

2. Click **Process Marked Headers** in the Server group.

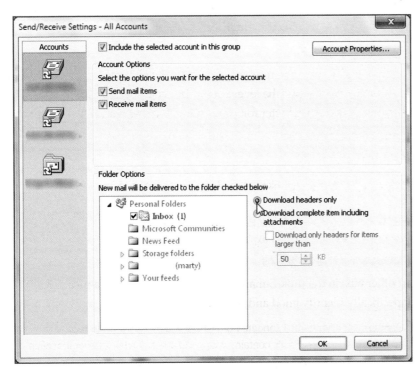

Figure 2-7: Outlook can be set up to download only headers for all messages.

The *domain* in a person's e-mail address is the part of the address after "@." In an Internet address (URL, or uniform resource locator), the domain is the part after the "http://www"—for example, "whidbey.net" (a local ISP) or "loc.gov" (the Library of Congress Web site).

One easy way to reduce the junk e-mail you get is to *avoid* replying to any suspicious message. If you reply and tell them to go away, they learn that they reached a valid address, which they will hit again and again.

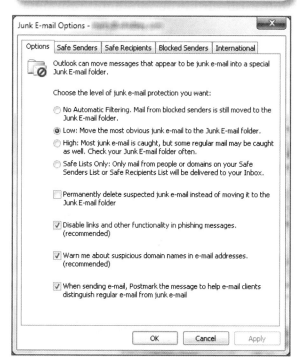

Figure 2-8: Blocking image and sound files protects your computer, but you can easily unblock a message by clicking in its top banner.

Filter Junk Mail

Outlook can automatically filter out a lot of annoying spam before you ever see it, and it can set aside suspicious-looking messages in a Junk E-mail folder. It does this in two ways: by analyzing message content based on a protection level you choose, and by having you identify good and bad senders.

Outlook also prevents pictures and sounds from being downloaded into messages that contain HTML formatting. Up to now, savvy spammers have been able to design messages that only download images when you open or preview the message. They plant *Web beacons* in the messages, which tell their server that they have reached a valid address so that they can send you even more junk. Outlook blocks both the external content, as shown in Figure 2-8, and the beacon, unless you tell it to unblock it.

CHOOSE A PROTECTION LEVEL

The amount of junk e-mail you receive suggests the level of protection you need. By default, Outlook sets the level at Low, but you might decide that another option would work better for you. Table 2-1 shows some considerations in choosing a level.

To set the protection level:

1. In the Home tab Delete group, click the **Junk** down arrow, and click **Junk E-mail Options**.

2. Beneath Choose The Level Of Junk E-mail Protection You Want, click the desired protection level. See Table 2-1 for explanations.

ADD ADDRESSES TO FILTER LISTS

The four other tabs in the Junk E-mail Options window provide a means for you to specifically identify good and bad e-mailers.

- **Safe Senders** specifies e-mail senders from whom you always want to receive messages. This list automatically contains your contacts, so Outlook never identifies their messages as junk, no matter how silly their jokes are. If you subscribe to a newsgroup or some other mass mailing, you might need to specifically add it to the list.

OPTION	RESULT	PROS	CONS
No Automatic Filtering	Only mail from blocked senders goes to the Junk E-mail folder.	You have total control.	Your Inbox could be stuffed; you or others might see unsolicited pornography.
Low (default)	Outlook scans messages for offensive language and indications of unsolicited commercial mailings.	The worst of the junk gets caught.	Some canny spammers will still find ways around the protections.
High	Pretty much all the junk e-mail gets caught.	Considerably fewer rude shocks in the Inbox.	Some regular mail will inadvertently get sent to the Junk E-mail folder.
Safe Lists Only	Only mail from Safe Senders and Safe Recipients lists goes to the Inbox.	Complete protection.	Lots of friendly mail will be junked.
Permanently Delete Suspected Junk E-Mail Instead Of Moving It To The Junk E-Mail Folder	Filtered junk mail never gets onto your computer.	You never have to inspect the Junk E-Mail folder.	Unless you chose the No Automatic Filtering option, you are sure to lose some friendly mail.
Disable Links And Other Functionality	Phishing mail is less dangerous.	You don't have to worry as much about phishing mail.	None.
Warn Me About Suspicious Domain Names	Warning message is produced with suspicious names.	Added level of protection.	May get an occasional unwanted warning.
When Sending E-Mail, Postmark The Message	Sent messages are not held up.	Your messages get to the addressee.	None.

Table 2-1: Junk E-mail Protection Levels

- **Safe Recipients** ensures that mailing lists you subscribe to treat you as a safe sender when you contribute messages to the list.

- **Blocked Senders** sends messages from specified senders straight to the Junk E-mail folder. It's especially useful to add obnoxious domains to this list so that no address from that source makes it to your Inbox (see Figure 2-9).

- **International** allows you to block international e-mails by foreign domain codes or by language.

UPDATE LISTS QUICKLY

1. Sender and recipient addresses can be added quickly to the Safe Senders, Blocked Senders, and Safe Recipients lists from an Outlook folder. Right-click a message whose sender you want to put on a list.

2. Point at Junk, and click the appropriate option.

Figure 2-9: *It is worth entering the addresses of senders you want to block if you think you'll otherwise see more of their mail.*

UNBLOCK PICTURE DOWNLOADS

By default, picture downloads are blocked to speed up the downloading of e-mail. To change that for specific items:

- For a **single opened message**, click **Click Here To Download Pictures** in the information bar at the top of the message, or right-click an individual picture.

- For **all mail from the source of the open message**, right-click a blocked item, point at **Junk**, and click **Never Block Sender's Domain (@example.com)**.

- For **all HTML mail** (not recommended), click **File**, click **Options**, click **Trust Center**, and clear the **Don't Download Pictures Automatically In HTML E-Mail Messages Or RSS Items** check box. Click **OK**.

Handle E-mail Messages

E-mail has a way of building up fast. Outlook lets you sort your messages just about any way you want. You will learn all about managing folders in Chapter 8. For now, we'll consider ways to sort and mark messages so that they don't get lost in the crowd.

Mark Messages as Read or Unread

A message is marked as "read" after you have selected it so that its contents display in the Reading pane for a designated time (see "Change the Time for Being Read"). The header in the Folder List changes from boldface to plain type. A message can get lost in the pile if it's accidentally selected and you don't notice or forget about it. You can easily mark it as unread again by right-clicking the message and clicking **Mark As Unread**.

Change the Time for Being Read

To change the time that a message must be selected before it is marked as read:

1. Click the **File** tab, click **Options**, and click **Advanced**.

2. In the Outlook Panes area at the top, click the **Reading Pane** button. The Reading Pane dialog box will appear.

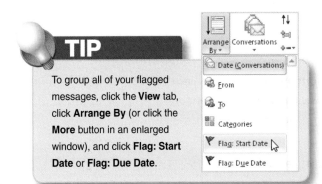
3. Click one of these options:

- **Mark Items As Read When Viewed In The Reading Pane** allows you to set the number of seconds that a message must be selected before being marked as read.

- **Mark Item As Read When Selection Changes** marks the message as read as soon as the pointer selects another message in the Folder pane. This is the default setting.

- Click **OK** to close the dialog box.

Flag Your Messages for Follow-up

You can place colored flags beside messages you want to do something with later. The flag will appear in the flag column of the Folder pane.

- Click the flag outline in the flag column of the message header in the folder pane to add the default red flag for a task that is due today. This is a toggle between the Follow-Up red flag and the Complete checkmark.

–Or–

- Select the message you want to flag, in the Home tab Tag group, click the **Follow Up** down arrow to open its context menu, and click the type of flag you want to insert.

–Or–

- Right-click the flag column of the selected message, and on the context menu, click the type of flag you want to insert.

FINE-TUNE YOUR FLAGS

You can fine-tune the follow-up actions of the flags and specify that a reminder be made so that an e-mail message can be responded to in a timely manner.

1. In the Folder pane, right-click the flag column, and click **Custom**.

–Or–

For a message open in the Reading pane, click **Follow Up** in the Tags group of the Home tab, and click **Custom**.

–Or–

Custom

Flagging creates a to-do item that reminds you to follow up. After you
follow up, you can mark the to-do item complete.

Flag to: Do not Forward

Start date: Tuesday, December 22, 2009

Due date: Tuesday, December 22, 2009

☐ Reminder:

Tuesday, December 22, 2009   4:00 PM

Clear Flag   OK   Cancel

NOTE

To remove a flag, or to indicate that the e-mail no longer
needs to be handled, right-click the flag and click either
Clear Flag or **Mark Complete**.

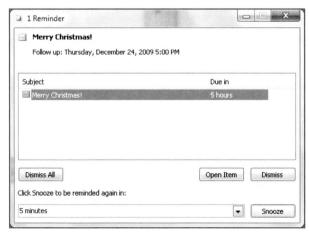

Figure 2-10: *You can set a flag to display a reminder with a
sound that alerts you that an important e-mail has not been
handled.*

For a message open in a message window, click
Follow Up in the Tags group of the Message tab,
and click **Custom**.

2. In the Custom dialog box, click the **Flag To** down
   arrow, and click an action.

3. Click the **Start Date** down arrow, and click a date
   to indicate when the message is to be flagged.

4. Click the **Due Date** down arrow, and click a date
   that indicates when the response to the e-mail is to be completed.

5. Click **Reminder** to place a check mark in the check box and to display the date when
   the reminder is to begin. Click the date down arrow, and click a date. Click the time
   down arrow, and click a time for the reminders to begin.

6. Click the **Sound** icon to remove the default setting in which a sound file is played
   when the reminder displays on the screen.

7. Click **OK**.

8. At the designated time, a reminder will be displayed, as shown
   in Figure 2-10. To repeat the reminder, click the snooze down
   arrow, click an interval until the next sound, and then click
   Snooze.

Arrange Messages in a Folder

Outlook contains 13 types of Inbox arrangements. You can
have Outlook organize messages by the date they were sent,
which Outlook uses by default; alphabetically by who sent
them or by first word in the subject line; or by clustering
those with attachments, colored flags you give them, or
categories you created for your own use. Outlook can even
group *conversations*, e-mail exchanges in which senders
clicked Reply, thus preserving the subject line. To arrange
messages:

1. Click **Inbox** or another specific mail folder in the navigation bar on the left side.

2. Click the **View** tab, in the Arrangement group, click **Arrange By** (or click the **More**
   button in an expanded window), and click one of the arrangements listed.

NOTE

The expand and contract symbols to the left of an item indicate that you can expand or contract a list by clicking the symbol. The symbols can be used for a group of folders in the Folder List of the Navigation pane or to group messages by day (such as messages for Tuesday) in the Folder pane.

◢ Favorites	◀
📄 Inbox	
📄 Sent Items	
📄 Deleted Items (1)	

◣ Favorites	◀
▷ Personal Folders	

| ▷ Personal Folders | |

NOTE

The first time you use a category, you are asked if you want to rename. If you do, type a name and click **Yes**. Otherwise, click **No**.

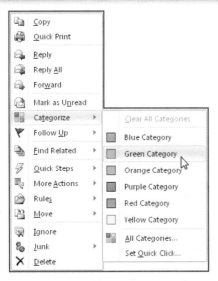

Figure 2-11: The Categorize menu shows colors, which you can define as categories according to your needs.

ADD COLORED CATEGORIES

Assigning categories to mail is one way of separating your messages by a colored code that you determine. You might categorize by project, priority, sender, etc. You determine what a color will mean when it is assigned to a message. Once your e-mail contains categories, it can be sorted and arranged so that you can find or track it more efficiently. The colors make the categories highly visible in lists. Mail is only one kind of item that you can categorize. You can assign categories to whatever you create in Outlook—tasks, appointments, contacts, notes, journal entries, and documents. You can also create new categories in the list.

1. Right-click a message header in the Folder pane, and click **Categorize**. The Categorize menu opens, as shown in Figure 2-11. (You can also click **Categorize** in the Tag group of the Home tab.)

2. Do one of the following:

   - Click a color category for the item.

   - Click **All Categories** to assign more than one category to a message (or to edit a category—see "Edit a Category" below). Click a color to select it (place a check mark in the check box), and then click **OK**.

Name
☑ 🟦 Blue Category
☐ 🟩 Green Category
☑ 🟧 Orange Category
☐ 🟪 Purple Category
☐ 🟥 Red Category
☐ ⬜ Yellow Category

3. View items sorted into categories by clicking the **View** tab, selecting **Arrange By** (or the **More** button), and clicking **Categories**.

EDIT A CATEGORY

You can edit a category to change its name, color, or assigned shortcut.

1. Right-click a message to be categorized, click **Categorize** from the context menu, and click **All Categories**.

2. Select from among these options:

   - To create a new category, click **New**. In the Add New Category dialog box, type a name; click the **Color** down arrow, and click a color; click the **Shortcut** key down arrow, and click a shortcut key if you want one. Click **OK**.

   - To rename a category, click a category, click **Rename**, and type the new name in the category name text box. ☑ 🟦 Blue Category

   - To delete a category, click the category and click **Delete**.

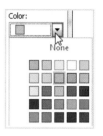

- To change the color, click the **Color** down arrow, and click a replacement color.

- To assign a shortcut key, click the **Shortcut Key** down arrow, and click a shortcut key combination.

3. Click **OK** to close the Color Categories dialog box.

Make Up Your Own Rules

When it comes to sorting e-mail, you can make up the rules as you go along, and Outlook will follow them. Or you can pick from a list of predefined rules for common situations, like having Outlook send a message to your cell phone if you win an eBay auction or flagging all messages from your son at college for follow-up. (This only works for POP3 server accounts.)

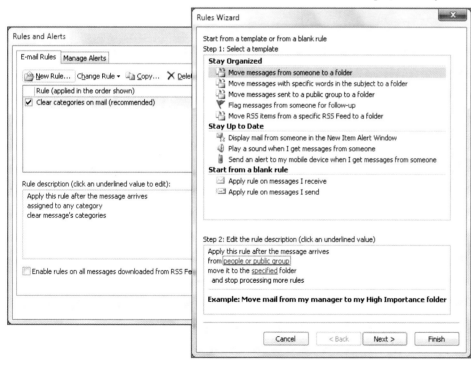

Figure 2-12: The Rules And Alerts dialog box's New Rule button opens the Rules Wizard, which is where you establish rules for handling e-mail, including alerts for the arrival of e-mail.

1. With Mail selected, click the **File** tab, and in the default Info view, click **Manage Rules & Alerts**. The Rules And Alerts dialog box appears, as shown in the background of Figure 2-12.

2. **Click New Rule** (shown in the upper-left area of Figure 2-12) to open the Rules Wizard, and click one of the options in the list under step 1 in one the following categories. In step 2, if desired, click the option link and complete the dialog box:

   - **Stay Organized** lets you move and flag messages in a variety of ways.

   - **Stay Up To Date** alerts you when new mail arrives by displaying it in a special window, playing a sound, or alerting your mobile device.

   - **Start From A Blank Rule** lets you build a completely custom rule for receiving or sending messages.

3. Click **Next**. Click all conditions under which you want the rule applied in step 1, clicking any underlined value in step 2 and changing it as needed. The information is added to the scenario. Click **Next**.

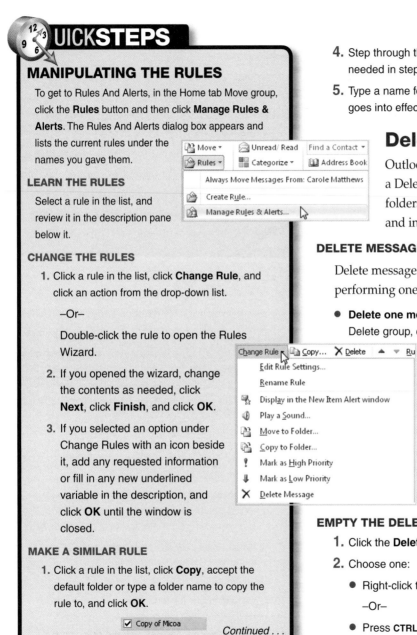

MANIPULATING THE RULES

To get to Rules And Alerts, in the Home tab Move group, click the **Rules** button and then click **Manage Rules & Alerts**. The Rules And Alerts dialog box appears and lists the current rules under the names you gave them.

LEARN THE RULES

Select a rule in the list, and review it in the description pane below it.

CHANGE THE RULES

1. Click a rule in the list, click **Change Rule**, and click an action from the drop-down list.

   –Or–

   Double-click the rule to open the Rules Wizard.

2. If you opened the wizard, change the contents as needed, click **Next**, click **Finish**, and click **OK**.

3. If you selected an option under Change Rules with an icon beside it, add any requested information or fill in any new underlined variable in the description, and click **OK** until the window is closed.

MAKE A SIMILAR RULE

1. Click a rule in the list, click **Copy**, accept the default folder or type a folder name to copy the rule to, and click **OK**.

Continued . . .

4. Step through the wizard, selecting circumstances and actions, changing values as needed in step 2, and clicking **Next**.

5. Type a name for the rule where requested, click an option specifying when the rule goes into effect, click **Finish**, and click **OK**.

Delete Messages

Outlook creates two stages for deleting messages by providing a Delete folder, which holds all the items you deleted from other folders. In the first stage, you remove deleted items to a separate folder, and in the second you remove the messages from your computer.

DELETE MESSAGES FROM THE INBOX

Delete messages by opening a folder in the Navigation pane and performing one of the following actions:

- **Delete one message** by clicking a message in the Folders pane and in the Home tab Delete group, clicking **Delete.**

   –Or–

   Right-clicking a message in the Folders pane and clicking **Delete**.

- **Delete a block of messages** by clicking the first message, holding down SHIFT, clicking the last message (all of the messages in between are selected as well), and in the Home tab Delete group, clicking **Delete**.

- **Delete multiple noncontiguous messages** by pressing CTRL while clicking the messages you want to remove and then in the Home tab Delete group, clicking **Delete**.

EMPTY THE DELETED ITEMS FOLDER

1. Click the **Deleted Items** folder.

2. Choose one:

   - Right-click the **Deleted Items** folder, and click **Empty "Deleted Items" Folder**.

      –Or–

   - Press CTRL+A to select all items in the folder, click **Delete**, and click **Yes**.

      –Or–

   - Select files to be permanently deleted as you did earlier, click **Delete**, and click **Yes**.

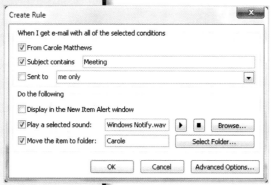

QUICKSTEPS

MANIPULATING THE RULES (Continued)

2. Double-click the copy.

3. Step through the wizard, changing settings as necessary and clicking **Next** as you go.

4. Give the rule a new name, and click **Finish**.

CANCEL A RULE

1. Select a rule in the list, and click **Delete**.

2. Click **Yes**.

REARRANGE THE RULES

You might want rules to be applied in a certain order.

1. Select a rule in the list that you want to move.

2. Click the **Move Up** or **Move Down** arrow until the rule resides where you want it in the sequence.

BASE A RULE ON A MESSAGE

1. In the Mail Folder pane, right-click the message, click **Rules**, and click **Create Rule**.

2. Check the desired options in the Create Rule dialog box.

3. To use the more detailed specifications in the Rules Wizard, click **Advanced Options**, step through the wizard (with information from the dialog box supplying some of the underlined values), click **Next** as needed, and then click **Finish**.

4. If using the Create Rule dialog box, click **OK**.

Manage Attachments

Messages that contain files, such as pictures and documents, display a paper clip icon in the second message line within the Folder pane to show that there's more to see. Attachments are listed in the message itself in the Reading pane, as shown in Figure 2-13. Since computer vandals like to broadcast debilitating viruses by way of attachments, you should be sure that you are dealing with a trusted source before you open any attachments. Also, it's important to have an up-to-date antivirus program running on your system, as well as any protection provided by your ISP. Make sure you have it, and keep your virus definitions up-to-date. If you are running Windows Vista or Windows 7, several Internet and e-mail protections are built into it.

When a message comes in with an attachment, you can preview the attachment, open it, or save it first.

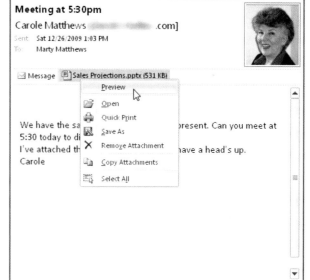

Figure 2-13: *A single message can contain one or many attachments, consisting of all kinds of files, which may be previewed before opening.*

QUICKFACTS

ARCHIVING MESSAGES

Archiving is for people who have a hard time throwing things away. Outlook is set up on a schedule, which you can see by clicking the **File** tab, clicking **Options**, clicking **Advanced**, and under AutoArchive, clicking **AutoArchive Settings**.

The AutoArchive dialog box that appears allows you to turn on AutoArchive, set the time interval between archive functions, determine when to delete old messages, specify the path to the archived file, and other settings. Click **OK** when you are finished.

If you selected **Apply These Settings To All Folders Now**, a dialog box appears, asking if you are ready to archive files; you can click **Yes** and be assured of finding the messages later. They are saved in a file structure that mirrors your Personal folders yet compresses the files and cleans up the Inbox.

To open archived files, click Expand ▷ beside Archive Folders in the Navigation pane, and click a folder.

OPEN ATTACHMENTS

The attachment can only be opened or viewed in the Reading pane.

● Double-click the attachment.

–Or–

● Right-click the attachment and click either **Preview** or **Open**.

SAVE ATTACHMENTS

If you have My Computer or Windows Explorer open to the folder where you want to save the attachment, you can drag the attachment there. Otherwise:

1. Right-click the attachment icon, and click **Save As**.
2. Use the Save Attachment dialog box to navigate to the desired folder.
3. Type a name in the File Name text box, and click **Save**.

OPEN SAVED ATTACHMENTS

1. Navigate to the folder where you saved the file.
2. Double-click the file.

Print Messages

Occasionally, you might receive something that you want to print and pass around or save as a hard copy. Outlook lets you print in a hurry with the default print settings, or you can control certain parts of the process.

PRINT QUICKLY

Right-click the message or an attachment, and click **Quick Print**. The message will be printed on your default printer.

CHOOSE PRINT SETTINGS

1. Select or open the message.
2. Click the **File** tab, and click **Print**. The Print window appears with a preview of what you will print and settings you can configure, as shown in Figure 2-14.

NOTE

If you preview an attachment, it will open in the Reading pane, where you can scroll through the document. To return to the message body, click the **Message** icon next to the attachment at the top of the message (see Figure 2-13).

TIP

To select multiple attachments in an e-mail at one time to copy or save them, for instance, right-click one attachment and click **Select All**. Then right-click one of the selected attachments, and choose the activity.

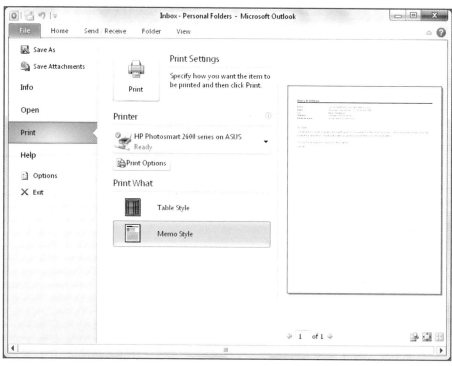

Figure 2-14: *You can customize how a message is printed.*

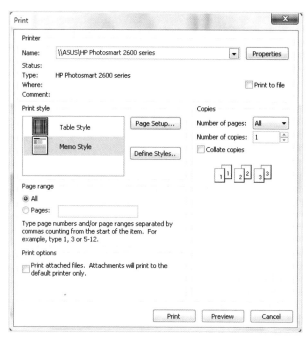

3. Open the **Printer** drop-down list, and choose the printer you want to use.

4. Click **Print Options** to open the Print dialog box.

5. Click **Properties**, select the layout or quality, and click **OK**.

6. Click **Page Setup** to open the Page Setup dialog box. Review the Format, Paper, and Header/Footer tabs for settings you may want to make, and click **OK**.

7. Click **Print** to begin printing.

Chapter 3

Creating and Sending E-mail

As the saying goes, you have to send mail to get mail. The beauty of Outlook e-mail is that the messages are so easy to send and respond to that you can essentially carry on conversations. Outlook also makes it just as easy to send a message to one person or to 50, bedeck messages with fancy backgrounds known as *stationery*, insert links to Internet sites, include pictures—even add a distinctive signature. In this chapter you will learn how to create and enhance messages, as well as how to send copies, respond to others, and control how and when e-mail is sent.

Write Messages

Creating an e-mail message can be as simple as dispatching a note or as elaborate as designing a marketing poster. It's wise to get used to creating simple messages before making an art project of one. Without your having to impose any guidelines, however, Outlook is set to create an attractive basic e-mail message.

Create a Message

One click starts a message, and the only field you have to complete is the address of the recipient. Normally, at least three fields are filled in before you send the message:

- **Recipient**   One or more e-mail addresses or names in your Address Book
- **Subject**   Words indicating the contents of the message (used by the Find tool in a search)
- **Message body**   Whatever you want to say to the recipient

To start a message:

With Outlook open and Mail selected in the Navigation pane, click the **New E-mail** button in the Home tab, New group. The new Message window opens, as shown in Figure 3-1.

Address a Message

Outlook is the lazy person's dream for addressing messages. Of course, the address itself is simple: *username@domain.extension* (such as "mary@someisp .com"). Once you have entered names in the Contacts workspace, however, you can address your messages with almost no typing. (See Chapter 4 for a complete explanation of how to add contacts to the Address Book.) In this chapter we will focus on what happens to the e-mail itself. The following alternatives come into play as soon as you create a new message by clicking **New E-mail** on the ribbon.

NOTE

The Outlook 2010 new Message window has many of the features of the Microsoft Word 2010 window and provides many of the tools available in Word.

TIP

To gain more working space, you can minimize the size of the ribbon. To do this, click the **Minimize Ribbon** button on the right next to the Help icon, or double-click the active tab name. Either click **Minimize Ribbon** or double-click the active tab again to restore the size of the ribbon. You can also press **CTRL+F1** to toggle the size of the ribbon.

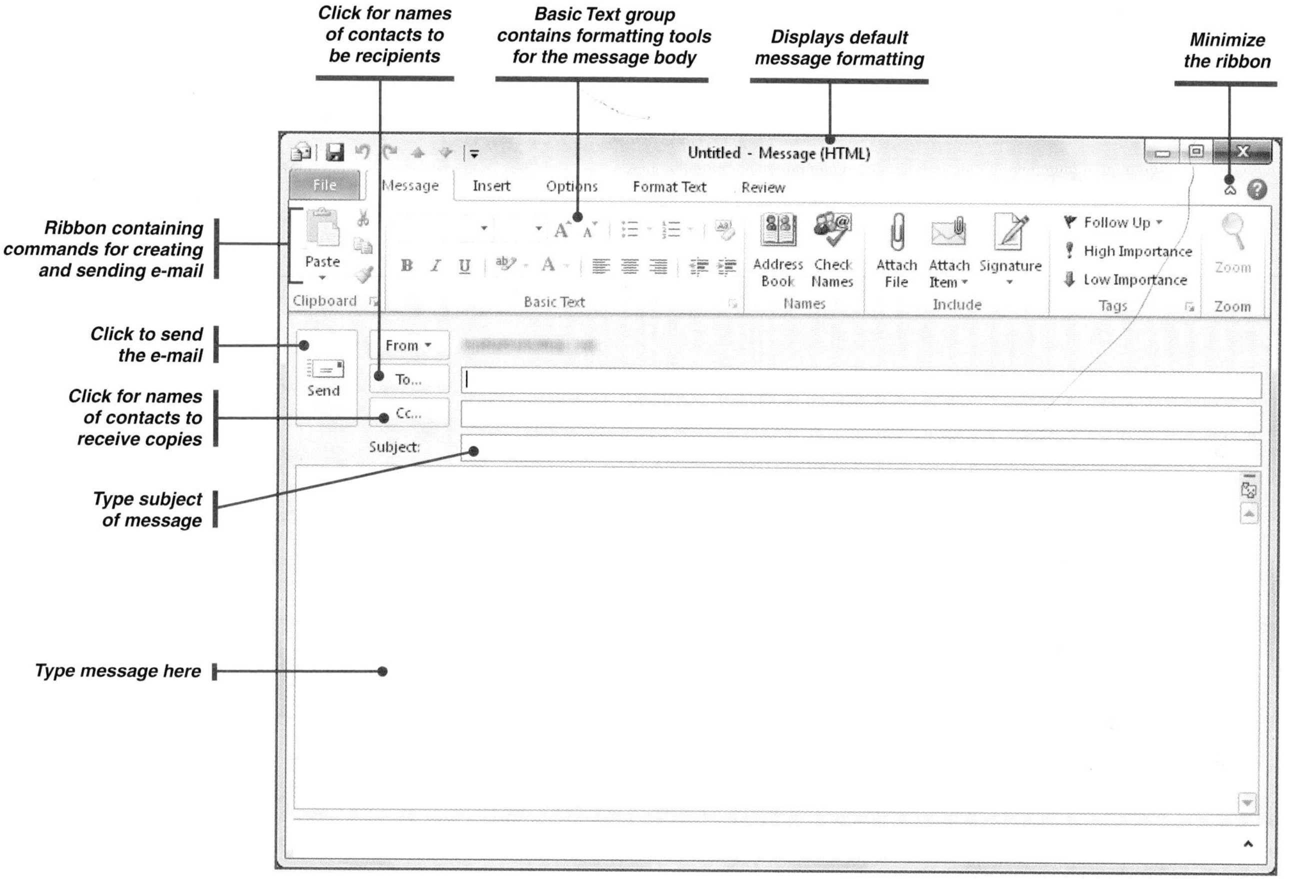

Click for names of contacts to be recipients

Basic Text group contains formatting tools for the message body

Displays default message formatting

Minimize the ribbon

Ribbon containing commands for creating and sending e-mail

Click to send the e-mail

Click for names of contacts to receive copies

Type subject of message

Type message here

Figure 3-1: The window for creating a message contains important differences from the one in which you read them.

TYPE THE ADDRESS

This is the most basic addressing technique. As soon as you click **New E-mail**, the cursor blinks in the To field on the message.

- For a **single recipient**, type the address.

- For **multiple recipients**, type each address, separating them with semicolons (;) and a space.

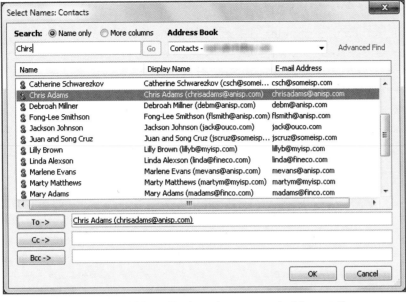

Figure 3-2: Your Outlook Address Book can become a valuable repository.

SELECT FROM THE ADDRESS BOOK

1. Click **To**. The Select Names dialog box displays your Address Book, shown in Figure 3-2.

2. Scroll through the list, and double-click the name you want.

3. For multiple names, if a comma or semicolon wasn't automatically added after a name you selected or entered, type one of those characters between names or e-mail addresses.

4. Repeat steps 2 and 3 as needed until all desired names are listed in the To text box. An alternate way is to hold down **CTRL** while you scroll manually and click all desired names. Then click **To**.

5. Click **OK**.

COMPLETE ADDRESSES AUTOMATICALLY

Outlook runs AutoComplete by default. As soon as you type the first letter of an address, Outlook begins searching for matches among names and addresses you've typed in the past.

1. Begin typing a name or address in the To field in the Message window. The closest names to what you have typed will be displayed in the Name list.

2. If the name you want appears in the list, click it, or press **DOWN ARROW** (if necessary) until the name is highlighted, and then click it or press **ENTER** to accept the address. The name displays, a semicolon follows it, and the cursor blinks where the next name will appear.

3. If you wish to add another recipient, begin typing another name, and repeat the process as needed.

4. Press **TAB** to go to the next desired field.

NOTE

You can turn off AutoComplete if you wish: Click the **File** tab, click **Options**, and click **Mail** in the left pane. Under Send Messages, clear the **Use Auto-Complete List To Suggest Names When Typing In The To, Cc, And Bcc Lines** check box. Click **OK** to close.

☐ Use Auto-Complete List to suggest names when typing in the To, Cc, and Bcc lines

Use a Contact Group

You can group your contacts into *contact groups* or distribution lists (see Chapter 4), giving you an even quicker way to add multiple addresses to messages. Use any of the preceding procedures to enter individuals in the Address Book, and enter or select the name of the contact group as it appears in the Address Book. After selecting the contact list, its name will have a plus sign next to it, which you can click to expand the contact list name and see the individuals in the list (you will be warned that once expanded, you can't contract it). When you send it, the message will go to everyone on the list.

| To... | ⊞ **Fineco**; |

Add Carbon and Blind Copies

You may never have seen a real carbon copy, but Outlook keeps the concept alive by way of this feature located just below the To field in the new Message window. Persons who receive a message with their e-mail address in the *Cc* (carbon copy) line understand that they are not the primary recipients—they got the message as an FYI (for your information), and all other recipients can see that they got it (see Figure 3-3). A *Bcc* (blind carbon copy) hides addresses entered in that line from anyone else who receives the message.

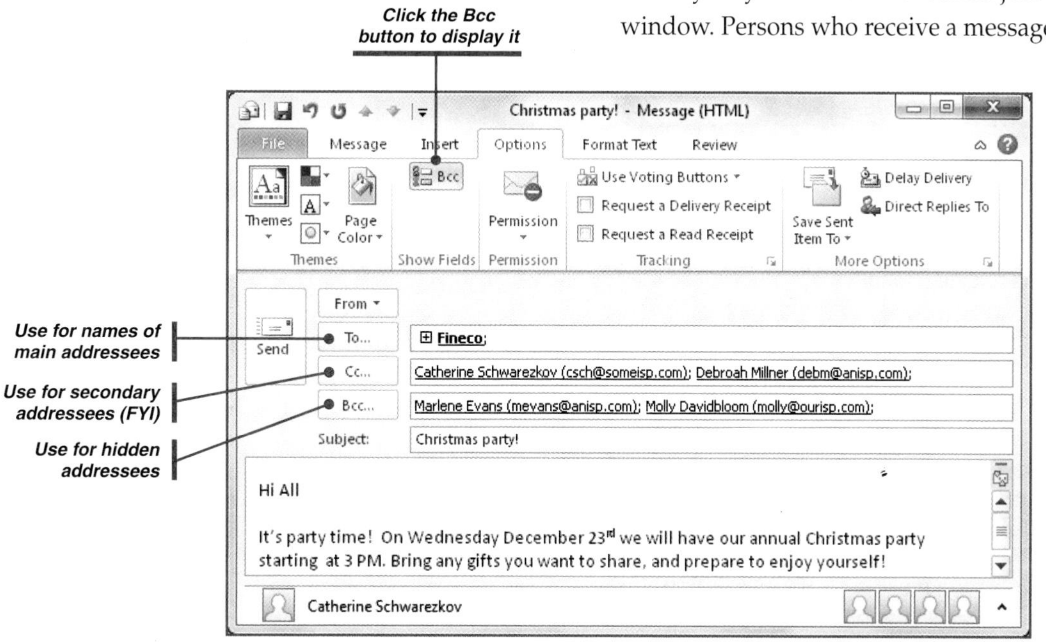

Click the Bcc button to display it

Use for names of main addressees

Use for secondary addressees (FYI)

Use for hidden addressees

Figure 3-3: The way a message is delivered suggests different roles for the various recipients.

INCLUDE OR REMOVE BCC ON NEW MESSAGES

1. In the Message window, click the **Options** tab.

2. In the Show Fields group, click **Bcc** to toggle the Bcc field on and off.

ADDRESS THE COPIES

Type addresses in the Cc and Bcc fields completely or with the aid of AutoComplete. You can also use the Address Book: click **Cc** or **Bcc** in the Message window, begin typing a name to scroll through the names, and double-click the name(s) in the Address Book you want to be copied.

Edit a Message

E-mail can be created in any of three formats and has the additional option of using the powerful formatting capability of Microsoft Word for composing messages. Outlook handles all three formats quite easily, but sometimes you need to consider your recipients' computer resources and Internet connections.

- **HTML** (HyperText Markup Language), the default format, lets you freely use design elements, such as colors, pictures, links, animations, sound, and movies (though good taste and the need to control the size of the message file might suggest a little discretion!).

- **Plain Text** format lies at the other extreme, eliminating embellishments so that any computer can manage the message.

- **Rich Text Format** (RTF) takes the middle ground, providing font choices—including color, boldface, italics, and underlining—basic paragraph layouts, and bullets.

With Outlook, you can edit messages you create as well as those you receive. Regardless which of the three formats you choose, some editing processes are always available, as shown in Table 3-1.

Using HTML or Rich Text Format provides a wide range of options for enhancing the appearance of a message. See the "Formatting Messages" QuickSteps for a rundown of additional formatting selections.

TO		DO THIS	
Insert new text in message body		Click where new text belongs, and type new text.	
Indent the start of a paragraph		Click before the first letter of the paragraph, and press **TAB**.	
Replace a	Word	Double-click the word.	Type new text.
	Line	Click to the left of the line.	
	Paragraph	Double-clicking to the left selects a paragraph. Triple-clicking to the left selects all the text in the message.	
Move a	Word	Double-click the word.	Drag to a new location in the message.
	Line	Click to the left of the line.	
	Paragraph	Double-click to the left of the paragraph.	
Delete a	Word	Double-click the word.	Press **DELETE**.
	Line	Click to the left of the line.	
	Paragraph	Double-click to left of the paragraph.	

Table 3-1: Standard Editing Operations

Finally, you can also create the message in another program and copy and paste it into a message body. HTML will preserve the formatting exactly, and Rich Text Format will come close.

SELECT A MESSAGE FORMAT

The type of message format being used is displayed in the title bar of the new Message window. You can either set a format for an individual message, or you can set a default for all message formats.

> Christmas party! - Message (HTML)

To set a default format for all e-mail:

1. In either the Outlook window or in a Message window, click the **File** tab, click **Options**, and click **Mail** in the left pane to open the Mail options, some of which are shown in Figure 3-4.

2. Click the **Compose Messages In This Format** down arrow, and select one of the choices.

3. Click **OK** to close the Options dialog box.

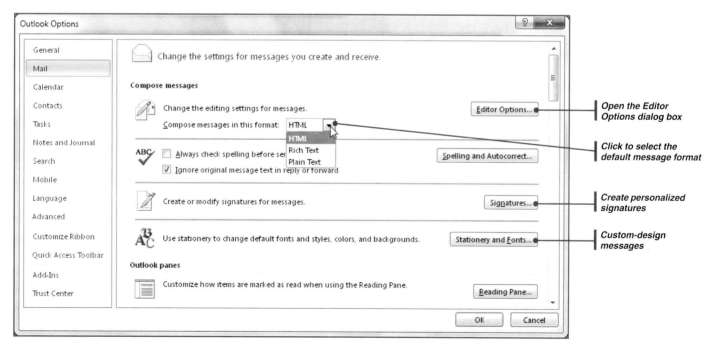

Figure 3-4: You can create personal message designs that distinguish you as the sender.

FORMATTING MESSAGES

To format text in the Message window, use the Format Text tab or the Message tab to access formatting commands. You can format text before you start typing, or you can select text and then format it after composing the message. See Table 3-1 for a list of selection methods.

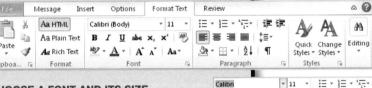

CHOOSE A FONT AND ITS SIZE

A font can immediately set the tone of your message.

● Select your text or paragraph.

● In either the Format Text tab Font group or the Message tab Basic Text group, click the **Font** down arrow, and move the pointer over several fonts and see how they affect your selected text. Select a font you want to use.

● Click the **Font Size** down arrow next to the font, and again move the pointer over several sizes and notice the effects. The default size is 11. Select a type size you want.

CREATE BOLD, ITALIC, UNDERLINED, AND STRIKETHROUGH

Select the text, and click the **Bold**, **Italic**, **Underline**, or **Strikethrough** effect in the Font group.

Continued . . .

To set formatting for an individual message:

1. In the Message window, click the **Format Text** tab.

2. In the Format group, click the formatting button you want.

Use Stationery

It's easy to choose stationery for a message. You can pick a different type of stationery for every new message or set a default style for all messages (until you change it).

SET A DEFAULT STATIONERY THEME

You can set a default for your stationery that will be used each time you write a new e-mail. You can also select a theme for your stationery and still have your own unique fonts. You can vary fonts as well, either for new e-mails or for those you reply to or forward. To set a default stationery:

1. Click the **File** tab, click **Options**, and click **Mail** in the left pane.

2. Make sure that **HTML** has been selected as the message format.

3. Click the **Stationery And Fonts** button. Click the **Personal Stationery** tab to open the dialog box shown in Figure 3-5. Select from these choices:

● Click the **Theme** button, and under Choose A Theme, click the theme you want, and click **OK**. When you choose a theme, the fonts will be automatically defined for you, and those buttons will become unavailable or grayed.

● If, after choosing a theme, you want to use another font, click the **Font** down arrow, and click either **Always Use My Fonts** or **Use My Font When Replying Or Forwarding Messages**. This will enable you to select a font for all new messages or for replying to and forwarding e-mails.

QUICKSTEPS

FORMATTING MESSAGES *(Continued)*

COLOR THE FONT

Select the text, click the **Font Color** down arrow, and select a color.

ALIGN PARAGRAPHS

Select the text and click an alignment, which, from left to right, provides a left-aligned margin, centered text, a right-aligned margin, or justified margins (where both the left and right margins end evenly).

CREATE NUMBERED, BULLETED, OR MULTILEVEL LISTS

Select the text to be affected, and click the **Bullets**, **Numbering**, or **Multilevel List** button (the latter is only in the Format Text tab Paragraph group).

SHIFT THE PARAGRAPH

The Decrease Indent and Increase Indent buttons move the selected paragraph in fixed increments. You can alternate clicking them until you are satisfied with the location. However, because they will not move the paragraph beyond the message margins, they have limited effect on centered paragraphs.

Click within a paragraph to be shifted, and click the appropriate button.

INSERT LINES OR BORDERS

Set off paragraphs with lines or borders.

1. Click where a line is desired (usually at the end of a paragraph), or select the paragraph(s) around which you want a border.

2. In the Format Text tab Paragraph group, click the **Borders** down arrow, and click the type of line or border that you want.

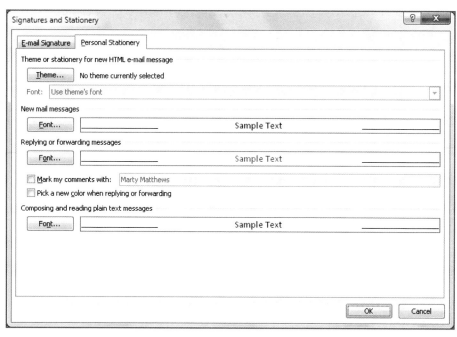

Figure 3-5: You can design custom stationery for your e-mail with your own theme, fonts, and colored replies and forwards.

- If you want to use your fonts, click the appropriate **Font** button, and select the font, font style, size, and color you want.

- If you want to insert your name, click the **Mark My Comments With** check box. Type over the default text, if desired.

- If you want your replies or forwards to be in a different color, click **Pick A New Color When Replying Or Forwarding**.

4. Click **OK** twice to close the Options dialog box.

APPLY STATIONERY TO A SINGLE MESSAGE

1. Click the **Insert** tab in the Outlook Message window, and click the **Signature** button in the Include group. Click **Signatures** on the menu. The Signature And Stationery dialog box appears.

2. Click the **Personal Stationery** tab.

3. Change the theme and fonts, as described in "Set a Default Stationery Theme."

4. Click **OK**.

TIP

You can also edit received messages when you forward them. This can be handy if you want to forward only the final comment and eliminate the original message text and other comments.

NOTE

If your Message window is not maximized, you may not see all available formatting buttons. In some cases, the commands will be available in menus. You can click the group down arrow to see the menu of commands, or click the **Maximize** button on the title bar to increase the size of the window.

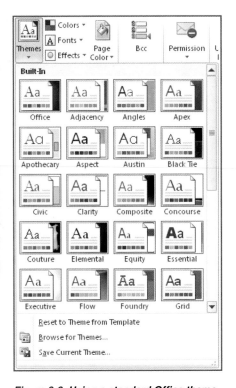

Figure 3-6: Using a standard Office theme allows you to coordinate your e-mail and regular Word correspondence.

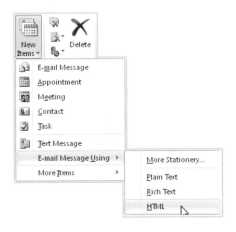

USE A STANDARD MICROSOFT OFFICE THEME

You can use a standard Microsoft Office theme in your e-mail that differs from the Outlook themes used for stationery. You might use these to coordinate your regular Word correspondence with your e-mail, thus creating a consistent and professional look. These themes are easy to use and available in your new Message window.

1. In the new Message window, click the **Options** tab if it is not already selected.

2. In the Themes group, if you can't see Colors, Fonts, and Effects, click **Themes**. Then, in any case, click the **Themes** down arrow, and click the standard theme you'd like to use for your e-mail, as shown in Figure 3-6.

   - Click **Colors** and click a combination of colors to change the color scheme.

   - Click **Fonts** and click a font style to change the fonts used.

   - Click **Effect** and click an effect to change the special effects of the graphics.

3. Type your new message and send it.

CHOOSE TO NOT USE STATIONERY

If you don't want to use your selected stationery for a single new message:

In the Outlook window Home tab New group, click **New Items**, click **E-Mail Message Using**, and select **HTML**. A new message will appear without your stationery.

To stop using stationery as a default:

1. In the Outlook window, click the **File** tab, click **Options**, and click **Mail** in the left pane.

2. Click the **Stationery And Fonts** button.

3. On the Personal Stationery tab, click **Theme** and click **(No Theme)** at the top of the theme list.

4. Click **OK** three times.

Attach Files

Sometimes you will want to send or receive a message that is accompanied by other files: pictures, word-processed documents, sound, or movie files. Creating attachments is like clipping newspaper stories and baby pictures to a letter. If you are editing or otherwise working on the item you want to attach, make sure that you save the latest version before you proceed. After that, click **New** to open the new Message window, and use one of the following attachment procedures.

DRAG A FILE TO A MESSAGE

Find the file to be attached by using My Computer or Windows Explorer, and drag it to the message.

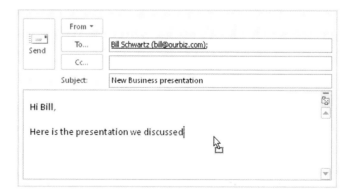

INSERT A FILE

When you attach a file to an e-mail message, it can either be attached as a file or entered as text into the body of the message. In some cases, it may be attached as a hyperlink. The attached file and its commands are identified with a paper clip icon.

1. To display the Insert File dialog box:

   ● Click the **Insert** tab, and then click **Attach File** in the Include group.

   –Or–

   ● In the Message tab, click the **Attach File** icon in the Include group.

2. The Insert File dialog box appears. Find and select the file to be attached. Then:

   ● Click **Insert** to insert the file as an attachment. If the e-mail format is HTML (HyperText Markup Language) or plain text, it will be attached in a field labeled "Attached" beneath the Subject field. If the format is Rich Text Format, the file attachment will be in the body of the message.

| Subject: | New Business presentation |
| Attached: | 📄 New Business Presentation.pptx (40 KB) |

Hi Bill,

Here is the presentation we discussed

New Business
Presentation.ppt...

Attachment identified for HTML or plain text format   ***Attachment identified for Rich Text Format***

   ● Click the **Insert** down arrow, and choose between inserting the file as an attachment and inserting it as text in the body of the message. If you choose **Insert As Text**, the file is entered as text in the message. The file content of certain file types, such as .txt, .doc, and .eml, and the source code of others, such as HTML or HTA (HTML Application), will become part of the message. Everything else—pictures, sound, and movies—will generate nonsense characters in the message body.

   ● Click **Insert As Hyperlink** to insert the selected file as a hyperlink. (This option is often not available from the Attach File command.)

   ● Click **Show Previous Versions** to list the previous versions of the files so that you can select the version you want to attach.

3. Complete and send the e-mail message.

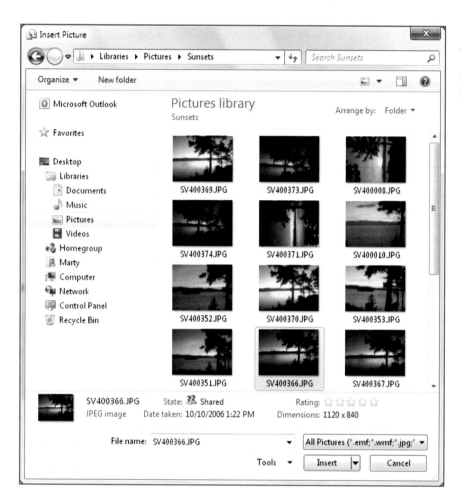

Figure 3-7: *You can insert a picture or a link to it using the Insert Picture dialog box.*

EMBED A PICTURE INTO A MESSAGE

Though any kind of file you save on your computer or on a disk can be sent by following the previous steps, you have the added option of placing pictures (.gif, .jpg, .bmp, .tif, and so on) right into the message body.

1. Click in the message body to set the insertion point.

2. Click the **Insert** tab, and click **Picture** in the Illustrations group. The Insert Picture dialog box appears, as shown in Figure 3-7.

3. Select the picture file you want, and click the **Insert** down arrow. From the submenu:

   - Click **Insert** to embed the picture in the message. You can then drag it to size it correctly for your message or right-click to display the Format Picture dialog box and edit the photo.

NOTE

If you link a picture to your message rather than embed it, you will need to either send the picture with the document or store the picture in a shared network folder available to the message recipient. Otherwise, your e-mail will be seen with a red X where the photo should be.

TIP

If you are on a Microsoft Exchange Server network, you can even insert voting options that the recipient has only to click for a response. To do this, create a message, click the **Options** tab, and click the **Use Voting Buttons** down arrow in the Tracking group. Select the kind of reply you need, or click **Custom** to type new options separated by semicolons (;) in the Use Voting Buttons text box.

NOTE

See Chapter 10 on how to create and use electronic business cards and insert them within a signature.

- Click **Link To File** to send a link to where the file is stored. This reduces the size of the message, but requires that the recipient have access to where the file is stored.
- Click **Insert And Link** to both embed the photo and send a link to its location.
- Click **Show Previous Versions** to list the previous versions of the files so that you can select the version you want to attach.

4. Complete and send the e-mail message.

Sign Messages

You can create closings, or signatures, for your e-mail messages. Outlook signatures can contain pictures and text along with your name. You can create signatures in different styles for the different kinds of messages you write: friendly, formal, or business.

CREATE A SIGNATURE

With Outlook open:

1. Click the **File** tab, and click **Options**. The Outlook Options window opens. Click **Mail** in the left pane.

2. Click **Signatures** in the right pane, and then click **New**.

3. Type a name for your signature, and click **OK**. This identifies the signature group that the signature serves. It will not be displayed on the message. The Signatures And Stationery dialog box appears with the E-mail Signature tab selected.

4. In the Edit Signature text box, type (or paste from another document) any text you want to include in your closing, including your name, as shown in Figure 3-8.

5. To apply formatting, select the text and click any of the formatting buttons in the toolbar. You can even insert a business card, picture, or hyperlink. Use the tips found earlier in the "Formatting Messages" QuickSteps. Plain text messages, by definition, cannot be formatted.

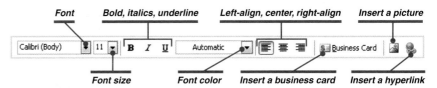

6. Click **OK** twice to close the dialog boxes.

QUICKSTEPS

USING SIGNATURES

You can use certain signatures for certain accounts, and you can still pick a different one for a particular message.

Click the **File** tab, click **Options**, and in the Outlook Options window, click **Mail** in the left pane.

ASSIGN SIGNATURES TO ACCOUNTS

1. Click the **Signatures** button, and then click the **E-mail Signature** tab.

2. Click the **E-mail Account** down arrow, and select an account.

3. Click the **New Messages** down arrow, and click the signature name to be used.

4. Click the **Replies/Forwards** down arrow, and click the signature name to be used.

5. Repeat steps 2–4 for each of your accounts, and then click **OK** twice.

INSERT A SIGNATURE IN A MESSAGE

Sometimes, you will want to replace a defined signature with another one or define a signature when you create a message.

1. Create an e-mail message.

2. Click in the body of the message where you want the special closing. Click the **Insert** tab, and click **Signature** in the Include group. Choose one of the following options:

Continued . . .

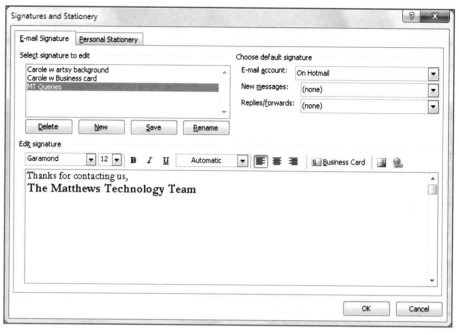

Figure 3-8: You can create one or more signatures with custom-designed characteristics that will be included in the bottom of your e-mail.

Use Digital Signatures

A *digital signature* certifies that everything contained in the message—documents, forms, computer code, training modules, whatever—originated with the sender. Computer programmers and people engaged in e-commerce use them a lot. To embed a formal digital signature, you need to acquire a *digital certificate*, which is like a license, from a certificate authority, such as VeriSign, GeoTrust, or GlobalSign.

Alternatively, you can create your own digital signature, although it is not administered by a certificate authority. A self-signed certificate is considered unauthenticated and will generate a security warning if the recipient has his or her security set at a high level.

QUICKSTEPS

USING SIGNATURES (Continued)

- Click the name of an existing signature, and it will be inserted in the message. If you already have a message that was inserted automatically, it will be replaced by the one you select.

- Click **Signatures**, and the Signatures And Stationery dialog box will appear. Create a new signature, as described in "Sign Messages." For the current message, once again click **Signature** in the Insert tab, and click the name of your new signature.

TIP

You can also do an Internet search on "Get a digital ID" and find other sources of digital IDs, some of which are free for an initial period.

Encrypted e-mail

- ☐ Encrypt contents and attachments for outgoing messages
- ☑ Add digital signature to outgoing messages
- ☑ Send clear text signed message when sending signed messages
- ☐ Request S/MIME receipt for all S/MIME signed messages

ACQUIRE A DIGITAL CERTIFICATE

If you do not already have a digital certificate, Outlook can lead you to a Web site where you can find a commercial certification authority to issue one. Make sure you are online before you begin.

1. Click the **File** tab, click **Options**, click **Trust Center**, and click **Trust Center Settings**. The Trust Center window opens. Click **E-mail Security** in the left pane.

2. Under Digital IDs (Certificates), click **Get A Digital ID**. A Microsoft Web page on digital IDs will open.

3. Follow the instructions on the page to select a vendor and obtain a certificate.

IMPORT OR EXPORT A DIGITAL ID

If you already have a digital ID in another application, you can import into Outlook or you can export your digital ID in Outlook so you can use it in another application.

1. Click the **File** tab, click **Options**, click **Trust Center**, and click **Trust Center Settings**. The Trust Center window opens. Click **E-mail Security** in the left pane.

2. Under Digital IDs (Certificates), click **Import/Export**. The Import/Export Digital ID dialog box appears.

3. Click **Import Existing Digital ID From A File** to import a digital ID, or click **Export Your Digital ID To A File** to export your own digital ID.

4. Fill in the requested information, and click OK three times.

ADD A DIGITAL SIGNATURE TO MESSAGES

1. Click the **File** tab, click **Options**, click **Trust Center**, and click **Trust Center Settings**. The Trust Center window opens.

2. Click the **E-mail Security** option.

3. Under Encrypted E-mail, click the **Add Digital Signature To Outgoing Messages** check box.

4. To make sure that recipients can read the message if they don't have Secure/Multipurpose Internet Mail Extensions (S/MIME) security, click the **Send Clear Text Signed Message When Sending Signed Messages** check box.

5. To receive a message confirming that your message got to the recipient, click the **Request S/MIME Receipt For All S/MIME Signed Messages** check box.

6. Click **OK** twice.

Check Spelling

Even though many abbreviations have emerged with e-mail, instant messaging, and texting, unintentional spelling errors still can be a problem. You can have Outlook check the spelling of your message when you finish, or you can have it automatically check messages as you are writing them.

CHECK A MESSAGE

Create a message and keep the cursor in the body when you are finished. Any spelling errors will be automatically flagged for you with a red wavy line. You will have these options:

- Right-click the flagged word, and if a correct spelling is suggested, click it.

- If you do not see the correct spelling, then the flagged word cannot be found in the dictionary. Either look it up in a reference source and type it in, or type another spelling to see if it is correct.

- If you know the flagged word is correct and you want to add it to the dictionary, right-click the word and click **Add To Dictionary**. Also, see "Add a Word to the Dictionary," next.

TIP

For exploring misspelled words, you will find a reference source by clicking **Research** in the Proofing group on the Review tab of the Message window.

ADD A WORD TO THE DICTIONARY

To add a flagged word to the dictionary so that it will not continue to be flagged as a potential misspelling:

1. Highlight the flagged word, and click **Spelling & Grammar** in the Proofing group of the Review tab. The Spelling And Grammar dialog box will appear, as seen in Figure 3-9.

2. Click **Add To Dictionary**.

3. Click **Close**.

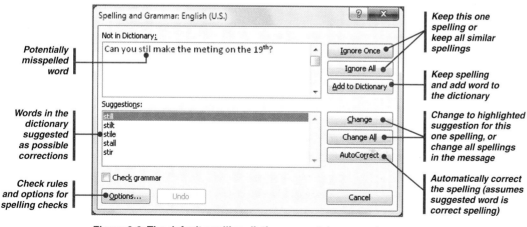

Figure 3-9: The default spelling dictionary contains everyday words rather than technical or scientific terms. You can add special words to it.

Potentially misspelled word

Words in the dictionary suggested as possible corrections

Check rules and options for spelling checks

Keep this one spelling or keep all similar spellings

Keep spelling and add word to the dictionary

Change to highlighted suggestion for this one spelling, or change all spellings in the message

Automatically correct the spelling (assumes suggested word is correct spelling)

CHECK MESSAGES BEFORE SENDING

To automatically check spelling in messages before sending them:

1. Click the **File** tab, and click **Options**. The Outlook Options window opens. Click **Mail** in the left pane.

2. Click **Always Check Spelling Before Sending**, and click **OK**.

Send Messages

No extra postage, no trip to the post office, no running out of envelopes. What could be better? Once a message is ready to go, you can just click a button. Outlook provides features that let you exercise more control over the process than you could ever get from the postal service, or "snail" mail.

Make sure that your message is complete and ready to send, and then click **Send** on the upper-left area of the message.

When you have more than one account, your Message window contains a From button that is not available otherwise. To send a message from a particular account:

Click **From** above the To button in the Message window, select an account, and click Send.

Reply to Messages

When you receive a message that you want to answer, you have three ways to initiate a reply:

- Open the message and click **Reply** in the Respond group on the Message tab.

  –Or–

- Right-click the message in the Folder pane, and select **Reply** from the context menu.

  –Or–

- Click the message in the Folder pane, and click **Reply** in the Home tab's Respond group.

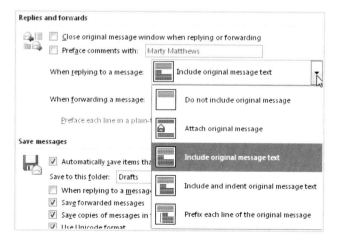

Figure 3-10: The Reply window uses the sender's message format and subject to make the e-mail conversation easy to track and respond to.

Whichever way you choose, a reply Message window opens, as shown in Figure 3-10. The message will be formatted using the same format the sender used, and the subject will be "RE:" plus the original subject in the Subject line. By default, the pointer blinks in the message body above the original message and sender's address (see also "Change the Reply Layout" below). Treat it like a new Message window: type a message, add attachments or links, and click **Send**.

REPLY TO ALL RECIPIENTS

If the To field in the message contains several recipients, all of whom should read your reply, Outlook makes it simple. Using any of the three ways just listed, select **Reply All**. The reply Message window will list all original recipients in the To and Cc fields. Send the message as usual.

CHANGE THE REPLY LAYOUT

You can select from five different ways to incorporate the original message. Also, if you'd rather just insert your responses into the original text, Outlook lets you decide how to identify your remarks.

1. Click the **File** tab, click **Options**, and click **Mail** in the left pane.

2. Beneath Replies And Forwards, click the **When Replying To A Message** down arrow, and select how you want the original message included.

3. Click the **Preface Comments With** check box, and type the label you want.

4. Click **OK**.

Forward Messages

When you forward a message, you send an incoming message to someone else. You can send messages to new recipients, using the same techniques as with the Reply feature.

When you receive a message that you want to forward to someone else, use one of these techniques:

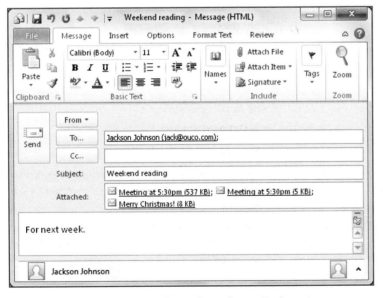

- Open the message and click **Forward** in the Respond group on the Message tab.

  –Or–

- Right-click the message in the Folder pane, and select **Forward** from the context menu.

  –Or–

- Click the message in the Folder pane, and click **Forward** on the Home group.

A Forward Message window opens, with the cursor blinking in the To field and a space above the original message for you to type your own. Once the Forward Message window opens, the simplest action is to enter the recipient(s) address(es), insert attachments as needed, and send as usual.

FORWARD MULTIPLE MESSAGES

Rather than forward a bunch of messages one by one, you can bundle them and forward them in one message.

1. Press **CTRL** while you click each message in the message list that you want to forward.

2. Right-click one of the messages in the group, and click **Forward**. A new mail message opens with the messages included as attachments, as seen in Figure 3-11. You may also see the attachments in the Attached box rather than in the message area.

3. Complete the message and send as usual.

Figure 3-11: You can group and forward e-mails as attachments.

Set Message Priority

If your recipient gets a lot of messages, you might want to identify your message as important so that it will stand out in his or her Inbox. Outlook includes a red exclamation point in the message list to call attention to messages set with high importance and a blue down arrow to indicate messages with low importance. In the Message window, you flag your e-mail messages with the appropriate flag.

1. Create a message. In the Options group on the Message tab, select one of these options:

   - Click **High Importance** to insert a red exclamation point to indicate high importance.

   - Click **Low Importance** to insert a blue down arrow to indicate low importance.

2. Send the message as usual.

Request Receipts

Anyone who has sent an important message and has not heard a peep from the recipient can appreciate receipts. When the addressee receives or reads the message, you are notified. You can request receipts for all your messages or on a message-by-message basis.

OBTAIN RECEIPTS FOR ALL MESSAGES

1. Click the **File** tab, click **Options**, and click **Mail** in the left pane.

2. In the Outlook Options window, scroll down to **Tracking**.

3. To request a receipt, click **Read Receipt Confirming The Recipient Viewed The Message, Delivery Receipt Confirming The Message Was Delivered To The Recipient's E-mail Server**, or both.

4. If you like, choose an option for responding to other senders' requests for a receipt—**Always Send A Read Receipt, Never Send A Read Receipt, or Ask Me Each Time** (the default).

5. Click **OK** three times.

Tracking

Delivery and read receipts help provide confirmation that messages were successfully received. Not all e-mail servers and applications support sending receipts.
For all messages sent, request:

☐ Delivery receipt confirming the message was delivered to the recipient's e-mail server
☐ Read receipt confirming the recipient viewed the message

For any message received that includes a read receipt request:

○ Always send a read receipt
○ Never send a read receipt
◉ Ask each time whether to send a read receipt

☑ Automatically process meeting requests and responses to meeting requests and polls
☑ Automatically update original sent item with receipt information
☐ Update tracking information, and then delete responses that don't contain comments
☐ After updating tracking information, move receipt to: [Deleted Items] [Browse...]

SENDING MESSAGES

You can fire off your messages now or later or on a schedule.

SEND MESSAGES MANUALLY

By default, as long as you are connected to the Internet, clicking **Send** in the Message window sends the completed message. You can turn this off so that clicking Send in the Message window only puts the message in the Outbox folder. You must then click **Send/Receive** in the Outlook standard toolbar to send all the messages in the Outbox folder.

TURN OFF AUTO-SEND

To prevent a message from being automatically sent unless you click Send in the Message window:

1. Click the **File** tab, click **Options**, and click **Advanced** in the left pane.

2. Under Send And Receive, clear the **Send Immediately When Connected** check box.

3. Click **Send/Receive**. Under Settings For Group "All Accounts," clear the **Schedule An Automatic Send/Receive Every** check box. Also clear the **Perform An Automatic Send/Receive When Exiting** check box.

4. Click **Close** and then click **OK**.

SEND MESSAGES AT A CERTAIN TIME

1. Create the message and click the **Options** tab.

2. Click the **Delay Delivery** button in the More Options group. The Message Options dialog box appears.

Continued . . .

OBTAIN A SINGLE RECEIPT

1. Create a message and click the **Options** tab in the Message window.

2. In the Tracking group, click **Request A Delivery Receipt**, **Request A Read Receipt**, or both. (If you have set these options for all mail, this message will reflect those settings.)

Delay Delivery with a Rule

You can create a rule to control when messages leave your system after you click Send.

1. In the Outlook window Home tab Move group, click **Rules**, and click **Manage Rules & Alerts**.

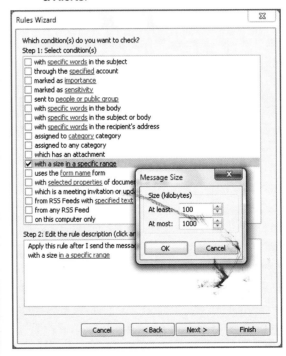

Figure 3-12: Outlook's rule-making feature has a large number of conditions that you can organize into rules.

2. If you are told that messages sent and received with HTTP (such as Hotmail, Gmail, and Yahoo!) cannot be filtered using rules and alerts, click **OK**.

3. In the Rules And Alerts dialog box, click **New Rule**.

4. In the Rules Wizard, under Start From A Blank Rule, click **Apply Rule On Messages I Send**, and click **Next**.

5. Click to select any desired conditions that limit which messages the rule applies to, and then click the link in the description pane (shown in Figure 3-12), which may display a dialog box to specify the exact criteria. Complete the dialog box, click **OK**, and click **Next**.

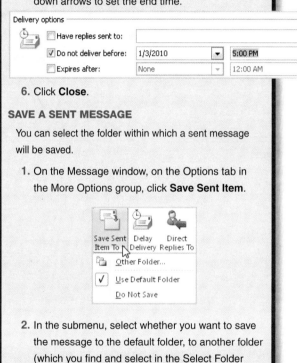
SENDING MESSAGES *(Continued)*

3. Under Delivery Options, click **Do Not Deliver Before**.

4. Click the date and time down arrows, and select a day and time.

5. Click **Expires After** and click the date and time down arrows to set the end time.

Delivery options		
☐ Have replies sent to:		
☑ Do not deliver before:	1/3/2010 ▼	5:00 PM ▼
☐ Expires after:	None ▼	12:00 AM ▼

6. Click **Close**.

SAVE A SENT MESSAGE

You can select the folder within which a sent message will be saved.

1. On the Message window, on the Options tab in the More Options group, click **Save Sent Item**.

```
Save Sent    Delay    Direct
Item To   Delivery  Replies To
☐  Other Folder...
✓  Use Default Folder
   Do Not Save
```

2. In the submenu, select whether you want to save the message to the default folder, to another folder (which you find and select in the Select Folder dialog box), or to not save the message at all.

6. Under Select Action(s), click **Defer Delivery By A *number* Of Minutes**.

7. In the description pane, click the link for *a number of* minutes, and in the Deferred Delivery dialog box, type the total minutes (up to 120) that you want messages delayed, click **OK**, and click **Next**.

8. Click any exceptions, specify them in the description pane, click **OK** if necessary, and click **Next**.

9. Type a name for the rule, and click **Finish**. You are returned to the Rules And Alerts dialog box, which will now show your new rule, as you can see in Figure 3-13.

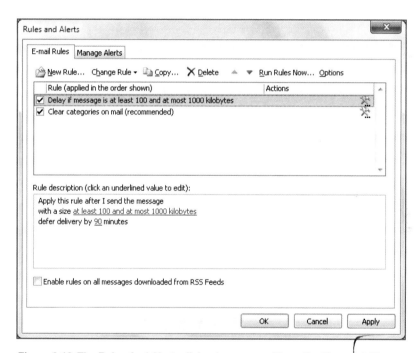

Figure 3-13: The Rules And Alerts dialog box, opened from the Home tab Move group, provides for the creation and management of rules.

Chapter 4
Managing Contacts

Taking a moment to create contacts can save you from typing—and later correcting—the whole e-mail address every time you send a message. Once you've entered a name as a contact, you can add business or personal information—like phone numbers, addresses, or an important anniversary—at your convenience. In this chapter, you will learn how to create and maintain your contacts, as well as different ways to use contact information.

Create Contacts

The kind of address books that fit in your pocket have spaces so tiny that you're forced to write phone numbers trailing down the margins. Often, entries get scratched out and replaced because people move. Other listings are almost unreadable because family members now have multiple phone numbers.

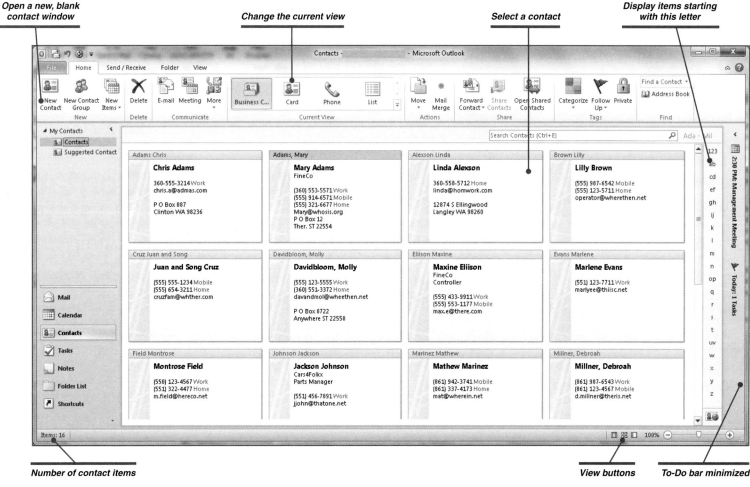

Open a new, blank contact window

Change the current view

Select a contact

Display items starting with this letter

Number of contact items

View buttons

To-Do bar minimized

Figure 4-1: The Contacts window, where you manage your contacts, displays current contact information for viewing, editing, or adding new ones.

Outlook Contacts provides a satisfying alternative, helping you keep everything straight and up-to-date, even information for acquaintances who don't have e-mail. You can create a new contact from within Outlook, from an e-mail message, from an electronic business card, and even from a public folder. Figure 4-1 shows an example of a list of contacts.

A name is all you need to save a contact. The New Contact window, shown in Figure 4-2, however, also provides a flexible layout that can store an immense amount of information, which you can use later for professional

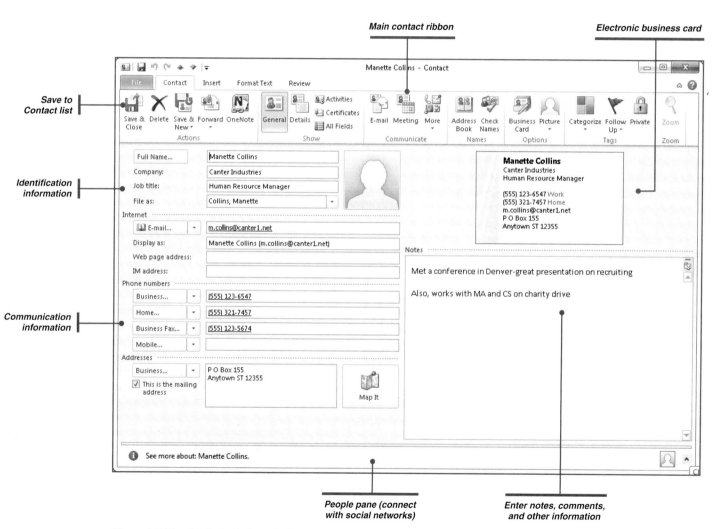

Figure 4-2: The Contact window displays fields into which you can enter information for reaching a contact in a variety of ways.

and social purposes. The ribbon provides for data entry and control in five different groups:

- **Actions** provide file management commands, including Save & Close, Delete, and Save & New. Click the **Save & New** down arrow, and click **Contact From The Same Company** to quickly add a new contact from the same company as the last entry you made. You can also forward the contact information to a third party or to OneNote.

- **Show** commands include all information about your new contact:

  - **General** contains basic information for identifying and getting in touch with the person (shown in Figure 4-2).

  - **Details** provides business and personal data.

  - **Activities**, a search tool, lists Outlook items (e-mail messages, notes, tasks, and so on) associated with the person.

  - **Certificates** imports and maintains a contact's digital ID. (See Chapter 3 for an explanation of digital certificates.)

  - **All Fields** lets you quickly look up the contents of a variety of fields completed for that contact.

- **Communicate** commands give you tools to send an e-mail message to the new contact, set up a meeting, send an instant message, telephone your new contact, connect to the contact's Web site, assign him or her to a task, create a journal entry about him or her, or see a map based on the contact's address.

- **Names** commands let you display the entire Address Book as well as verify names and e-mail addresses to ensure you have typed the information correctly.

- **Options** commands allow you to add or modify the contact's electronic business card and add a picture to your Contact dialog box.

- **Tags** commands let you categorize your contact with any one of six categories that you can customize, create follow-up flags and reminders for this contact, and mark an item as private.

- The **Zoom** command lets you zoom in on the data in the Notes section of your contact.

Add a New Contact

To add a new contact to Outlook 2010:

1. Open Outlook and choose **Contacts** from the Outlook View, if it is not already selected.

> **NOTE**
>
> There is a significant distinction between the "Contacts window" (plural) that lists the people in a Contacts list (shown in Figure 4-1) and the "Contact window" (singular) where you enter and edit a contact (shown in Figure 4-2).

Mail
Calendar
Contacts
Tasks
Notes
Folder List
Shortcuts

2. On the Contacts Home tab, click **New Contact**.

–Or–

Press **CTRL+N**.

–Or–

From anywhere in Outlook, press **CTRL+SHIFT+C**.

In any case, the Contact window opens.

3. If you don't see the Contact window shown in Figure 4-2, in the Contact tab Show group, click **General**. This opens a number of fields that allow you to enter basic contact information. Use the **TAB** key to move through the fields, or click in the desired fields.

   a. Full Name   Click the button to enter separate fields for title, first, middle, and last name; or type a full name in the text box. This is all that is required to create a contact.

   b. Company   Type the name of the company or organization with which the person is affiliated.

   c. Job Title   Type any title that you need to remember.

   d. File As   Click the down arrow beside the text box to select the combination of name and company that will dictate its place in the Contacts window. You need to enter the name and company first before you can access this information.

   e. Internet fields allow you to enter:

      i. E-mail   Click the down arrow to select up to three e-mail addresses to be associated with the person. For each one, type an address in the text box.

      ii. Display As   Press **TAB** or drag to select the default display, and, if desired, type a new name. This is the field that determines how the person's name will appear in the To field in an e-mail message.

      iii. Web Page Address   Type the person's URL.

      iv. IM Address   Type the Internet mail address that the person uses for instant messaging.

   f. Phone Numbers   Click the down arrow beside each button to select among 19 number types, and then click the label button to enter detailed information about it; or type the number in the text box.

   g. Addresses   Click the down arrow beside the button to select among three types of addresses, and then click in the text box to enter detailed information; or type the address in the text box. If you have more than one address for a contact, click **This Is The Mailing Address** to specify the address to be used for mail.

   h. Notes   Type any comments or notes in the large text box.

TIP

A quick way to create an e-mail message from the Contacts window is to right-click the contact, select **Create**, and click **E-mail**.

4. In the Contact tab Show group, click **Details** to display the Detail fields.

a. **Specific Office Information**   Complete the text fields as needed, such as department, manager's name, etc.

b. **Personal Information**   Type information such as the person's nickname, spouse's name, and birthday, selecting from drop-down date boxes, as appropriate.

c. **Internet Free-Busy**   Type an Internet address (Uniform Resource Locator, or URL) that has information about the person's schedule availability.

5. In the Contact tab Show group, click **Activities**, click the **Show** down arrow, and select an area from which to list items related to the person. The search can take quite a while before producing a list.

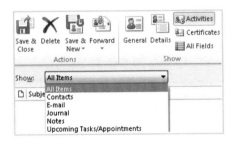

6. In the Contact tab Show group, click **Certificates**, and click **Import** to browse for the person's digital certificate. (See Chapter 3 for information about digital certificates.) Click a certificate in the list, and click **Properties** to review details. Click **Set As Default** to use the selected certificate by default.

7. In the Contact tab Show group, click **All Fields**, select a type of field from the drop-down list, and review the contents of the associated fields.

8. In the Contact tab Actions group, click **Save & Close** when finished. If you need to enter another contact, click **Save & New** to open a new Contact window.

ADD A CONTACT FROM THE SAME COMPANY

If you already have a contact for someone in a company and you want to add another, Outlook helps you out by filling in the company information.

1. Open an existing contact from the company.

2. In the Contact tab Actions group, click the **Save & New** down arrow. Click **Contact From Same Company**. A new Contact window opens with the company data displayed.

3. Fill in any other information, save the contact, and close the window.

Copy Contacts from E-mail

When you copy an address in the From or Cc e-mail message fields, the Contact window opens with the name and e-mail address fields filled in.

1. Open an e-mail message you have received.
2. Right-click the name in the message window, and click **Add To Outlook Contacts**. Fill in any additional information you want.
3. Click **Save & Close**. The name and e-mail address are added to your contacts.

CREATE CONTACTS BY DRAGGING

Any Outlook item, like an e-mail message, turns into a contact if you drag it onto the Contacts view bar in Outlook View. This is especially useful with important e-mail messages whose senders you need in your contacts. The name and e-mail address go into their respective fields, and the important message displays in the Contact window Notes text box. The New Contact window opens in back of the Mail window, and when it is saved, it closes automatically.

CREATE A CONTACT FROM AN ELECTRONIC BUSINESS CARD

Electronic business cards pack contact information into a small, easy-to-share package. If another Outlook user sends you an electronic business card attached to an e-mail message, you can automatically create a new contact when you save the message.

1. Open the e-mail message.
2. Double-click the electronic business card attachment (it should be a .vcf file). You might see a warning about only opening trustworthy attachments. If so, click **Open** if this is a business card you trust.
3. The Add A Contact dialog box appears. You may modify the information. To save the contact, click **Add Contact**. If you do not want to save the information, click **Cancel**.

Create a Contact Group

Avoid entering the address for each member of an organization to which you send messages. Instead, create and name a contract group for the organization,

UICKSTEPS

EDITING CONTACTS

Once you have created a contact, you can change the information as much as you want. Just open the contact and change or enter new information. The following tasks all begin with an open Contact window and end with clicking **Save & Close**.

ADD A PICTURE

To insert an image into your electronic business card:

1. In the Contact tab Options group, click **Business Card** to open the Edit Business Card dialog box.
2. Click **Change** in the Image field.
3. Locate the photo file on your computer, and double-click the image to select it.
4. Click **OK**.

Continued . . .

UICKSTEPS

EDITING CONTACTS *(Continued)*

ADD A FILE

To place a copy of a photo, document, spreadsheet, or any other kind of file in the contact:

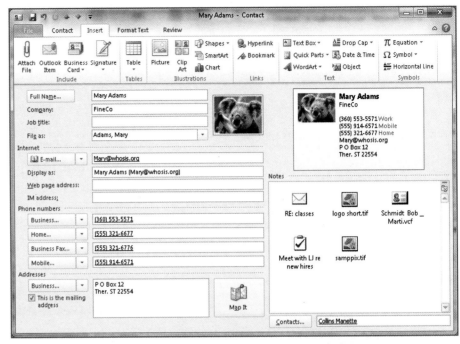

Figure 4-3: Attach any type of file in your Contact window for easy reference.

1. From the Contact window's Insert tab Include group, click **Attach File**. The Insert File dialog box will appear.

2. Select the file you want to attach by double-clicking the file name. A link to the file is displayed in the Notes section, as shown in Figure 4-3.

3. Double-click the file to open it.

4. Reopen the Contact tab to save and close the contact.

ADD AN ITEM

You can place a copy of an Outlook item (e-mail message, task, appointment, and so on) in the contact.

1. Open the contact and in the Insert tab Include group, click **Outlook Item**. The Insert Item dialog box appears.

2. Select the item you want to include with your contact. You may insert the item as:

   - Text only
   - An attachment
   - A shortcut to the item

3. When you are done, click **OK**.

TIP

To select more than one name at the same time, in the Add Members dialog box, hold down the **CTRL** key as you click each name you want to include.

as shown in Figure 4-4. It will appear as an entry of its own in your Contacts list, so sending a message to the group will send a message to each member. Review Chapter 3 to see how to send e-mail messages using a contact group.

1. From the Contacts window, in the Home tab, select **New Contact Group**. The Contact Group window opens.

2. Type a name for the group in the Name text box. In the ribbon's Contact Group tab Members group, click **Add Members** to choose the location of the members you want to include.

3. Click **From Outlook Contacts** or **Address Book** to choose names.

4. Click **New E-mail Contact** to enter a name and e-mail address. The Add New Member dialog box appears.

   - Click **Add To Contacts** if you want to include the name in your regular Contacts list.
   - Clear the **Add To Contacts** check box if you only want this name included with this contact group.

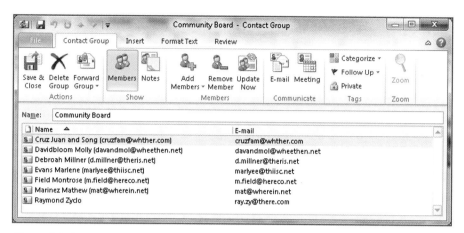

Figure 4-4: Contact groups make it easy to send a message to every member of your organization.

• Click **OK** to close the Add New Member dialog box.

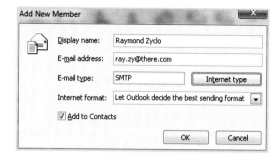

5. You may add notes to your group. In the Contact Group tab Show group, click **Notes** to display the Notes window. Type any notes that pertain to this contact group.

6. In the Contact Group tab Actions group, click **Save & Close** to save your new list.

Remove a Name from a Contact Group

You can count on change affecting the people in your list. To keep your messages going to the right places, you can add or remove members and update current information directly from your contacts.

1. To remove a name, open the Contact window, and locate the contact group. Double-click the list to open it.

2. In the Contact Group tab Show group, click **Members** to display the list of members, if it isn't already displayed.

3. Click the member name you want to remove. In the Members group, click **Remove Member**. The name is removed from your contact group. This does not remove the name from your Contacts list, only from the contact group.

4. In the Actions group, click **Save & Close** to save your changes.

TIP

When you send e-mail to a contact group, you don't have to let the members see who's on it—enter the name of the list into the Bcc field. To display the Bcc field from the e-mail message window, in the Options tab Show Fields group, select **Bcc**.

NOTE

You can create a new contact group from anywhere in Outlook 2010. Press **CTRL+SHIFT+L** to open a new Contact Group window.

Use Contacts

Once you enter a contact, you can do a lot with it besides fill in e-mail addresses quickly and accurately—though that alone makes it worth far more than any effort involved. You can share contact information, sort contacts, flag them for future action, use an automated telephone dialer built into the contact, and even create a Postal Service letter using the contact.

Add Contacts to E-mail

The information you have for a contact may be useful to someone else. Whether it's a business associate or a relative, sharing the information by way of e-mail prevents typos, copying errors, and tedium. You can send the contact as an item—both in text and as an attachment—or as an electronic business card, which you can send to other Outlook users, or you can send a vCard (.vcf file) to those who don't use Outlook. No matter how you send it, the recipient treats the contact like any other attached file.

ADD A CONTACT TO E-MAIL

You can include an Outlook contact as an attachment to an e-mail message, as plain text, or as an electronic business card.

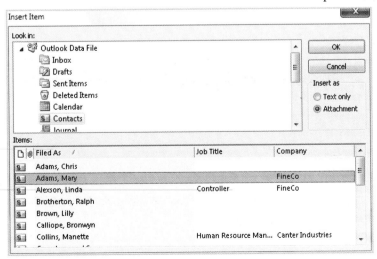

To include a contact with your e-mail as an attachment or as plain text:

1. In the e-mail message window, in the Message tab Include group, click the **Attach Item** down arrow. A menu is displayed.

2. Click **Outlook Item**. The Insert Item dialog box will appear.

3. Under Look In, click **Contacts** and under Items, select the contact you want to include.

4. Click **Attachment** to send the information as an attachment.

   –Or–

   Click **Text Only** to send the information as plain text. All of the contact's information will appear in the body of the e-mail message.

5. Click **OK** to close the Insert Item dialog box.

To include a contact as an electronic business card:

1. In the e-mail message window, in the Insert tab Include group, click **Attach Item.**

2. From the drop-down menu, click **Business Card**.

3. Click **Other Business Cards** to display the Insert Business Card dialog box.

4. Click the contact name you want to include. The electronic business card will appear in the body of the e-mail message as seen in Figure 4-5.

5. Click **OK** to close the dialog box.

If you choose to send your contact as an electronic business card, the way your e-mail recipient sees it depends on his or her computer system.

● If your recipient uses Outlook 2010, she will see the card exactly as you see it, with all of its graphics and color. She may save the information on the card by right-clicking it and saving it to her Contacts list.

● If the recipient uses an e-mail application that views e-mail as HTML (HyperText Markup Language), he will see the electronic business card as an image. The same recipient receives the information in the form of a .vcf file that is attached to the e-mail. He can save the contact information to his Address Book from that .vcf file.

● If the recipient uses a plain-text e-mail viewer, she will not see the graphic electronic business card. Instead, the recipient will receive an attached .vcf file from which the information can be saved.

Figure 4-5: You can insert any business card in your Contacts list into an e-mail message.

SEND A CONTACT GROUP

You can send a contact group through e-mail.

1. Open the Contacts window, and locate and select the contact group you want to send.

2. Press **CTRL+F**. This opens an e-mail message window. The contact group appears as an attachment.

3. Create and send the message as usual.

Arrange Contacts

You probably create contacts for different reasons, to serve various purposes, with some more important than others. Therefore, Outlook provides different ways for you to organize and look at them.

NOTE

Chapter 10 has a discussion about creating and using electronic business cards.

NOTE

You can select multiple contacts using the keyboard and mouse. Hold down **CTRL** while you click all desired contacts. Or hold down **SHIFT** while you click the first contact in a sequence, and then click the last contact.

QUICKSTEPS

WORKING WITH COLOR CATEGORIES

Outlook 2010 color categories give you a way to organize your contacts and other items. You can assign a color category not just to a contact, but also to e-mail messages, calendar items, and so forth. There are 25 colors you can use to designate a category, including the 6 standard colors that are displayed. Only the 10 most recently viewed color categories are displayed on the Categorize menu, but you can see the rest by clicking **All Categories** in the Categorize menu.

CREATE A NEW COLOR CATEGORY

To create a new color category:

1. In the Contacts ribbon Home tab Tags group, click **Categories.**

2. Click **All Categories** to display the Color Categories dialog box.

3. Click **New**. The Add New Category dialog box appears.

    a. Enter the name you want for this category.

    b. Click the **Color** down arrow, and click a color from the palette. You can use any of the 25 colors.

    c. Click the **Shortcut Key** down arrow, and click a keyboard shortcut. You have 11 choices of keyboard shortcut keys.

    d. Choose one of the keyboard shortcuts displayed, or leave the default selection (None).

    e. Click **OK** to complete the process and close the Color Categories dialog box.

Continued . . .

CATEGORIZE YOUR CONTACT GROUP

If you use color categories to organize Outlook 2010, you can easily assign one or more to your contact group. See the "Working with Color Categories" QuickSteps for further information.

1. To assign one color category to your contact group, open the Contacts window, and locate the contact group. Double-click the list to open it.

2. In the Contact Group tab Tags group, click **Categorize** to display the Categorize menu.

3. Click the category you want. The category is displayed above the name of your contact group. The menu closes automatically.

4. To assign more than one color category, follow steps 1–3, except click **All Categories** at the bottom of the Categorize menu. The Color Categories dialog box appears.

5. Click the check boxes for the categories you want.

6. Click **OK** to close the dialog box and return to your contact group. All of the color categories you chose appear above the name of your contact group.

7. In the Contact group tab Actions group, click **Save & Close** to close the Contact group window.

CATEGORIZE MULTIPLE CONTACTS

After you have created a number of contacts, you might want to group them into their respective categories.

1. In the Contacts window, select the contacts you wish to place in a specific category.

2. Right-click any of the selected contacts to open a menu.

3. Click **Categorize** and select the color category into which you want them grouped.

4. The menu closes automatically, and the color category is added to your contact grouping.

QUICKSTEPS

WORKING WITH COLOR CATEGORIES *(Continued)*

RENAME A COLOR CATEGORY

To rename an existing color category:

1. Open the Color Categories dialog box, as described in the previous section, or by clicking **Categorize** on the ribbon and clicking **All Categories.**

2. Select the category and click **Rename**.

3. Type a new name for this category in the text box that is now selected.

4. Press **ENTER** to complete the process.

5. Click **OK** to close the Color Categories dialog box.

DELETE A COLOR CATEGORY

To delete an existing color category:

1. Open the Color Categories dialog box in either of the two ways described previously.

2. Select the category and click **Delete.**

3. A warning message will appear, informing you that deleting the category removes it from your list but does not affect previously categorized items.

4. Click **Yes** to delete the category, or click **No** to leave it on the list.

CHANGE THE VIEW OF CONTACTS

Just as you can select and customize the view of other parts of Outlook, you can choose from four standard views of the Contacts window, and you can change the view to suit your needs.

- **Business Cards** shows the electronic business cards for each contact.

- **Cards** shows names, e-mail addresses, phone numbers, mailing addresses, and notes for the contact.

- **Phone List** gives each contact one line in a table, with telephone and fax numbers displayed, as seen in Figure 4-6.

- **List** displays each contact on one line in the same manner as Phone List. However, the contact's e-mail address is displayed first.

Manage Your Contact Views

It's easy to try the various views to find which one works best for you and then to customize that view.

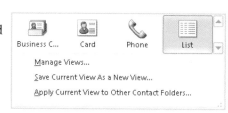

1. From the Contacts window Home tab, click the **More** button on the lower-right area of the Current View group.

		Full Name	Company	File As ▲	Business Phone	Business Fax	Home Phone	Mobile Phone	E-mail	Journal	Categories	
		Click here to add a new ...										
										☐		
		Chris Adams		Adams Chris	360-555-3214	360-555-1438			chris.a@admas.com	☐		
		Mary Adams	FineCo	Adams, Mary	(360) 553-5571	(555) 321-6776	(555) 321-6677	(555) 914-6571	Mary@whosis.org	☐		
		Linda Alexson		Alexson Linda			360-558-5712		linda@homwork.com	☐		
		Lilly Brown		Brown Lilly			(555) 123-5711	(555) 987-6542	operator@wherethen.net	☐		
		Manette Collins	Canter Industries	Collins Manette	(555) 123-6547	(555) 123-5674	(555) 321-7457		m.collins@canter1.net	☐		
		Community Board		**Community Board**						☐	**Personal Errands/Tasks,...**	
		Juan and Song Cruz		Cruz Juan and Song			(555) 654-3211	(555) 555-1234	cruzfam@whther.com	☐		

Figure 4-6: Displaying Outlook Contacts in Phone List view gives quick access to both work and home phone numbers.

Figure 4-7 Dialog Box

Manage All Views

Views for folder "Contacts":

View Name	Can Be Used On	View Type
<Current view settings>	All Contact folders	Table
Business Card	All Contact folders	Business Card
Card	All Contact folders	Card
Phone	All Contact folders	Table
List	All Contact folders	Table

Buttons: New... | Copy... | Modify... | Rename... | Reset

Description

Fields:	File As, Full Name, Last Name, E-mail, Home Phone, Mobile Phone,
Group By:	None
Sort:	Last Name (ascending)
Filter:	Off

☐ Only show views created for this folder

OK | Apply View | Close

Figure 4-7: Use the Manage All Views dialog box to customize the way you view your contacts.

–Or–

From the Contacts window's View tab, click **Change Views** in the Current View group.

2. In either case, choose **Manage Views** from the context menu that displays. This will open the Manage All Views dialog box, seen in Figure 4-7.

CREATE A NEW VIEW

If none of the preset views meet your needs, you can create a new view.

1. In the Manage All Views dialog box, click **New**. The Create A New View dialog box appears.

2. Type a name for your new view.

3. Select the type of view you want. There are several from which you can choose.

- **Table** displays your information in a list, such as the Phone or List views.

- **Timeline** displays your contacts in a timeline format, showing the contact name on the date you added the contact. For example, you might have added a new contact at the last company conference, but you don't remember the person's name. Use a timeline view to see the names you added around the date of the conference.

- **Card** view displays your contacts with all of the information entered for each contact.

- **Business Card** view displays only that information shown on a business card, such as name, address and phone numbers.

- **Day/Week/Month** views show the same information as the Timeline view, but in a calendar grid with the Task pane visible.

- **Icon** view shows each contact as a small icon in your Contact window.

Create a New View Dialog Box

Create a New View

Name of new view:
New view

Type of view:
- Table
- Timeline
- Card
- Business Card
- Day/Week/Month
- Icon

Can be used on
- ○ This folder, visible to everyone
- ○ This folder, visible only to me
- ● All Contact folders

OK | Cancel

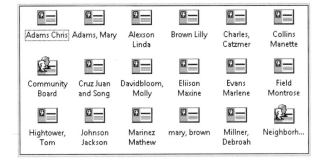

Icons: Adams Chris | Adams, Mary | Alexson Linda | Brown Lilly | Charles, Catzmer | Collins Manette | Community Board | Cruz Juan and Song | Davidbloom, Molly | Eliison Maxine | Evans Marlene | Field Montrose | Hightower, Tom | Johnson Jackson | Marinez Mathew | mary, brown | Millner, Debroah | Neighborh...

4. Click **OK**. The Advanced View Settings dialog box appears for your new view.

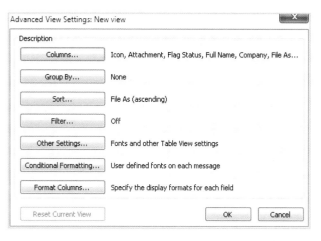

5. Each element on the Advanced View Settings dialog box has its own dialog box. You click a button to edit each element of the view. The availability of each element depends on the view type you chose in Manage All Views.

- **Columns** displays available fields on the left side of the Show Columns dialog box and fields that are actually used on the right. The fields displayed on the right are in the order in which they appear in the view you selected.

- **Group By** allows you to choose how your items are grouped.

- **Sort** alphabetically orders the contents. If Group By is also used, Sort will provide a secondary ordering within the groups.

- **Filter** lets you filter by words, categories, and other advanced options.

- **Other Settings** control how the data looks, such as the font style and size.

- **Conditional Formatting** lets you set rules for the selected view.

- **Format Columns** lets you change the format and labels of columns within a view.

6. Make your selections for each element, and click **OK** to close the dialog box. When you have completed your selections, click **OK** at the Advanced View Settings dialog box to return to the Manage All Views dialog box.

7. Click **OK** to save your new view. Your new view will appear on the list of available views.

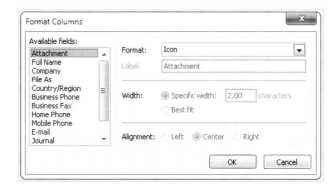

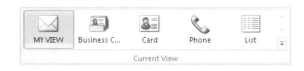

MODIFY A VIEW

You can modify an existing view to meet your needs.

1. Open the Manage Views dialog box as described earlier. Select an existing view, and click **Modify**. The Advanced View Settings dialog box appears.

2. Follow steps 5–7 in "Create a New View."

3. Click **OK** as required to close the dialog boxes.

RESET A VIEW

If you have made changes to an existing view, you can reset that view to its original settings.

1. Open the Manage Views dialog box as described in "Manage Your Contact Views" earlier in this chapter.

2. Select the view you modified. Click the **Reset** button.

3. A warning appears asking if you are sure you want to restore the view to its original settings. Click **Yes** to restore the original settings.

SORT CONTACTS BY FIELDS OR COLUMNS

When you work with either the Phone or List view, you can change how your contact information displays from the list without using the Manage All Views dialog box.

1. From your Outlook window, click **Contacts** in the Outlook View. Your Contacts list displays in the Contacts window.

2. In the Contacts window, click the column name by which you want to sort. A small arrow appears to the right of the column you selected.   `Last Name  ▲`

3. The default is to sort by ascending sequence—lowest number to highest number and then by A to Z. Click the column name a second time to reverse the sort order in descending sequence from highest number to lowest number and then by Z to A.

CHOOSE OTHER SORTING OPTIONS

You can arrange your list views in other ways as well.

1. Open Outlook Contacts and click the **View** tab. Go to the Arrangement group.

   - Click **Date** to arrange your list by the date the contact was entered.

   - Click **Company** to sort your list by company name. Any contacts that do not include a company name appear at the top of the list.

- Click **Categories** to organize your list by category. Again, any contacts without a category are shown at the top.

- Click **Location** to organize the list by geographic location.

- Click the **More** arrow at the lower-right area of the Arrange group to open a context menu. From this menu, click **Show In Groups** to organize the contacts by groups.

- Click **Reverse Sort** to sort the column in Z–A order rather than the default A–Z.

- Click **Add Column** to open the Show Columns dialog box and add columns to your list.

2. To move one column to another location on your list, click the column name you want to change, hold down your left mouse key and drag it to its new location. Red arrows above and below the column names indicate where the dragged column will be inserted.

3. Right-click any column heading to see a context menu.

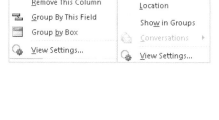

- Click **Arrange By** to open an additional context menu that allows you to specify how the column is sorted.

- Click **Reverse Sort** to sort from Z–A.

- Click **Field Chooser** to add fields (columns) to this list view.

- Click **Remove This Column** to delete the current column from this list.

- Click **Group By This Field** to group this list by the selected column.

- Click **Group By Box** to open a box above the column headers. Then drag a column header into the box in order to sort the contacts by that column.

- Click **View Settings** to open the Advanced View Settings dialog box.

Find a Contact

While you may use the Address Book that appears in the new message window for e-mail messages, you need to know how to find a contact for the other information it contains. The method you use will probably depend on how many contacts you have and the views you use. As with your e-mail items, the number of contacts you have in your Contacts folder is displayed on the lower-left corner of the Contacts window.

USE THE SCROLL BAR

If you have fewer than 50 contacts, scrolling will probably work just fine. When you use the Business Card view, the contacts move vertically when you drag the scroll button or click the scroll bar or scroll arrows. The Card view uses a horizontal scroll bar, which works in the same way as the vertical scroll bar.

USE THE SEARCH TOOL

With the Search tool, you don't have to know the contact's whole name to start sifting through your contacts. This can be useful when you work with hundreds of contacts.

- Click in the **Search Contacts** text box above the column headers. Type as much of the name as needed to get the contact you want, and press **ENTER**. If there are several contacts with that name, the Choose Contact dialog box will appear. Double-click the contact you want to open that person's Contact window.

Search Contacts (Ctrl+E)	🔎

- You can use the Search Contacts box to search for any information that is included in your Contacts list. For example, to find all of your contacts in a certain city:

    1. Click in the **Search Contacts** box at the top of the Contacts list.

    2. Type in the name of the city.

    3. All of the contacts that meet the criteria you typed will immediately display without you needing to press **ENTER**.

    4. Click **X** to clear the search.

USE THE ALPHABETIC INDEX TO FIND A CONTACT

If you have a hundred or more contacts and the current view is one of the card views, you'll find the alphabet bar handy. The alphabet bar searches by the File As name. To use the alphabet bar:

1. In the Contacts window, click a letter button on the alphabet bar to display the first name in your list beginning with that letter.

2. Use either the horizontal or vertical scroll bar (depending on the view you are in) to scroll to the name you want to use.

123
ab
cd
ef
gh
ij
kl
mn
op
qr
s
t
uv
w
x
y
z

USE FIND A CONTACT

The Find tool, located in the Contacts window Home tab Find group, is another useful way of locating a contact.

- Click in the **Find A Contact** text box in Outlook View, and type the name you want. A small text box of possible matches will be displayed. Double-click the one you want. Find A Contact is also available on the title bar next to the Quick Access toolbar.

- Click **Address Book** in the Find group. The Address Book: Contacts window appears as search box.

  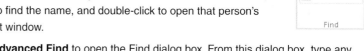

  1. Choose whether you want to search using the name only or more columns. Enter the name you want, and click **Go**. In the results, scroll to find the name, and double-click to open that person's Contact window.

  2. Click **Advanced Find** to open the Find dialog box. From this dialog box, type any part of the name you want to find, and click **OK**.

Print Contact Information

Outlook lets you print contacts to fit a variety of standard organizers, as well as a standard list.

1. Sort your contacts, as described in "Arrange Contacts" earlier in this chapter, so that you print only the group you want in the order you want.

2. Click the **File** tab, and click **Print**. The Print Settings dialog box appears, as seen in Figure 4-8.

3. Click the **Printer** down arrow to choose the printer you want to use.

4. Click **Print Options** to open the Print dialog box. Choose the print style in which you want to print. Not all options are available in every view. The options are:

   - **Card Style** prints your selected items on the selected paper size, grouped with each contact immediately following the one before it.
   - **Small Booklet Style** prints your list in a ⅛-sheet booklet format.
   - **Medium Booklet Style** prints in a ¼-sheet booklet format.
   - **Table Style** prints each chosen record in a columnar style.
   - **Memo Style** prints only one contact.
   - **Phone Directory Style** prints on an 8½ × 11-inch sheet of paper.

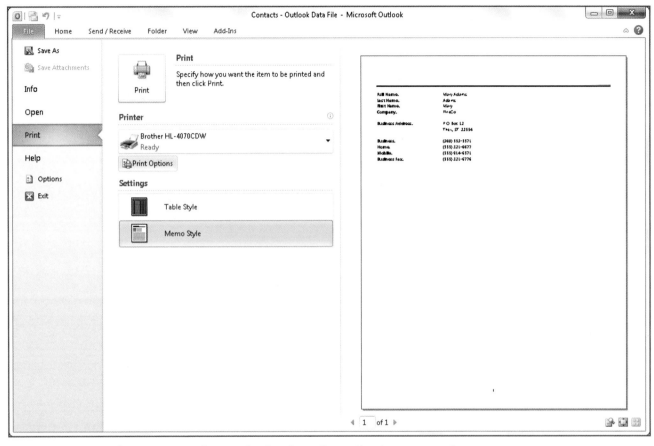

Figure 4-8: You may print your contacts in several styles, depending on the view you are using.

5. Click **Copies** to tell Outlook how many copies to print and so forth, as shown in Figure 4-9.

6. Click **Page Setup** to open the Page Setup dialog box for the style you have chosen.

   a. Click **the Format** tab to:

   • See a preview of how your list will look when it is printed

   • Choose how the sections will print

   • Set the number of columns and any blank forms to be printed at the end of the list

   • Set the font face and size for both the headings and the body of your list, as well as choose to have gray shading to make the list easier to read

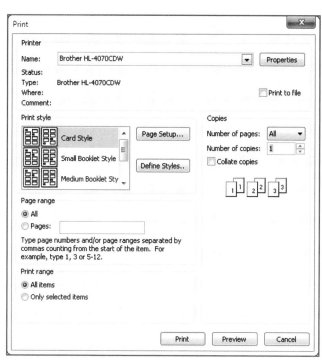

Figure 4-9: Use Print Options to tell Outlook where to print your contact list and which style to use.

b. Click the **Paper** tab to:

- Select the paper size. The default is letter-size paper, 8½ × 11 inches.
- Set the margins for your printed list
- Define the orientation: Portrait or Landscape
- Define what paper tray on your printer to use

c. Click **Header/Footer** to:

- Create a header and set its font
- Create a footer and set its font
- Delete the page number that appears on each page of your list by default by clicking the center **Footer** box, highlighting **[Page #]**, and pressing **DELETE**.

d. Click **OK** to close the Page Setup dialog box and return to the Print Options dialog box.

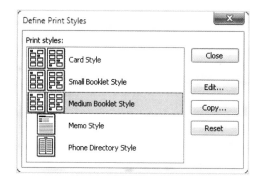

7. Click **Define Styles** to make any changes to your selected print style.

    a. Click **Edit** to make changes.

    b. Click **Close** when you have completed your changes.

8. Click **Page Range** to select which pages to print.

9. Click **Print Range** to select the items you want to print.

10. Select the number of pages and copies you want to print.

11. Click **Preview** to see how your list will look when printed.

12. When you are satisfied with all of the settings, click **Print** to print your page.

PRINT A SINGLE CONTACT

1. From the Contacts window, double-click a contact to open the Contact window.

2. Click the **File** tab, and choose **Print** to open the Print Settings dialog box.

3. Click the **Printer** down arrow to choose a printer, and click **Print Options** to review the settings. Make any changes you want, and click **Print** to print the information.

   –Or–

   On the Print Options dialog box, click **Preview** if you want to see how the information will look when printed.

4. From the Print view, click **Print** to print the information.

Phone a Contact

If your computer has a modem and is connected to a phone line, you can have Outlook dial your contacts. If you have to dial up to connect to the Internet or use e-mail, then the modem is probably set up for automatic phone dialing. (Many new computers do not have a modem.) Give it a try and find out.

1. Make sure you are not online if you have a dial-up connection.

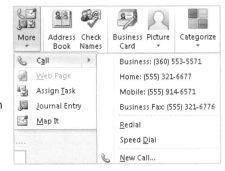

2. In the Contacts window, double-click a contact for whom you have entered a phone number. From the Contact tab Communicate group, click the **More** down arrow.

3. Click **Call**. The list of telephone numbers for this contact is displayed.

4. Click a phone number. The New Call dialog box appears with the selected phone number in the Number field.

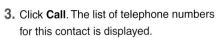

5. Click **Start Call** to dial the number. The Call Status dialog box appears. You are directed to lift the receiver and click **Talk**.

6. A message appears if Outlook cannot locate a dial tone. Click **OK** to close the message box.

7. When you are finished with your call, hang up, click **End Call**, and click **Close**.

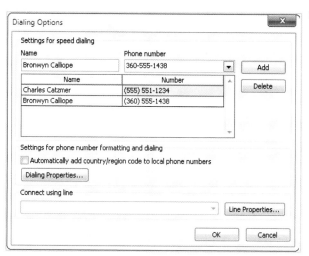

USE SPEED DIALING

For faster connections, there's speed dialing. Of course, you first need to enter the numbers.

1. From your Contacts window, double-click any contact to open the Contact window.

2. In the Contact tab Communicate group, click **More** and then click **Call**.

3. In the New Call dialog box, click **Dialing Options** to open the Dialing Options dialog box.

4. Type a name and phone number in the text boxes.

5. Click **Add** to add this number to the speed dialing settings.

6. Enter any additional information required.

7. Click **OK** and click **Close**.

8. To place a speed dial call, in the Communicate group, click the **More** down arrow. From the context menu that appears, click the **Call** arrow to display the Call submenu.

9. Click **Speed Dial** and choose a number. The New Call dialog box appears.

10. Proceed as described earlier in "Phone a Contact."

See a Map for a Contact's Address

If you have an Internet connection, you can use Outlook 2010 to obtain a map and get directions to an address you have recorded in your list of contacts. To see a map:

1. Open the Contact window for your selected contact.

2. Click the **Addresses** down arrow, and select the address you want from the menu that appears.

3. Click **Map It** to the right of the Address field.

4. A map displays, as seen in Figure 4-10.

5. By default, the map is displayed in two dimensions. On the top edge of the map, click **3D** to see the map in a three-dimensional format.

6. Click **Road** to view the map as a standard road map.

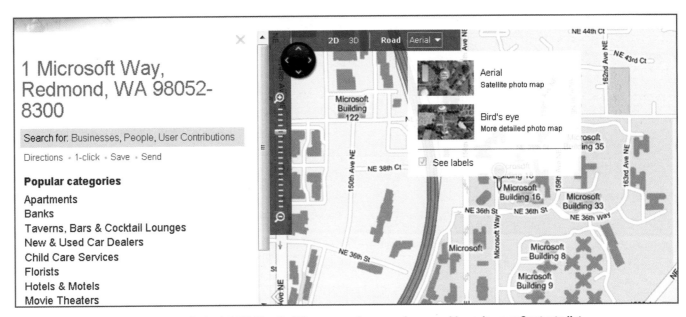

Figure 4-10: Using the Internet, the Outlook 2010 Map It utility can create a map for any address in your Contacts list.

7. Click **Aerial** to open a menu with two choices.

   ● Click **Aerial** to see a satellite photo of this address.

   ● Click **Bird's Eye** for details that you might see if you were flying over the address.

8. Click **Close** to close the map and return to your Contact window.

GET DRIVING DIRECTIONS TO A CONTACT'S LOCATION

On the map of the location:

1. On the left navigational pane, click **Directions**. Type the address from which you want to start into the A field. The B field displays your contact address.

2. Click **Shortest Time**, **Shortest Distance**, or **Get A Route Based On Traffic**, depending on which option you want.

3. Click **Miles** or **Km**.

4. If you choose not to save your destination history, clear the **Destination History** check box.

5. Click **Get Directions**. A driving map appears with the driving directions on the left side of the map.

USING KEYBOARD SHORTCUTS WITH CONTACTS

To save time in Outlook 2010, you can use keyboard shortcuts. A keyboard shortcut usually requires that you hold down one or two keys and then press another. Some of the most popular contact-related shortcuts in Outlook are shown in the following table.

SHORTCUT	ACTION PERFORMED
CTRL+N	Creates a new contact from anywhere in Contacts
CTRL+SHIFT+C	Creates a new contact from anywhere else in Outlook 2010
CTRL+D	Deletes a contact from any view
CTRL+1	Switches to your Mail folder
CTRL+2	Switches to your Calendar folder
CTRL+3	Switches to your Contacts folder from anywhere else in Outlook
CTRL+4	Switches to your Tasks folder
CTRL+SHIFT+L	Creates a new contact group (Inside a mail message, this shortcut produces a bullet)

6. Click the **Print** icon at the bottom of the driving directions to open the Print Settings dialog box.

Map and text | Map only | Text only   🖶 Print   ❓ Help

Bing Maps

A: **Space Needle, WA**
B: **1 Microsoft Way, Redmond, WA 98052-8300**
Route: **13.0 mi, 19 min**

Type your route notes here (up to 120 characters).

FREE! Use **Bing 411** to find movies, businesses & more: **800-BING-411**

🚩	**Space Needle, WA**	**A–B: 13.0 mi** 19 min
	1. Depart from **Space Needle, WA**	0.0 mi
⬅	2. Turn **left** onto **Broad St**	0.1 mi
↰	3. Bear **left** onto **5th Ave N**	0.3 mi
⮕	4. Turn **right** onto **Mercer St**	0.6 mi
↰	5. Take ramp **left** and follow signs for **I-5 North**	1.3 mi
⮥	6. At exit **168B**, take ramp **right** for **SR-520 East** toward **Bellevue / Kirkland**	9.9 mi

- Click **Map And Text** to print both.
- Click **Map Only** to print just the map.
- Click **Text Only** to print just the driving directions.
- Click **Print** to open the Print dialog box. Choose the printer you want to use, and click **Print**.

7. Click **Close** twice to close the map and return to Outlook.

Create a Mail-Merged E-mail

From time to time, you might want to send a personalized message to several different contacts. You can use the Outlook Mail Merge feature, which works with Microsoft Word, to easily accomplish this task.

Actions

1. Open any Contacts view, and select the contacts you want to receive the e-mail.

2. From the Home tab, click **Mail Merge** in the Actions group.

3. The Mail Merge Contacts dialog box appears, as seen in Figure 4-11.

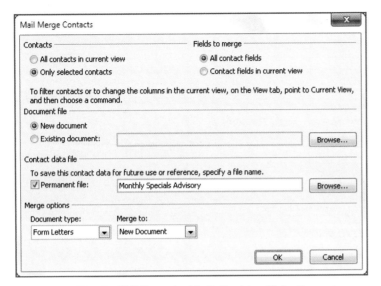

Figure 4-11: Use the Mail Merge tool in Outlook to efficiently create *personalized messages*

4. From the Contacts section:

   ● Click **All Contacts In Current View** to choose all the contacts in your current view.

   ● Click **Only Selected Contacts** to send the e-mail message to only the contacts you selected in step 1.

5. Depending on your choices in step 4, make any changes in the Fields To Merge section.

6. In the Document File section:

   ● Click **New Document** if you are creating a message for the first time.

   ● Click **Existing Document** and **Browse** to find a document you have already created.

7. In the Contact Data File section, specify a file name to save this contact data.

   ● Click the **Permanent File** check box to save the set permanently.

   ● Click **Browse** to find a file elsewhere on your computer and replace it with the information in this file.

8. In the Merge Options section:

   ● Click the **Document Type** down arrow to choose what type of document you are creating: Form Letters, Mailing Labels, Envelopes, or Catalog.

   ● Click the **Merge To** down arrow to choose between:

     ● **New Document**, which creates a Word document that you can e-mail

     ● **Printer** to send the messages directly to the printer

     ● **E-Mail** to create a group of e-mails to be sent at the same time. If you choose to merge to e-mail, you are prompted to insert a message subject.

9. Click **OK** to continue.

   If you have chosen either Mailing Labels or Envelopes, a Mail Merge Helper dialog box appears.

10. Continue through the Mail Merge Helper to complete your document. A new Word document appears, with the Mailings tab displayed.

11. Click **Start Mail Merge**. From the context menu, choose between the following types of documents:

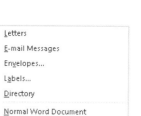

- Letters
- E-mail Messages
- Envelopes
- Labels
- Directory
- Normal Word Document

12. Click **Start Mail Merge**, and from the menu, click **Step By Step Mail Merge Wizard** to begin the mail merge. The Mail Merge task pane appears at the right side of your Word window.

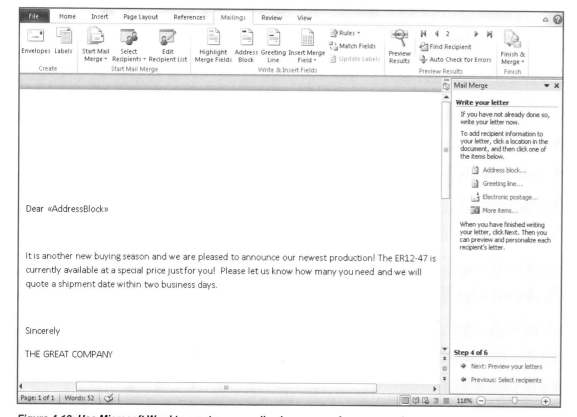

Figure 4-12: *Use Microsoft Word to create personalized messages for a group of contacts.*

13. In the Select Recipients section, **Use An Existing List** is selected by default. This is the list you designated in step 1.

14. At the bottom of the pane, click **Next: Write Your Letter**.

15. Write your letter. Make sure you leave a space for the address and name for each letter, as shown in Figure 4-12.

16. Click **Address Block** to enter the recipients' information. The Insert Address Block dialog box appears.

Select the format in which you want the recipient's name to appear. At the right of the dialog box, the preview area displays how the information will be shown on the document.

Click **Match Fields** to correct any problems with the elements of your address block.

Click **OK**.

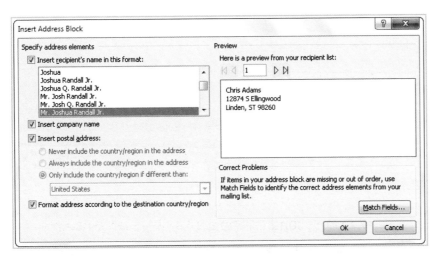

17. Click **Next: Preview Your Letters** to see how the merged document will appear. You can go through the letters one by one to verify their merges by clicking the back and next arrows in the Preview Results group.

18. Click **Next: Complete The Merge** to continue.

19. Click **Print** to print your letters.

Chapter 5

Scheduling and the Calendar

The Calendar is second only to mail in its importance in Outlook. The Calendar works closely with Contacts and Tasks to coordinate the use of your time and your interactions with others. The Calendar lets you schedule appointments and meetings, establish recurring activities, and tailor the Calendar to your area, region, and workdays.

In this chapter, you will see how to use and customize the Calendar, schedule and manage appointments, and schedule and track meetings and resources.

Use the Calendar

The Calendar has a number of unique items in its Outlook window, as seen in Figure 5-1.

- Buttons allow you to quickly switch the view of your calendar between daily, weekly, and monthly views, as well as to show or hide details of your activities.

- The current date and each appointment are displayed on the calendar in Normal view.
- Your tasks appear at the bottom of each day in the Day, Work Week, and Week views.

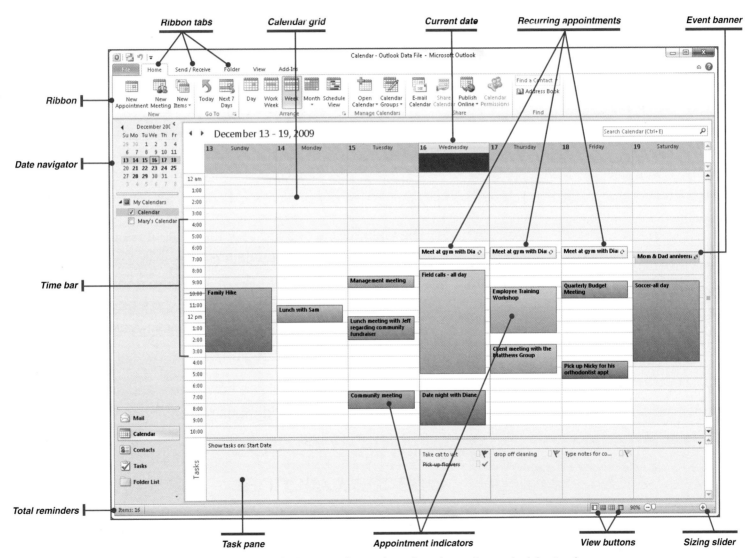

Figure 5-1: *The Outlook Calendar displays your day, week, work week, month, or schedule at a glance.*

Appointments	Appointments only involve you.	
Meetings	Meetings happen at a scheduled time, just like an appointment. The difference is that other people are involved. You invite others via e-mail, and the meeting displays in your calendar with the location and organizer's name.	
Events	Events last all day. Events that you put on your calendar do not block out time like a meeting or an appointment, so you can have other entries for that day display on your calendar.	
Tasks	Tasks are activities that do not need time scheduled for them and are your own personal tasks, even if they are part of a larger project of which you are a team member. Your tasks will display in the Day and Week views of your calendar, as well as on your To-Do bar.	

Table 5-1: Common Calendar Activities

Explore the Calendar

The Calendar is designed for you to easily keep track of appointments, meetings, events, due dates, anniversaries, birthdays, and any other date-related happening. You can schedule several different types of activities, as shown in Table 5-1.

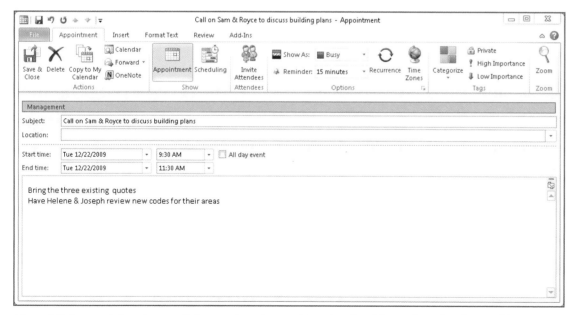

Figure 5-2: An appointment or an all-day event can be any date-related activity, such as due dates or birthdays.

To open your calendar, start Outlook in one of the ways described in Chapter 1. Then:

1. Click **Calendar** in Outlook View.

   –Or–

   Press **CTRL+2** on the keyboard.

2. Click a date on the Calendar Navigator, and that day displays in Day view. If the calendar shows in Work Week, Week, or Month view, double-click any date on the calendar.

3. A new Appointment window opens, as shown in Figure 5-2. See "Create Appointments" later in this chapter for more information.

QUICKSTEPS

NAVIGATING THE CALENDAR

The Date Navigator, which by default is in the upper-left corner of the Outlook View, allows you to pick any date from April 1, 1601, to September 30, 4500. To cover this almost 2,900-year span, Outlook provides several efficient tools.

◄	December 2009					►
Su	Mo	Tu	We	Th	Fr	Sa
29	30	1	2	3	4	5
6	7	8	9	10	11	12
13	14	15	16	17	18	19
20	21	22	23	24	25	26
27	28	29	30	31	1	2
3	4	5	6	7	8	9

- **Display a day** by clicking it in the Date Navigator. Or, from anywhere in Outlook, click **Calendar** on the Outlook View.

- **Display a day with appointments** by clicking a boldface day in the Date Navigator.

- **Display a week** by clicking to the left of the first day of the week.

- **Display several weeks** by holding down **CTRL** while clicking to the left of the weeks.

- **Display a month** by dragging across the weeks of the month.

- **Change the month from one to the next** by clicking the left or right arrow in the month bar.

- **Scroll through a list of months** by clicking the month name in the Calendar Navigator to display a month list, and moving the pointer up or down to select an individual month.

- **Directly display any date** by clicking the **Go To Date** Dialog Box Launcher at the right of the Go To group in the Home tab. This opens the Go To Date dialog box. Type in the date, and click **OK**. You can also open the Go To Date dialog box by pressing **CTRL+G**.

4. After you have entered your information, click **Save & Close** to close the Appointment window.

5. In the ribbon's Home tab, click **New Items** and **Task** to open a Task window. In Outlook, a task is an item you track until it is completed. It may not have a specific timetable, but is something you want to monitor.

6. After you have entered the task, click the appropriate choice in the Task ribbon's Follow Up group. Click Save & Close to close the Task window.

Customize the Calendar

As you have seen with the rest of Outlook, there are many ways you can customize the calendar to meet your needs. You can change the way the calendar displays time intervals, the font size and face, the background color, and any additional options you require.

CHANGE THE TIME SCALES

The default display of time intervals, or *scales*, on your Calendar grid is 30 minutes. If you want to change these scales to reflect another time interval:

1. In the Calendar grid, right-click any blank area.

2. Click **View Settings** to open the Advanced View Settings | Calendar dialog box.

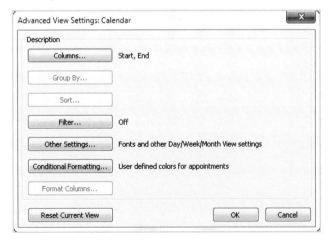

3. Click **Other Settings** to open the Format Day/Week/Month View Settings dialog box.

4. Click the **Time Scale** down arrow to display a list of choices.

5. Click the scale you want to show in the calendar.

6. Click **OK** to close the Format Day/Week/Month dialog box, and click **OK** again to close the Advanced View Settings Calendar dialog box.

CHANGE THE FONT FACE AND SIZE

You can change the font in both your calendar and your Task list.

1. Right-click any blank area in the Calendar grid.

2. Click **View Settings** to open the Advanced View Settings Calendar dialog box.

3. Click **Other Settings** to open the Format Day/Week/Month View dialog box.

–Or–

In the ribbon's View tab, click **View Settings** to open the Advanced View Settings Calendar dialog box, and click **Other Settings**.

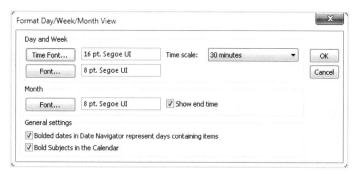

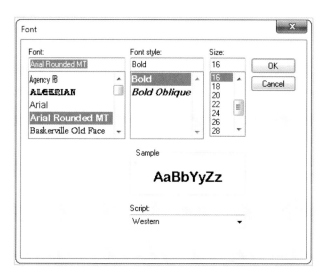

4. Click **Time Font** to open the Font dialog box to change the font face and size for times in the Day, Work Week, and Week views.

   a. Click **Font** to change the font face.

   b. Click **Font Style** to choose from the various font styles, such as Regular, Italic, Bold, and so on. The styles available will vary, depending on which font face you have chosen in step 4a.

   c. Click **Size** to set the size of the font that will show the times on your calendar in Day, Work Week, and Week view.

   d. Click **OK** to close the Font dialog box and save your choices.

5. Click **Font** to open the Font dialog box to change how information other than the time displays in Day, Work Week, and Week views.

6. Click **OK** to close the Font dialog box and save your choices.

7. Click **Font** under Month, and follow steps 5–7.

8. Click **OK** to close the Format Day/Week/Month View dialog box. Click **OK** once more to close the Advanced View Settings Calendar dialog box.

SET ADDITIONAL SETTINGS

You can open the Advanced View Settings dialog box in two different ways:

- From the Calendar ribbon's View tab, click **View Settings** in the Current View group

  –Or–

- Right-click any blank section of the Calendar grid, and click **View Settings** at the bottom of the context menu.

From the Advanced View Settings dialog box, you can tell Calendar how to display the items in your Calendar and Date Navigators.

1. In the Format Day/Week/Month View dialog box, under General Settings, **Bolded Dates In Date Navigator** is set by default. If you do not want these dates to appear in bold text, clear this check box.

2. Clear the **Bold Subjects In The Calendar** check box to have the headings or subjects of your activities appear in regular font in your Calendar grid.

3. Click **OK** to close the dialog box.

UNDERSTANDING THE VIEW TAB

The View tab includes several options, some of which are also available when you display a menu by right-clicking in a blank area of the Calendar grid

1. Open the Outlook Calendar, and click the **View** tab. The ribbon displays various options.

2. In the Arrangement group, you see several button options, including:

   - **Day** displays detailed information about each appointment in Day view.

   - **Work Week** displays all the appointments you have set on this calendar for the days you have set in your work week, normally Monday through Friday.

   - **Week** displays a seven-day work week, including Sunday, shown on the left of the week's Calendar grid, and Saturday, shown on the right.

   - **Month** shows an entire month on the Calendar grid. If you click the down arrow, a menu opens with options for displaying appointments in various degrees of details—from low detail to high detail.

USING THE NAVIGATION AND READING PANES

While the default views in Outlook Calendar are designed to display your information in the way many users need to see it, you can change how the Navigation and Reading panes display information.

USE THE OUTLOOK VIEW

By default, the Outlook View appears at the left of the Calendar grid. However, you can choose to minimize it, turn it off entirely, or change the buttons that display on it. To make these changes:

1. On the View tab Layout group, click **Outlook View** to open a drop-down menu.

    a. Click **Minimized** to minimize the Outlook View's display.

    b. Click **Off** to turn it off entirely.

2. Click **Options** to open the Outlook View Options dialog box from which you can choose which buttons appear on the Outlook View and the order in which they appear.

3. Click **OK** when you are finished making changes.

USE THE READING PANE

In Outlook Calendar, the Reading Pane is available when you want to see the contents of the appointments, meetings, and tasks displayed on your Calendar. By default it is turned off, but you can change this. From the Layout group in the View tab, click **Reading Pane** to open a drop-down menu.

1. Choose **Right** to display the Reading pane at the right side of the Calendar grid.

2. Select **Bottom** to display it at the bottom of the grid.

Continued . . .

- **Schedule** displays your appointments, meetings, and other commitments in a timeline format.

- **Time Scale** opens a menu on which you can change how time intervals in the time bar display on your Calendar grid, as well as a link to change the time zone.

3. Click **Color** in the Color group to change the default grid colors.

4. The Layout group lets you tell Outlook how to display the information you have entered.

    - Click **Daily Task List** to tell Outlook how to display your tasks in the Day, Work Week, and Week views.

    - Click **Outlook View** and **Reading Pane** to choose which buttons are displayed and in which order. See "Using the Navigation and Reading Panes" QuickSteps for more information.

    - Click **To-Do Bar** to tell Outlook how to display the To-Do bar.

5. The People Pane group connects Outlook to online social networks such as LinkedIn and Facebook. You can connect with both your business and personal contacts without leaving Outlook. Click the down arrow to set your options.

    - Click **Normal** to display the People pane at the bottom of the Calendar grid.

    - Click the **Minimized** setting to shrink the People pane.

    - Click **Off** to turn off the Internet connection.

    - Click **Account Settings** to add new settings or modify your current settings.

6. The Window group has several buttons.

    - Click **Reminders Window** to see a list of open reminders.

    - Click **Open In New Window** to open your calendar in a new window.

    - Click **Close All Items** to open the Close Meeting dialog box.

Customize Calendar Views

As with Mail and Contacts, you can create customized calendar views, either by modifying an existing view or by creating a new one. You create or modify a view from the ribbon's View tab Current View group.

MODIFY A DAY, WORK WEEK, WEEK, OR MONTH VIEW

1. In Outlook, click **Calendar** in Outlook View to open the Calendar.

3. Click **Off** to turn off the Reading pane entirely.

4. If the Options button is grayed out (unavailable), click **Right** or **Bottom** again to make the Options choice available. Click **Options** to open the Reading Pane dialog box to make the following choices:

   a. Click **Mark Items As Read When Viewed In the Reading Pane** to have each item marked as being read.

   b. Type the number of seconds you want Outlook to wait before marking the item.

   c. Click **Mark Item As Read When Selection Changes** to show items as having been read without any time delay.

   d. Clear the **Single Key Reading Using Space Bar** to turn off the ability to read through items one key at a time by pressing the space bar on your keyboard.

5. Click **OK** to close the Reading Pane dialog box.

---

2. From the View tab, click **Change View** in the Current View group.

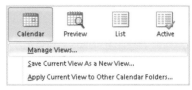

3. From the drop-down menu, click **Manage Views** to open the Manage All Views dialog box.

4. Select the view name you want to modify. Click **Modify** to open the Advanced View Settings dialog box for your selection as seen in Figure 5-3. To simplify your choices, click **Only Show Views Created For This Folder**.

5. Click the **Columns** button to open the Date/Time Fields dialog box. Select a field from the Available Date/Time Fields list. The Start and End fields set how each date and time item is displayed within the current view. Choose from the following:

   a. Click **Created** if you want the start or end time to be the time and date the item was created.

   b. Click **Due By** to have either the start or end time be the date and time at which the item must be completed.

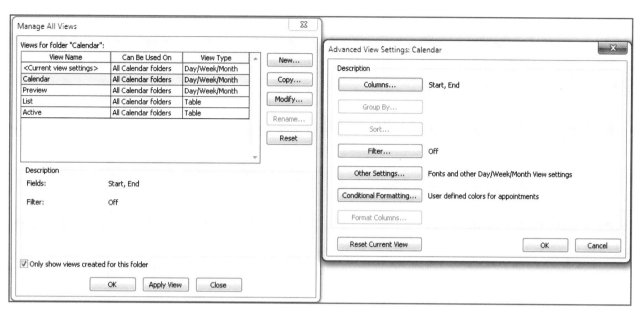

Figure 5-3: *You can modify existing views as well as create new views to suit your needs.*

c. Click **End** to display the ending time or date in either the Start or End field.

d. Click **Recurrence Range End** or **Recurrence Range Start** to show when a recurring appointment starts or ends.

e. Click **Start** to show when an appointment begins.

f. Click **End** if the new field is to replace the End field.

g. Click **OK** to close the dialog box.

6. After you have made your selection from the Available Date/Time Fields list, click **Start** to have your choice appear in the Start field.

7. Click **End** to have it appear in the End field.

8. Click the **Select Available Fields From** down arrow to open a list of other field lists from which you can choose.

9. Click **OK** when you have completed your choices. You are returned to the Advanced View Settings dialog box.

10. Click **Filter** to open the Filter dialog box. You can use filters to create a customized view that shows only specific types of appointments. For example, you can create a view that shows only management meetings or family events.

    a. In the Appointments And Meetings tab, enter any words by which you want to filter your calendar entries for this view.

    b. In the More Choices tab, click **Categories** to select the category or multiple categories that you want to display.

    c. Select what types of items you want to include in this view, as well as the size of the items to display.

    d. In the Advanced tab, you can enter specific criteria to display in your view, as well as set conditions.

    e. After you have finished making your choices, click **OK** to save your view and return to the Advanced View Settings dialog box.

    f. Click **OK** one more time to return to the Manage All Views dialog box.

    g. Click **Apply View** to set your new view.

    h. Click **OK** or **Close** to close the dialog box.

11. Click **Other Settings** to open the Format Day/Week/Month View Settings dialog box as described in "Customize the Calendar" earlier in this chapter.

12. Click **Conditional Formatting** to open the Conditional Formatting dialog box.

    a. Click **Add** to create a new rule.

    b. Click in the **Name** text box, and type a name for this rule.

    c. Click the **Color** down arrow to choose a color for this rule.

    d. Click **Condition** to open the Filter dialog box. Type the word or words to create this filter.

    e. Click **In** to choose where Outlook is to find the words you are searching for.

    f. Enter any additional filter information you require.

    g. Click **OK** to close the Filter dialog box.

    h. Click **OK** to close the Customize View dialog box.

13. Click **OK** to save your changes.

14. If you want to undo a change you made to the current view, click **Reset Current View** in the Advanced View Settings dialog box.

NOTE

You can also open the Advanced View Settings dialog box from a Day, Work Week, Week, or Month view by right-clicking an empty part of your Calendar grid and clicking **View Settings**.

Figure 5-4: *The Advanced View Settings: List dialog box offers more choices than the Calendar view.*

NOTE

The Active view displays all of your current events and items in a table. You can change how the items display in the Advanced View Settings dialog box.

MODIFY A LIST VIEW

1. In Outlook, click **Calendar** on Outlook View to open the calendar.
2. Click **Change View** in the Current View group to view your choices.
3. Select **List** and **Manage Views** to open the Manage All Views dialog box, and click **Modify.**
4. The Advanced View Settings: List dialog box will appear, as seen in Figure 5-4.
5. Click **Columns** to set the columns that will display in this modified view. Choose from the Available Columns list, and click **Add** to add them to your list.
   - Select an item in the Show These Columns In This Order list, and click **Move Up** or **Move Down** to change its position in your modified list.
   - Select an item in the Show These Columns In This Order list, and click **Remove** to delete the item from the list.
6. Click **Group By** to set how items are grouped.
7. Click **Sort** to determine how the items are sorted. You can select up to four fields, and each field can be sorted either A–Z (ascending) or Z–A (descending).
8. Click **Filter** to set filters for this view.
9. Follow the same steps as described in "Modify a Day, Work Week, Week, or Month View" earlier in this chapter for the Other Settings, Conditional Formatting, and Format Columns fields.
10. Click **OK** to close the Advanced View Settings: List dialog box.

CREATE A NEW VIEW

1. In Outlook, click **Calendar** on Outlook View to open the calendar.
2. Click **Change View** in the Current View group to view your choices.
3. Select **Manage Views** to open the Manage All Views dialog box, and click **New.**
4. The Create A New View dialog box appears.
   a. Type a name for this new view.
   b. Click the type of view this will be from the six options displayed.
   c. Click **This Folder, Visible To Everyone** if you want to make your new view available in this folder to everyone. Choose one of the other two options, if required.
   d. Click **OK** to open the Advanced View Settings dialog box for your new view.

      Depending on the view you are creating, options in the Advanced View Settings dialog box vary. Not all the options described in the "Modify a Day, Work Week, Week, or Month View" section are available for every type of view.
   e. Click **OK** to save the new view and close the dialog box.

5. Your new view will appear on the Manage All Views dialog box.

6. Click **Apply View** to immediately see the new view, or click **Close** to close the dialog box and stay in the current view. The next time you click Change View, the new view is included on the list.

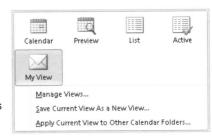

Outlook Options

Change the settings for calendars, meetings, and time zones.

General
Mail
Calendar
Contacts
Tasks
Notes and Journal
Search
Mobile
Language
Advanced
Customize Ribbon
Quick Access Toolbar
Add-Ins
Trust Center

Work time

Work hours:
Start time: 8:00 AM
End time: 5:00 PM
Work week: ☐ Sun ☑ Mon ☑ Tue ☑ Wed ☑ Thu ☑ Fri ☐ Sat
First day of week: Sunday
First week of year: Starts on Jan 1

Calendar options

☑ Default reminders: 15 minutes
☑ Allow attendees to propose new times for meetings
Use this response when proposing a new meeting time: ? Tentative
Add holidays to the Calendar: Add Holidays...
Change the permissions for viewing Free/Busy information: Free/Busy Options...
☐ Enable an alternate calendar
English / Gregorian
☑ When sending meeting requests outside of your organization, use the iCalendar format
☐ Show bell icon on the calendar for appointments and meetings with reminders

Display options

Default calendar color:
☐ Use this color on all calendars
Date Navigator font:
Font... 8 pt. Segoe UI
☑ Show Click to Add prompts in calendar
☐ Show week numbers in the month view and in the Date Navigator
☐ When in Schedule View, show free appointments
☑ Automatically switch from vertical layout to schedule view when the number of displayed calendars is greater than or equal to: 5 calendar folders
☑ Automatically switch from schedule view to vertical layout when the number of displayed calendars is fewer than or equal to: 1 calendar folder(s)

OK   Cancel

Figure 5-5: **You can set Calendar options, such as defining your work week and displaying week numbers, the time zone, and holidays.**

Set Up the Calendar

Calendar allows you to define your normal work week in terms of the days it contains and when it starts, the normal start and end of your working day, the holidays you observe, and what you consider the first week of the year. To set up your calendar:

1. Click **Calendar** in the Outlook View. From the ribbon's Arrange group, click the **Calendar Options Dialog Box Launcher** at the bottom-right area to open the Outlook Options dialog box.

2. In the Outlook Options dialog box, click **Calendar** to display the Calendar Options view, if it does not already appear, as shown in Figure 5-5.

3. Click the **Start Time** down arrow to choose the normal start time for your working day if it is other than 8:00 A.M. Click the **End Time** down arrow to change the end of your working day if it is other than 5:00 P.M.

4. Click the days of the week you consider workdays if they are different from the default of Monday through Friday.

5. Click the **First Day Of Week** down arrow to select the day of the week you want considered the first day of the week if it is a day other than Sunday. The weeks in the Date Navigator will begin with this day.

6. Click the **First Week Of Year** down arrow to choose a definition for the first week of the year if it does not begin January 1. If you turn on week numbering, week number 1 is defined in this manner.

7. Under Calendar Options, change the **Default Reminder** times to other than the 15 minutes that shows, if necessary.

8. Click **Allow Attendees To Propose New Times For Meetings** if you choose to allow this.

9. Click the **Use This Response When You Propose New Meeting Times** down arrow to change the automatic response to new meetings.

10. Click **Add Holidays** to open the Add Holidays To Calendar dialog box.

   a. Click the check box for the country and/or religious holidays you want added.

   b. Click **OK** to close the dialog box.

11. Click the **Free/Busy Options** button if you want to make changes to how your time is displayed to others. See "Set Free/Busy Options" later in this chapter.

12. Click **Enable Alternate Calendar**, if desired, and use the drop-down lists to choose them.

13. Under most circumstances, it is best to leave the **When Sending Meeting Requests** check box selected.

14. Clear the **Show Bell Icon** check box if you do not want this reminder icon to display.

15. Clear **Show "Click To Add" Prompts On The Calendar** if you do not want this default prompt to display.

16. Under Display Options, click the **Default Color** down arrow to choose from a list of colors other than the default blue for the background on your Calendar grid.

17. Click **Use This Color On All Calendars** if you want this new color to be used on all calendars you create.

18. Click the **Font** button to change the Date Navigator font.

19. Click **Show Week Numbers In The Month View And Date Navigator** to display week numbers.

20. Make any necessary changes to remaining options, including when you want to show your free time in Schedule View and to vary views when more than one calendar is displayed.

21. Under Time Zones, make any changes necessary in the Time Zones section. You can define and name your current time zone, as well as an additional one, if you choose.

   a. If you are going to use two time zones, click in the **Label** text box, and type a name that will identify the current time zone appearing in the Time Zone drop-down list.

   b. Click **Show A Second Time Zone** to add a second time zone.

   c. Click in the **Label** text box, and type a name identifying this second time zone.

   d. Click the **Time Zone** down arrow to display a list of time zones from which you can choose.

   e. Click **Adjust For Daylight Saving Time** if it applies to either time zone you've selected.

   f. Click **Swap Time Zones** to swap which time zone displays on the left of the time bar.

22. Make any necessary adjustments in the Scheduling Assistant and Resource Scheduling sections to display calendar details or to manage resources, such as conference room or automobile availability.

23. Click **OK** to save your changes.

SET FREE/BUSY OPTIONS

If you and your coworkers are part of a Microsoft Exchange network, are willing to share your schedules over the Internet, or can all access a common server, you can store your free/busy times and make them available to each other to schedule meetings and other times together. In this case, requests for meetings are handled automatically. The request will be matched against the group's free/busy schedule, and meetings will be scheduled at available times. For an individual to set up his or her free/busy options:

1. From the File tab, click **Options** and click **Calendar.**

2. In the Calendar Options section, click **Free/Busy Options**. The Free/Busy Options dialog box appears.

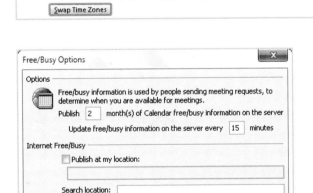

3. Click in the **Publish** box to type the number of months of free/busy information you want to store on the server.

4. Click the **Update Free/Busy Information** text box to enter how often you want the server to update your information.

5. In the Internet Free/Busy section, click **Publish At My Location**, and enter the URL (Uniform Resource Locator, or Web address) of your Internet calendar if that applies to your situation. See the "Understanding Internet Calendars" QuickFacts later in this chapter.

6. Click **Search Location** and type the URL of servers you want Outlook to search for the free/busy information of others.

7. Click **OK** to return to the Outlook Options dialog box.

Maintain Multiple Calendars

If your calendar is becoming cluttered and hard to use, you might try separating it into two side-by-side calendars. For example, create one for business appointments and one for family appointments.

1. Click **Calendar** in the Outlook View.

2. On the Folder tab, click **New Calendar** in the New group.

3. Click **Name** and type a name for your new calendar.

4. Click the **Folder Contains** down arrow, and select the type of information the calendar will contain.

5. In the Select Where To Place The Folder area, determine where the calendar will be created.

6. Click **OK** to close the Create New Folder dialog box. Your new calendar displays in the Outlook View.

7. Click the check box to the left of your new calendar to display it side by side with your original calendar, as seen in Figure 5-6.

VIEW MULTIPLE CALENDARS

You can view a calendar in a new window, side by side with other calendars, or stack transparent calendars over each other to find a common free time slot on several different calendars.

CAUTION

At least one calendar must always be displayed, but you can create up to 30 calendars if you choose.

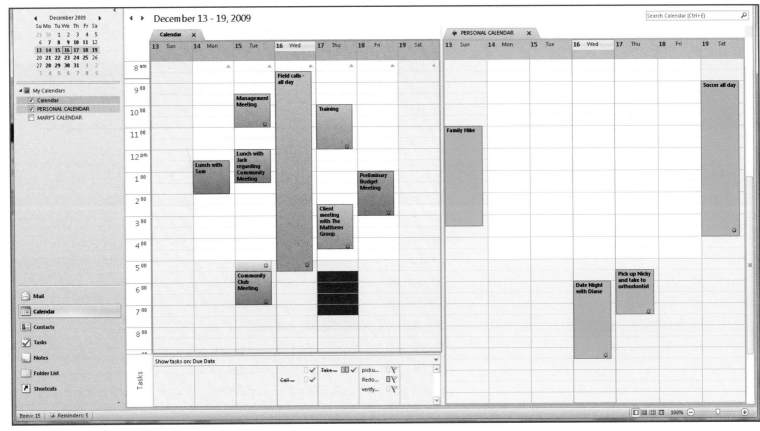

*Figure 5-6: **By displaying two calendars side-by-side, you can, for example, show personal appointments that have no effect on your work calendar.***

To view a second calendar in a new window:

1. Click **Calendar** in the Outlook View, and right-click the name of the second calendar in the Outlook View under My Calendars.

2. In the resulting menu, click **Open In New Window**.

To open several calendars side by side:

1. In the Calendar Outlook View, click the check box for each calendar you want to view.

2. All the calendars will be displayed next to each other in your Calendar grid.

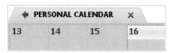

To overlay your calendars:

1. In the Calendar, from the Outlook View, click the check box for each calendar you want to stack. The calendars display next to each other in your Calendar grid.

2. On the tab of each calendar you want to stack, click the arrow that points to the left.

3. All of the calendars are stacked atop each other, and you can see any dates that may be free on all calendars.

4. To undo the stack, click the right-pointing arrow on the tab of each calendar. The calendars are once again displayed side by side.

Share a Calendar

There are several ways to share your Outlook 2010 Calendar with others. You can send a calendar via e-mail, publish your calendar to Microsoft Office Online, or share your default Microsoft Exchange Calendar with others on the same server.

SEND A CALENDAR IN E-MAIL

You can send any calendar you own to another person in the body of an e-mail message. The person receiving the calendar will see a snapshot of it at a given moment in time. If the recipient uses Outlook 2010, he or she can open the calendar snapshot as an Outlook Calendar and display it either side by side or as an overlay with any other calendars. The downside of using a calendar snapshot is that the calendar you send is not automatically updated when you make changes. If the e-mail recipient needs a regularly updated calendar, consider publishing your calendar to Microsoft Office Online, using a calendar-publishing Web service, or, if your office has it, sharing your calendars via an Exchange server.

To share a calendar:

1. In Calendar's Outlook View, select the calendar you want to share.

2. On the Home tab, click **E-mail Calendar** in the Share group.

–Or–

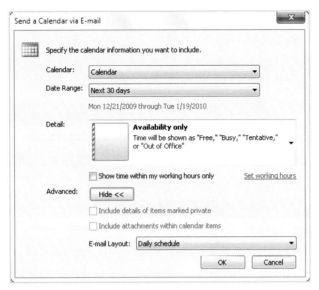

In the Outlook View, right-click the calendar you want to share. From the context menu, click **Share** and click **E-mail Calendar.**

In either case, an e-mail message box opens with the Send A Calendar Via E-Mail dialog box in the message portion of the e-mail window.

3. Click the **Calendar** down arrow, and click the calendar you want to e-mail.

4. Click the **Date Range** down arrow, and click the time period of the calendar that you want to send.

5. Click the **Detail** icon, and select the type of calendar information you want to send.

6. If you chose Availability Only in step 5, click **Show Time Within My Working Hours Only** if that is what you want.

7. Click **Advanced** and, if desired, click **Include Details Of Items Marked Private** and/or click **Include Attachments**.

8. Click **E-mail Layout** and click either the **Daily Schedule** or **List Of Events** format.

9. Click **OK** to close the dialog box.

10. Click **To** and type the recipient's e-mail address.

11. Click **Send** to send the e-mail.

PUBLISH A CALENDAR TO MICROSOFT OFFICE ONLINE

Microsoft offers a publishing service for your calendars. This method does not require Microsoft Exchange for either the user or the owner of the calendar. The first time you use the service, you must register using your Microsoft Windows Live ID account. If you don't yet have an account, you may follow the instructions on the screen to obtain one for free.

1. In Calendar's Outlook View, right-click the calendar you want to share.

2. Click **Share** and click **Publish to Office.com**. Go through the registration procedure, if needed. The Publish Calendar To Office.com dialog box appears.

3. Click a **Time Span** button to choose whether you want to send a section of the calendar (recommended) or all of it. If selecting a time range, click the **Previous** and **Through Next** down arrows to set the time span for the calendar.

4. Click **Only Invited Users Can Subscribe To This Calendar** if you want to restrict access to your calendar.

5. Click **Anyone Can Subscribe To This Calendar** if you want to share your Calendar with anyone.

CAUTION

Be careful when you set the date range of a calendar snapshot. If you set it for a long period, the e-mail file might be too big for the recipient's e-mail Inbox.

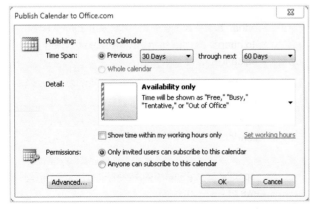

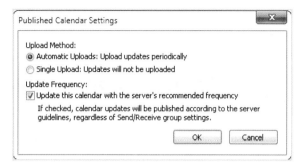

6. Click **Advanced** to open the Published Calendar Settings dialog box.

7. Click **Automatic Uploads** if you want Outlook 2010 to periodically update your published calendar automatically.

8. Click **Single Upload** if you do not want to have your calendar updated.

9. Click **OK** to publish your calendar.

10. After your calendar has been successfully published, you are prompted to create an e-mail announcing this fact. Click **Yes** to create the e-mail, or click **No** to close the dialog box.

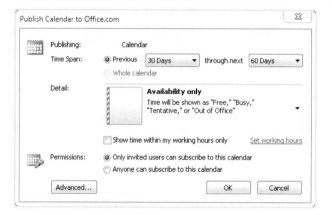

Use the Calendar

Within the calendar, you can enter several types of activities.

- **Appointments** take time on your calendar, are less than 24 hours long, and do not require inviting others within Outlook to attend. Examples include a sales call, lunch with a buyer, or time you want to set aside to write a report.

- **Meetings** are appointments that require that others be invited and/or that resources be reserved. Meetings are set up using e-mail.

- **All Day Events** are 24 hours or longer, do not occupy time on your calendar, and appear as a banner on each day's calendar. Examples are conferences, birthdays, or your vacation.

- **Tasks** are activities that do not need specific time periods for them. Your tasks display in the Day, Work Week, and Week views of your calendar.

All types of activities can be entered in several ways and with a number of options.

UNDERSTANDING INTERNET CALENDARS

There are several types of Internet calendars. We've discussed sharing the calendar via e-mail and publishing it to Microsoft Office Online. There is another type of Internet calendar that is downloaded from calendar publishing services or special Web sites that host calendars. This downloaded calendar is created and saved in Outlook. Most Internet calendar companies charge a subscription fee for this service. While calendar snapshots are not updated with any regularity, a subscription to an Internet calendar means that your calendar is synchronized on a regular basis with a calendar saved on a Web server. The updates that result from the synchronization are downloaded to your Internet calendar.

TIP

Try using text dates, as described in the "Entering Dates and Times" QuickSteps, and you'll be amazed at how Outlook can interpret what you enter.

ENTERING DATES AND TIMES

The Outlook Calendar allows you to enter dates and times as text and convert that text to numeric dates and times. For example, you can type "next tue" and be given next Tuesday's date, or you can type "sep ninth" and see that date. You can type this way in any date or time field in Outlook, such as the Go To Date dialog box, reached by pressing **CTRL+G**, or right-clicking any empty spot on the Calendar grid while in Day, Work Week, Week, or Month view. Likewise, you can type in the Start and End date and time fields in the appointment and event views or the Meeting dialog box. Some of the things you can do include:

- Abbreviate months and days (for example, *Dec* or *fri*).

- Ignore capitalization and other punctuation (for example, *wednesday, april,* and *lincolns birthday*).

- Use words that indicate dates and times (for example, *noon, midnight, tomorrow, yesterday, today, now, next week, last month, five days ago, in three months, this Saturday,* and *two weeks from now*). Words you can use include *after, ago, before, beforehand, beginning, end, ending, following, for, from, last, next, now, previous, start, that, this, through, till, tomorrow, yesterday, today,* and *until*.

- Spell out specific dates and times (for example, *August ninth, first of December, April 19th, midnight, noon, two twenty p.m.,* and *five o'clock a.m.*).

- Indicate holidays that fall on the same date every year (for example, *New Year's Eve, New Year's Day, Lincoln's Birthday, Valentine's Day, Washington's Birthday, St. Patrick's Day, Cinco de Mayo, Independence Day, Halloween, Veterans' Day, Christmas Eve, Christmas Day,* and *Boxing Day*).

Create Appointments

Appointments can be entered in any view and in several different ways. Independent of the view you are using, the different ways can be grouped into direct entry and window entry. *Direct entry* means simply typing directly on the calendar, while *window entry* uses a window to gather the information, which is then displayed on the calendar. Direct entry is fast if you want to make a quick notation. Window entry allows you to select and set a number of options.

ENTER APPOINTMENTS DIRECTLY

You can directly enter an appointment on the calendar in any view by clicking a date or time and typing the description. If you want the entry longer or shorter than the default half hour (or whatever standard duration you have selected), just drag the top or bottom border up or down to change the time. If you want to move the appointment, simply drag it to where you want it in the current day or to another day in either the calendar itself or the Date Navigator. To change the properties of an appointment, double-click the appointment, which opens the context menu, where a number of properties can be set.

To directly enter appointments:

1. Click any date and time in the Calendar grid in the Day, Work Week, Week, Month, or Schedule view. Type a short description of the appointment, and press **ENTER**.

2. Place the mouse pointer on the sizing handle at the bottom border of the appointment. Drag the border down until the end of the appointment time.

3. If you need to change the beginning time of your appointment, drag the top border up or down until the proper time is reflected in the calendar.

ENTER ALL-DAY EVENTS DIRECTLY

An all-day event is an activity that normally lasts at least 24 hours, although you can designate something as an event that lasts less than 24 hours but takes most of your time that day, such as a company picnic. Examples of events are conferences, seminars, and holidays. If events are tied to specific dates, they are considered annual events, such as a birthday or holiday. When you enter an event, it is considered free time, not busy. You create events differently than appointments.

All events appear in the banner at the top of the daily schedule, while all appointments are on the calendar itself. To directly enter an event:

1. With the Outlook Calendar open in Day, Work Week, or Week view, select a day in the Calendar grid when the event will take place.

2. Click in the dark blue area at the top of the daily schedule, just under the date header, type the event name, and press **ENTER**.

ENTER APPOINTMENTS IN A WINDOW

As an alternative to directly entering appointments and events, you can use a New Appointment window, seen in Figure 5-7, to accomplish the same objective and immediately be able to enter a lot more information. To open a New Appointment window:

1. In the Outlook Calendar, in the Home tab, click **New Appointment** in the New group.

2. Click **Subject** and type the subject of the appointment. This text becomes the description in the calendar, with the location added parenthetically and the date and time determining where the appointment goes on the calendar.

3. Press **TAB**. Type the location, if relevant, in the Location text box.

4. Click the **Start Time** down arrow on the left to display a small calendar in which you can choose a date.

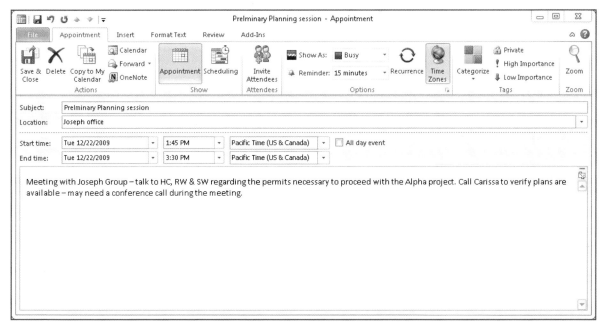

Figure 5-7: **The Appointment window is used to set up or change an appointment.**

5. Click the down arrow on the right, and select a start time.

6. Click the **End Time** down arrow, and select the end date and time. By default, the end date for an appointment is the same date as the start date unless you have selected All Day Event.

7. If you have selected more than one time zone, select the appropriate time zone for this appointment.

8. Type any notes or other information necessary in the message section of the Appointment dialog box.

9. In the Appointment tab Options group, click the **Show As** down arrow, and tell Outlook how to display this time slot on your calendar.

   - **Free**   This time is available to be scheduled for an appointment.

   - **Tentative**   This time is potentially scheduled, but is currently not finalized.

   - **Busy**   This time is now unavailable to be scheduled for anything else.

   - **Out Of Office**   This time is unavailable and cannot be scheduled.

10. In the Appointment tab Options group, click the **Reminder** down arrow, and set the reminder time. See "Use Reminders" later in this chapter for more information.

11. In the Appointment tab Actions group, click **Save & Close** to save your appointment.

ENTER AN EVENT IN A WINDOW

To enter an all-day event:

1. In the Outlook Calendar, from the ribbon's Home tab, click **New Items** in the New group.

2. Click **All Day Event**. The New Event window opens.

3. Click **Subject** to enter text describing the event as it will appear on your calendar.

4. Click **Location** to type information about the location. By default, All Day Event is selected.

5. Repeat steps 8–11 from "Enter Appointments in a Window." The start and end times become unavailable; the reminder, by default, goes to 18 hours; and Show Time As changes to Free, as seen in Figure 5-8.

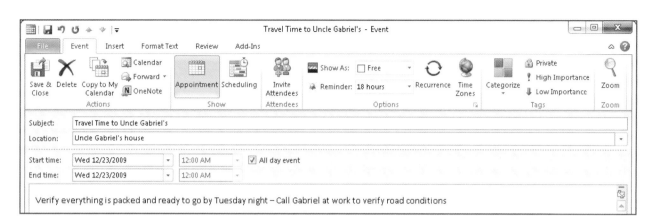

Figure 5-8: *An Event window looks much like the Appointment window, except All Day Event is selected.*

Enter Recurring Appointments

Often, you'll have appointments and events that recur predictably, for example, a weekly staff meeting, a monthly planning meeting, a monthly lunch with a friend, and birthdays. You obviously do not want to re-enter these every week, month, or year. Outlook has a feature that allows you to enter these activities once and have them reappear on a given frequency for as long as you want.

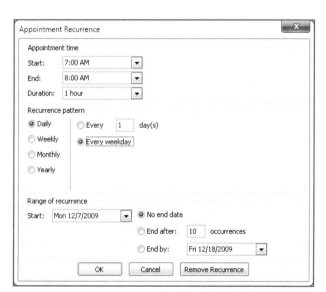

Figure 5-9: *Use the Appointment Recurrence dialog box to schedule recurring appointments automatically.*

1. Create a new appointment as described in "Enter Appointments in a Window."

2. In the Appointments tab Options group, click **Recurrence**. The Appointment Recurrence dialog box appears, as shown in Figure 5-9.

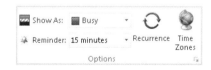

3. Click the **Start** down arrow, and select the start time of this recurring appointment.

4. Click the **End** down arrow, and select the end time.

5. Click the **Duration** down arrow, and select the length of time this appointment lasts.

6. Click **Recurrence Pattern** and choose how often this appointment occurs. The specific fields you enter to complete the pattern will differ, depending on the appointment interval you choose.

7. Under Range Of Recurrence, click the down arrow, select the date this appointment starts, the number of times it occurs, and its ending date.

8. Click **OK** to close the Appointment Recurrence dialog box.

9. Click **Save & Close**.

EDIT RECURRING APPOINTMENTS

To change one instance of a recurring appointment:

1. In the Outlook Calendar, locate and double-click a recurring appointment in any calendar view. The Open Recurring Item dialog box appears.

2. Click **Open This Occurrence** if you want to make a change to only this instance of the appointment.

3. Click **OK** to open the Appointment window and make the necessary changes to this occurrence of the appointment.

4. In the Appointment Occurrence tab Actions group, click **Save & Close**.

To change all instances of a recurring appointment:

1. In the calendar, locate and double-click the recurring appointment in any calendar view. The Open Recurring Item dialog box appears.

2. Click **Open The Series** if you want to make a change to the recurring appointment itself.

3. Click **OK** to open the Appointment window.

4. In the Appointment Occurrence tab Options group, click **Recurrence** (if you forgot to click Open The Series in step 2, you will see "Edit Series" in place of "Recurrence"). The Appointment Recurrence dialog box appears.

5. Make the necessary changes to this appointment, and click **OK**.

6. In the Appointment Occurrence tab Actions group, click **Save & Close**.

Move Appointments

If an appointment changes times within a day, you can move it to its new time by simply dragging it to that new time, as you saw earlier. If you entered an event on the wrong day, or if an appointment changes days, you can drag it to the correct day in the Work Week, Week, or Month view or in the Date Navigator. You cannot drag a recurring appointment to a date that skips over

TIP

You can delete a single instance of a recurring activity without affecting the rest of the series. If you choose to delete a recurring activity, the dialog box asks if you want to delete the current instance of the activity or the entire series.

another occurrence of the same appointment. You can, however, change a recurring appointment to another date before the next one occurs. The different ways to move appointments or events are:

- Drag the appointment to the day you want in a Work Week, Week, or Month view; Calendar Navigator; or Date Navigator. You can drag an appointment anywhere in the Calendar grid by dragging from anywhere in the appointment, except at the expansion points on the middle of the sides.
- When you drag an appointment to a new day, it will be placed in the same time slot. You can change the time by dragging it to the new time, either before or after you move it to the new day.

Use Reminders

When you have set a reminder for an appointment, the Reminder dialog box appears at the time you have set before the appointment. You have several choices in the dialog box.

- Click **Dismiss All** to close the reminder and tell it not to appear again.
- Click **Snooze** to tell the dialog box when to remind you again but close the reminder for now.
- Click **Open Item** to open the Appointment window so that you can make changes to the appointment, the reminder, or both.
- Click **Dismiss** to close only the highlighted reminder.

Print Calendars

When you have completed making entries on your calendar, you may want to take it with you, away from your computer, for reference and to jot new appointments on. For this reason, Outlook includes a number of printed formats to fit your needs.

To print your calendar:

1. In any view in Outlook Calendar, click the **File** tab.
2. Click **Print** to open the Print Setting dialog box, as seen in Figure 5-10.

TIP

You can copy an activity by right-dragging it (use the right mouse button) to where you want the copy and selecting **Copy** from the context menu that appears when you release the right mouse button.

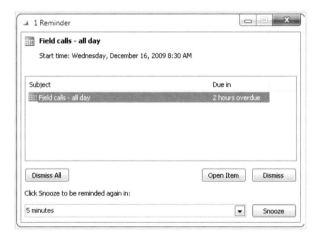

NOTE

Reminders are wonderful if they are used sparingly. If they are constantly going off and you dismiss them, then they are of little value. The default is for a reminder to be automatically turned on, so you must turn it off in a new appointment if you don't want it.

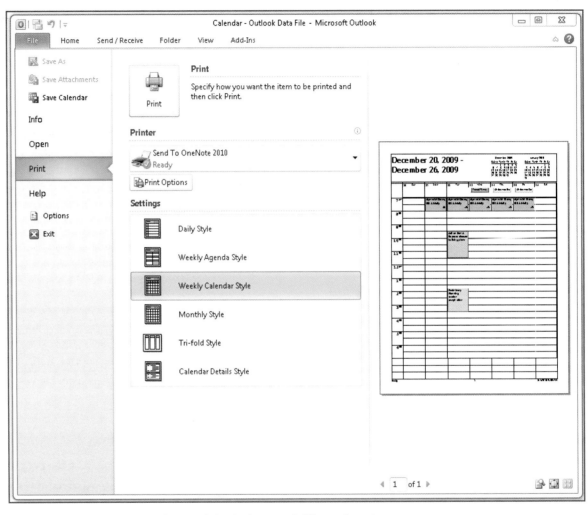

Figure 5-10: You can print your Outlook Calendar in several different formats.

3. In the Settings area, select the format for your printed calendar. There are several from which to choose, and each style will display in the Preview area.

4. Click **Print Options** and click the print style you want to print. Your choices are determined by the Calendar view you have chosen.

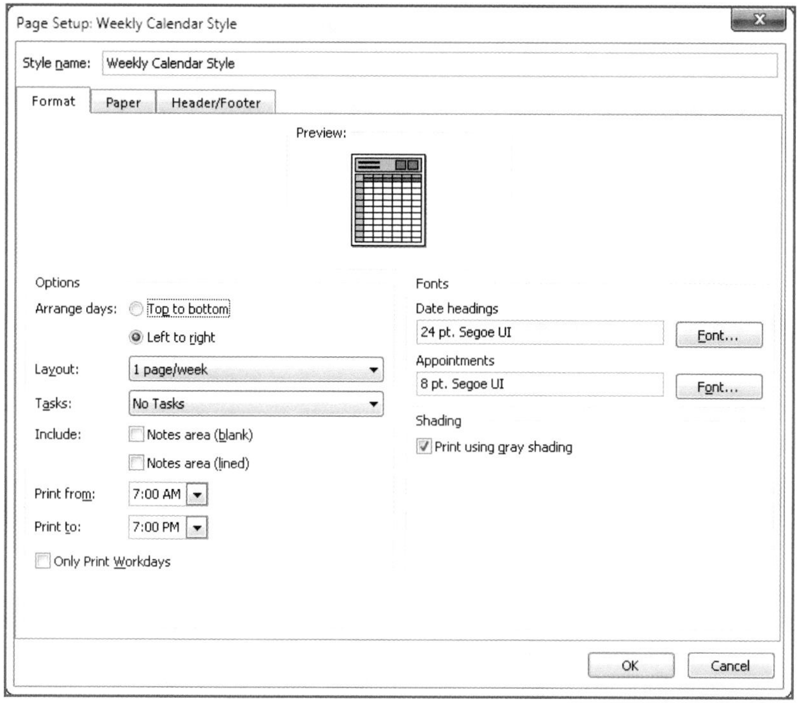

Page Setup: Weekly Calendar Style

Style name: | Weekly Calendar Style

| Format | Paper | Header/Footer |

Preview:

Options

Arrange days: ○ Top to bottom
               ◉ Left to right

Layout: 1 page/week

Tasks: No Tasks

Include: ☐ Notes area (blank)
           ☐ Notes area (lined)

Print from: 7:00 AM ▼

Print to: 7:00 PM ▼

☐ Only Print Workdays

Fonts

Date headings
| 24 pt. Segoe UI | Font... |

Appointments
| 8 pt. Segoe UI | Font... |

Shading
☑ Print using gray shading

| OK | Cancel |

*Figure 5-11: **The Print Setup dialog box gives you considerable flexibility with regard to the print style, the format, paper specifications, and header/footer information.***

5. Click **Page Setup** to open the Print Setup dialog box shown in Figure 5-11.

   a. Click the **Format** tab, and make any changes in the Options and Fonts sections.

   b. Click the **Shading** check box if you want gray shading to be used in your printed calendar.

   c. Click the **Paper** tab to choose the paper specifications.

   d. Click the **Header/Footer** tab to add the professional touch of a header and/or a footer.

   e. When you are ready, click **Preview** to see how your printed calendar will look.

   f. Click **Print** to print your calendar.

Plan Meetings and Request Attendance

In addition to using Outlook 2010 for scheduling appointments and events, you can use Outlook to plan and schedule meetings. In Outlook, a meeting is an appointment to which others are invited.

Schedule a Meeting

You create a meeting by identifying the people you want to invite and picking a meeting time. You e-mail a meeting request to people in your Outlook Contacts who you want to attend.

1. Open the calendar.

2. From the Home tab, click **New Meeting** in the New group.

   –Or–

   Press **CTRL+SHIFT+Q**.

   In either event, the New Meeting window opens, as seen in Figure 5-12.

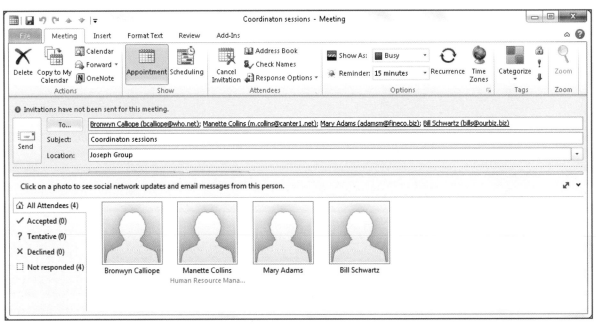

Figure 5-12: The Meeting window allows you to send out invitations, track who can attend, and schedule resources for the meeting.

3. Click **To**, double-click your attendees from your Contacts list, and click **OK.**

4. Click in the **Subject** text box, and type a description for your meeting. This description will appear on all calendars.

5. Click in the **Location** text box, and type the location information, if necessary.

6. Click the **Start Time** down arrow, and select the date and time the meeting is to start.

7. Click the **End Time** down arrow, and select the date and time the meeting is scheduled to end.

8. Click **All Day Event**, if necessary.

9. Enter any additional information in the Notes section of the Meeting window that may be needed by the attendees.

10. In the Meeting tab Show group, click **Scheduling**. In the All Attendees column, click **Click Here To Add A Name** to include others in the meeting. (If you don't see it, enlarge the window.) If necessary, click **Add Others** to add names.

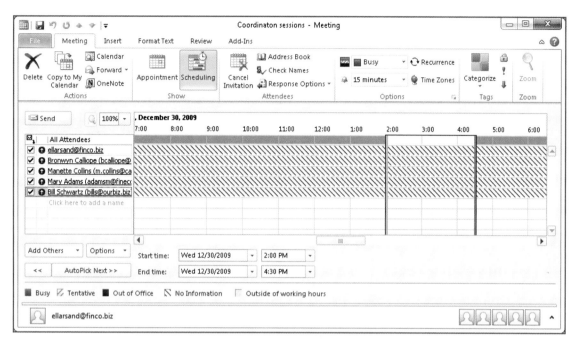

11. If you want to change the meeting times, you can enter the start and ending times, or you can drag the edges of the vertical meeting line, as shown in Figure 5-13.

12. Click **Close** to open the Close Meeting dialog box. Choose to save your changes and either send or not send the meeting announcement or not to save changes.

Figure 5-13: The Scheduling dialog box allows you to send out invitations, track who can attend, and schedule resources for the meeting.

Respond to an Invitation

When you receive a meeting request, a message appears in your Inbox with an icon that is different from the normal e-mail icon.

1. In Outlook, open the meeting notification or request.

2. On the Message tab Respond group, click one of the following:

- Accept
- Tentative
- Decline

3. To send your response with no comments, click **Send The Response Now**. Click **OK**.

4. To include comments with your response, click **Edit The Response Before Sending**.

5. Type your comments and click **Send**.

6. To send no response, click **Don't Send A Response**, and click **OK**. The meeting is added to your calendar.

Chapter 6

Using Tasks

Keeping organized and meeting appointments and deadlines is important to us all. Outlook can help you stay organized and can even alert you to events and appointments. Outlook defines a task as something you create and track until the item is complete. Any incomplete tasks appear on the To-Do bar, along with other Outlook items you have marked for follow-up. The To-Do bar appears in every Outlook 2010 area, so you can see what you need to accomplish at a glance. An Outlook item can be an e-mail you need to answer, a contact you have marked to call back next week, or some other uncompleted task. In this chapter, you will learn how to create and manage tasks, mark items for follow-up by both you and e-mail recipients, modify and delete tasks, and share task information with others.

Use the Task Window

Tasks are Outlook items, just like e-mail and calendar entries, and when you create tasks, they are stored in a specific Outlook window. The Tasks window keeps all of your tasks in one place and automatically keeps them organized for you. In this section, you'll see how to use the Tasks window and how to view tasks.

Explore the Tasks Window

You can easily access the Tasks window and view your tasks.

1. Open Outlook as described in Chapter 1 if it is not already open.

2. From the Outlook View, click **Tasks**.

   –Or–

   Press **CTRL+4**.

In all cases, the Outlook Tasks view opens with your tasks listed in the center of the window, as shown in Figure 6-1. The window contains a listing of any existing tasks, which also appear in the Tasks section of the To-Do bar on the right side of the window.

View Tasks

By default, Outlook gives you a simple list view of your tasks in the Outlook Tasks view. You see the name of the task, the due date, the category, and any flags you have assigned to the task. However, you can re-sort these tasks in various ways using several different views, depending on the information you need, which can make your work easier.

1. Click the **View** tab to see the ribbon's groups.

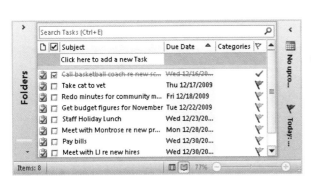

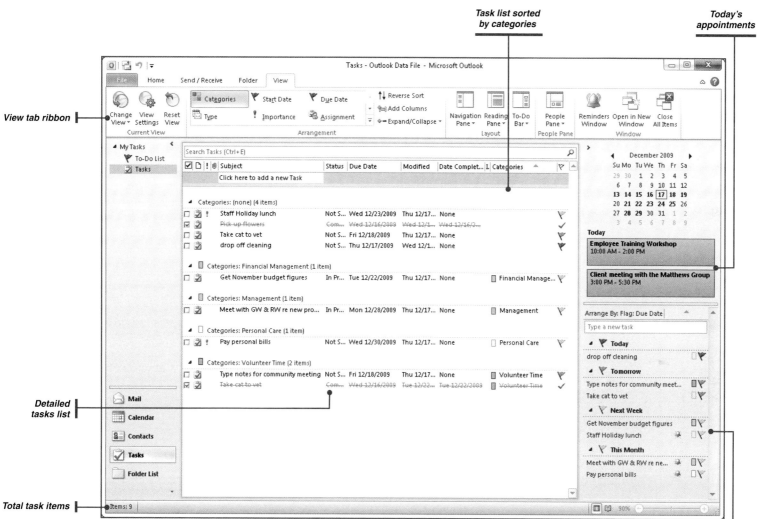

Task list sorted by categories

Today's appointments

View tab ribbon

Detailed tasks list

Total task items

To-Do bar with tasks displayed

Figure 6-1: **The Tasks window displays a listing of your tasks in both the center pane and in the To-Do bar.**

2. In the Current View group, click **Change View**. You can change your view of the tasks by clicking the different options.

- **Simple List** displays a listing of your tasks with the subject, due date, categories, and flags shown.

- **Detailed** displays the subject, status, due date, date modified, folder location, categories, and flags, as shown in Figure 6-2.

- **Active** is the same as Detailed, but only shows tasks that are currently active—that is, tasks that have not been deferred or completed.

- **Overdue** is the same as Detailed, but only shows tasks that are overdue.

- **Completed** shows you all tasks that have been completed.

- **Assigned** shows you tasks that have been assigned to others. This view shows you the task, the owner, the due date, and the status of each task.

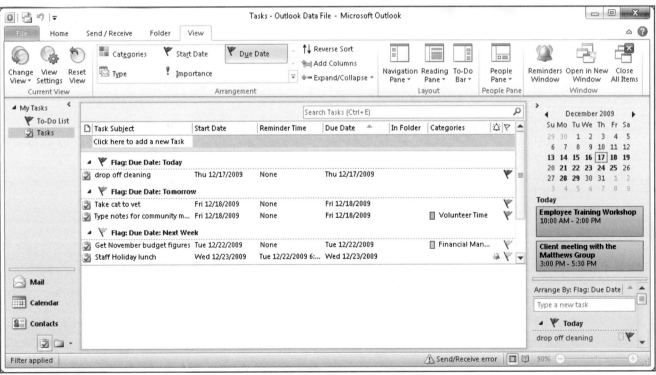

Figure 6-2: Viewing your tasks in to-do list format can help you set daily priorities.

- **To Do List** shows the task subject, its start date, reminder time, due date, folder, categories, and flags. This view groups the tasks by start date.

- **Today** is the same as Detailed, but only shows tasks for today.

- **Server Tasks** are used with Microsoft Exchange accounts. This view includes the name of the person to whom the task has been assigned.

- **Prioritized** shows the list grouped by priority.

- **Next 7 Days** is the same as Detailed, but only shows tasks for the next seven days.

CREATE A NEW TASK VIEW

You can modify any task view to fit your needs.

1. Click the **View** tab to see the ribbon's View groups.

2. In the Current View group, click **Change View**. Click **Manage Views** to open the Manage All Views dialog box.

3. Click **New** to open the Create A New View dialog box.

4. Type a name for your new view. Choose the type of view you want to create.

   - Click **Table** to create a view that displays the standard views in a table format.

   - Click **Timeline** to create a view that shows your tasks in a timeline format, as shown in Figure 6-3.

   - Click **Card** to display your tasks in a card format.

     - Click **Business Card** to display your tasks in the same format as a business card.

     - Click **Day/Week/Month** to display tasks in a calendar format.

   - Click **Icons** to display tasks as icons.

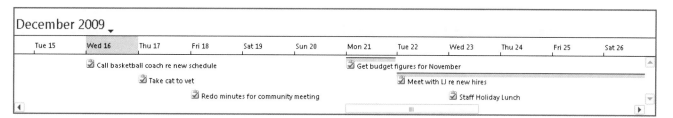

Figure 6-3: **Using the Timeline view can help you see your scheduled tasks according to calendar dates.**

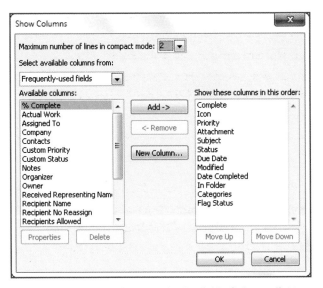

Figure 6-4: *Choose items from the Available Columns list to create a personalized task view.*

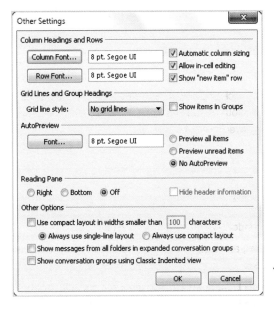

5. Once you have chosen the type of view and clicked OK, the Advanced View Settings dialog box appears.

a. Click **Columns** to select the columns to display in your customized view, as seen in Figure 6-4.

b. Choose the fields you want displayed in your Tasks window. Click **OK** when you are finished.

6. Click **Group By**, click the **Group Items By** down arrow, click the item on which to group, click **Ascending** or **Descending**, and choose whether to show the field. Repeat this process for up to three more subgroupings, and then click **OK**.

7. Click **Sort**, click the **Sort Items By** down arrow, click the item on which to sort, and click **Ascending** or **Descending**. Repeat this process for up to three more subsorts, and then click **OK**.

8. Click **Filter**, click in the **Search For The Word(s)** text box, type the words to search on, click the **In** down arrow, click where you want to search, and use the other fields to locate just tasks you want to work with. Enter any other criteria, and click **OK**.

9. Click **Other Settings** to set font size, font face, and other visual settings for your view. In the AutoPreview section, choose how you want to use AutoPreview, if and where you want the Reading pane, and make any desired changes in the Other Options section.

10. Click **Conditional Formatting**. Set your desired rules, change the font if you desire, and click **OK**.

QUICKSTEPS

CUSTOMIZING TASK SETTINGS

You can customize options in the Outlook Tasks view by changing the default settings for it. To change the Tasks options:

1. With Tasks selected on the Outlook View, right-click anywhere on the ribbon or the tabs. Click **Customize The Ribbon**.

> Add to Quick Access Toolbar
>
> Customize Quick Access Toolbar...
>
> Show Quick Access Toolbar Below the Ribbon
>
> Customize the Ribbon...
>
> Minimize the Ribbon

2. Click the **File** tab, and then click **Options**. On the Outlook Options dialog box, click **Tasks**.

3. In the Tasks view, click the **Set Reminders On Tasks With Due Dates** check box to have the option to set reminder times each time you create a task.

4. Click the **Default Reminder Time** down arrow, and if you want an alternate time other than the default of 8:00 A.M., click your choice.

> **Task options**
>
> ☐ Set reminders on tasks with due dates
> Default reminder time: 8:00 AM ▾
> ☑ Keep my task list updated with copies of tasks I assign to other people
> ☑ Send status report when I complete an assigned task

5. Clear the **Keep My Task List Updated** check box if you do not want to track tasks you've assigned to others.

Continued . . .

11. Click **Format Columns**; click the field (or column) to format; and change the format, label, width, and alignment of the field you selected.

12. Click **Reset Current View** if you want to return to the view's default settings.

13. When you have made all of your changes, click **OK** to close the dialog box. Click **Apply View** to continue making changes, or click **OK** to close the Manage All Views dialog box.

Create Tasks

To use the Outlook Tasks feature, you'll have to create tasks. As new appointments, jobs, and other tasks come your way, you can simply create a task in the Tasks window to organize your work. In this section, you'll see how to create a task from several different locations, change a task, make a recurring task, and more.

Create a New Task from the Ribbon

The ribbon, now an established part of Microsoft Outlook, is where new tasks are added. You'll see that Outlook 2010 continues this approach, making this familiar and easy.

1. In the Outlook Tasks view Home tab New group, click **New Task**.

   –Or–

   From the Task pane, double-click **Click Here To Add a New Task** at the top of the pane. In the To-Do List view, you will see "Task Subject" above the new task field instead of "Subject," as displayed in the other views.

   Either way, the new Task window opens, as shown in Figure 6-5.

2. Click in the **Subject** text box, and type a name for this task. This is all the information you must enter for your task.

3. If you choose, click the **Start Date** down arrow to display a calendar from which you can choose the starting date for this task, or simply type a date.

CUSTOMIZING TASK SETTINGS

(Continued)

6. By default, the **Send Status Report When I Complete An Assigned Task** check box is selected. If you want, clear the check box by clicking it. Both of these items are used primarily by those users on Microsoft Exchange Server.

7. Click the **Overdue Task Color** down arrow to display a drop-down list of other colors from which you can choose. Click the color you want to use instead of the default red.

8. Click the **Completed Task Color** down arrow, and change the color of completed tasks to the color you want to use.

9. Click the **Quick Click** button to assign flags to tasks with a single click.

10. Set the number of working hours per day and per week using the up and down arrows in the spinners.

11. Click **OK** to close the Outlook Options dialog box.

TIP

To create a new task from anywhere in Outlook, press **CTRL+SHIFT+K**.

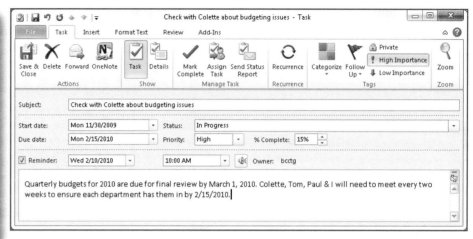

Figure 6-5: **The new Task window helps you enter information about a job you must complete.**

4. If you have chosen to enter a start date, the due date is automatically the same date. Click the **Due Date** down arrow to display a calendar from which you can choose the date this task is to be completed.

5. You can keep track of the progress of this task with the Status, Priority, and %Complete boxes.

   - Click the **Status** down arrow to choose the current stage of this task.
   - Click **Priority** to set the importance of this task to low, normal, or high.
   - Click **%Complete** to enter what percentage of the task is currently complete. You can also use the up and down arrows to scroll among 25%, 50%, 75%, and 100%.

6. If you want to be reminded of this task, click the **Reminder** check box and then the down arrow, and choose a date on which to be reminded. Type a time for the reminder or choose one from the drop-down list.

7. Click the 🔊 to open the Reminder Sound dialog box.

   - Click **Play This Sound** to hear the sound that will play.
   - Click **Browse** to look for and select another sound file that you want to play as a reminder.
   - Click **OK** to close the dialog box.

8. Click in the task body to add any information or notes about this task.

9. To save the task, click **Save & Close** in the Actions group.

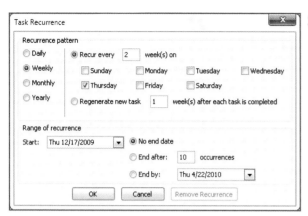

Figure 6-6: *The Task Recurrence dialog box is used when you create repeating tasks.*

Set Recurring Tasks

If you want to have a task reappear in your To-Do bar on a regular basis, such as paying your bills each month on the tenth, you need to tell Outlook.

1. From the Tasks pane, double-click the task you want to recur. The Task window opens.

2. On the Task tab Recurrence group, click **Recurrence** to open the Task Recurrence dialog box.

3. Click **Monthly** if you want to have this task appear on a monthly basis. Choose one of the other options if they apply. The choices displayed will vary depending on the recurrence pattern you choose.

4. Click **Day** to set the day of the month on which this task is to appear, and enter how many months. For example, if you want your task to appear on the 30th of every month, type 30 and 1, as seen in Figure 6-6.

5. Alternately, you can designate the first, last, or other week and corresponding day of the month.

6. Click **Regenerate New Task _ Month(s) After Each Task Is Completed**, and enter the number of months between appearances if this is a monthly, quarterly, or other repeating task, such as paying your bills.

7. Click **No End Date** if the recurrence of the task is permanent—as in paying bills. If the task occurs for only a specific amount of time, choose the option that applies.

8. Click **OK** to close the dialog box. In the Task tab Actions group, click **Save & Close**.

SKIP A RECURRING TASK

1. From the Tasks pane, double-click the recurring task with which you want to work. The Task window opens.

2. On the Task tab Recurrence group, click **Skip Occurrence**. The current occurrence of this task will be skipped, and the due date is set to the next regular occurrence.

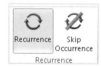

3. Click **Save & Close** from the ribbon to save your change.

4. If you have set a specific number of occurrences for this task, the number is reduced by one.

END A RECURRING TASK

If you wish to end a recurring task:

1. From the Tasks pane, double-click the recurring task you want to end. The Task window will open.

2. On the Task tab Recurrence group, click **Recurrence** to open the Task Recurrence dialog box.

3. Click **Remove Recurrence** at the bottom of the dialog box. Remove Recurrence

4. Click **Save & Close** from the ribbon.

Categorize a Task

If a task belongs with other Outlook items in a specific category:

1. From the Tasks pane, double-click the task you want to categorize.

2. On the Task tab Tags group, click **Categorize** to open the Color Category menu.

3. Click the category to which this task belongs. The category appears at the top of the Task window.

4. From the ribbon, click **Save & Close**.

CREATE A TASK IN THE TO-DO BAR

By default, the To-Do bar appears in most Outlook views. However in the Calendar, you must choose Classic view to display the To-Do bar. You can easily create a new task in the To-Do bar itself.

1. In any Outlook view, click the task input panel. (You may see this as the Type A New Task text box.)

2. The text box changes to an outlined box with a blinking cursor. Type a quick description for the task, and press **ENTER**.

3. The new task will appear immediately in your Outlook Tasks view with today as both the start and due dates. The new task also appears under Today in the To-Do bar.

4. Double-click the new task in the To-Do bar to make any changes to it.

NOTE

To change or remove the color category of an existing task, in the Task pane, right-click the **Categories** field, and choose **Clear All Categories** or choose another color category.

CREATE A NEW TASK IN CALENDAR

When you are working in the Day, Work Week, or Week view in the Outlook Calendar view, you can choose to display the Tasks list at the bottom of the Calendar grid. You can quickly add a new task from this list.

1. In the Outlook Calendar view, click **Day, Work Week**, or **Week**. The Tasks list appears beneath the Calendar grid.

2. Position your mouse pointer in a blank area of the Tasks list, and click the **Click To Add Task** message that appears under your mouse pointer. A text box appears.

3. You may also right-click in a blank area to open a context menu. Click **Task** to open a Task dialog box.

4. Type a name or subject for your task, and press **ENTER**. The task will be assigned the same start and end dates of the day in which the Tasks list appears.

5. To change these dates, you can drag the task to the proper date or double-click the task and make the changes.

ADD A NEW TASK FROM AN E-MAIL MESSAGE

From time to time, you may receive an e-mail that you need to make into a task.

1. In Outlook, from the Mail view, click the e-mail to select it.

2. Hold down the mouse button and drag the e-mail message to the Task button on the Outlook View.

3. The New Task window opens with a copy of the e-mail appearing in the task body. It may be placed beneath your e-mail window. If so, minimize the e-mail window so you can see the Task window. Make any changes or additions you need, as described in "Create a New Task from the Ribbon" earlier in this chapter.

4. From the Task ribbon, click **Save & Close** to save the new task.

CHANGE A TASK

Some of the tasks that you create will change. The report that was due in a month is suddenly due in a week, and the conference call you had planned for 10:00 A.M. changes to 4:00 P.M. You can easily change and edit your tasks. To change a task:

1. Double-click your selected task from the Outlook Tasks view.

   –Or–

   Double-click the selected task in the To-Do bar.

   In either case, the Task window will open.

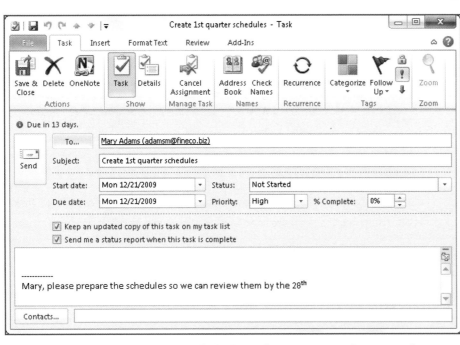

Follow up. Start by Monday, December 21, 2009. Due by Tuesday, December 29, 2009.
Due in 12 days.

Financial Tasks

Subject: Get budget figures for November

Start date: Mon 12/21/2009   Status: In Progress

Due date: Tue 12/29/2009   Priority: High   % Complete: 15%

Reminder: None   None   Owner: Ellar Sands

Check with each department head on the 21st to ensure their preliminary figures will be to the section managers by the 29th. (Note, offices are closed the 30th and 31st)

Figure 6-7: **You can make many changes to a task.**

2. Make any desired changes to the task. For example, in Figure 6-7, we have changed the due date for the task, changed the status to In Progress, and changed its percentage complete to 15%. We have also added a note to remind us that the office will be closed on the 30th and 31st of December.

3. When you're done, click **Save & Close** from the ribbon.

Assign a New Task

You can easily create a task and assign it to someone else who is using Microsoft Outlook.

1. In the Outlook Tasks view, on the Home tab New group, click **New Task**. The Task window will open, as shown in Figure 6-8.

2. From the Task tab Manage Task group, click **Assign Task**.

3. Click **To** and enter the name or e-mail address of the person to whom you are assigning the task.

4. Click **Subject** and enter a name for this new task.

5. If you choose, click the **Start Date** and **Due Date** down arrows, and enter the beginning and due dates of this task, respectively.

6. If you choose, click the **Status** and **Priority** down arrows to enter the current status and priority level of this task.

7. If any part of the task has been completed, indicate the percentage in the **% Complete** field.

8. Clear the **Keep An Updated Copy Of This Task On My Task List** check box (which is selected by default) if you do not want to have this task updated.

9. Click the **Send Me A Status Report When This Task Is Complete** check box (also selected by default) if you don't want to receive a status report.

10. Click in the body of the task, and type any additional information needed by the assignee.

Figure 6-8: **Assigning a task to another Outlook user is as easy as sending an e-mail.**

TIP

You can assign the same task to several people by simply typing all e-mail addresses in the To text box, just as you would with any e-mail.

TIP

The recipient must accept the task that you send in order for it to be added to his or her Task window. You will receive an e-mail receipt from the recipient once the task is accepted.

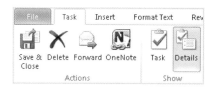

11. If you want this task to be recurring, in the Task tab Recurrence group, click **Recurrence** and follow the steps outlined in "Set Recurring Tasks" earlier in this chapter.

12. Click **Send** to send the task request.

ASSIGN AN EXISTING TASK

1. In the Outlook Tasks view, double-click the task you want to assign. The Task window opens.

2. In the Task tab Manage Task group, click **Assign Task**. The Assign Task window will open.

3. Click **To** and type the e-mail address or name of the person to whom you are assigning this task. The e-mail subject will be the same name as the existing task.

4. Follow steps 5–12 in "Assign a New Task" earlier in this chapter.

TRACK ASSIGNED TASKS

You can track assigned tasks in three ways: automatically keep copies, view assigned tasks, and view a list of people who have received assigned tasks.

To automatically keep copies:

1. In Outlook Tasks, right-click anywhere on the ribbon, and select **Customize The Ribbon**.

From the Outlook Options dialog box, click **Tasks** to open the Tasks view. Choose **Keep My Tasks List Updated With Copies Of Tasks I Assign To Other People**.

2. Click **OK** to close the Outlook Options dialog box.

VIEW ASSIGNED TASKS AND RECIPIENTS

To view tasks you have assigned to others:

1. In the Outlook Tasks view, from the View tab Current View group, click **Change View**.

2. Click **Assigned**. The list of assigned tasks is displayed in your Task window.

To view a list of people who have received tasks:

1. In the Outlook Tasks view, double-click the assigned task you want to view.

2. From the Task tab Show group, click **Details** to see a list of people who have accepted the task. The names will appear in the Update List box.

3. In the Task tab Actions group, click **Save & Close**.

Make a Task Private

In networks that use Microsoft Exchange Server, you can give other people access to your tasks. For example, let's say you are a team leader for a department. Within your department, several department coordinators may need to access your tasks and enter tasks that you need to complete. This allows others to manipulate and change your tasks, which you can, of course, also work on yourself.

However, in some instances, you may create a task that you want to keep private in an environment like this. This action will keep people who have permission to view your tasks from seeing that particular task. To make a task private:

1. In the Outlook Tasks view, double-click a selected task to open it.

2. From the Task tab Tags group, click **Private**.

3. Click **Save & Close**. Your task is no longer visible to others.

Manage Tasks

After you have created a task, Outlook provides several tools you can use to manage them, including marking them as completed, choosing whether to display them, deleting, and renaming them, as well as creating status reports on your tasks.

Mark a Task as Complete

Once you finish a task, you can mark it as having been completed. The task will be attached to the day on which you marked it complete, and it will appear with a line drawn through it.

There are several ways in which you can mark a task as complete.

MARK A TASK AS COMPLETE FROM THE TASK WINDOW

1. From the Outlook Tasks view, double-click the selected task.

2. On the Task tab Manage Tasks group, click **Mark Complete**. The task will be marked as complete, and the Task window will close. The task will appear on your Task list with a line drawn through it.

CHANGE A TASK'S PERCENTAGE OF COMPLETION

1. From the Outlook Tasks view, double-click the selected task to open it.

2. Click the **% Complete** down arrow to change the percentage of complete.

3. Click **Save & Close** to close the task.

MARK A FLAGGED TASK AS COMPLETE FROM THE TASKS WINDOW

1. On the Outlook Tasks view, locate the task you want to mark as complete.

2. Click the flag. The flag turns into a check mark, and a line is drawn through the task.

MARK A TASK AS COMPLETE FROM THE TO-DO BAR

1. On the To-Do bar in any view of Outlook 2010, locate the task.

2. Right-click the task that you want to mark as complete.

3. Click **Mark Complete** on the context menu.

Choose to Not Display a Completed Task

Normally, when you complete a task, it remains on the Task list with a line through it. However, a task does not appear on the To-Do bar after it has been marked as complete.

SET COMPLETED ITEMS NOT TO DISPLAY IN A TASK LIST

1. In Outlook Tasks view, from the View tab Current View group, click **Change View**.

2. From the dialog box that appears, click **Active Tasks**. Only the active items will display on your list.

NOTE

If you want to change the status of a task you have marked as complete, click the item's **Status** field in Detailed List view to see a drop-down menu. Choose the status to which you want to change.

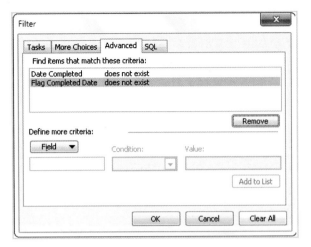

SHOW COMPLETED ITEMS IN THE TO-DO BAR

By default, the To-Do bar does not display completed items. To change this:

1. In the To-Do bar, right-click **Arrange By** to open its context menu.
2. Click **View Settings** to open the Advanced View Settings: To-Do List dialog box.
3. Click **Filter** to display the Filter dialog box.
4. Click the **Advanced** tab.
5. Select **Remove** or **Clear All** to clear the default choices.
6. Click **OK** to close the Filter dialog box.
7. Click **OK** once more to close the dialog box.

SHOW COMPLETED ITEMS IN THE DAILY TASK LIST

1. In the Outlook Calendar Day, Work Week, or Week view, click the **View** tab.
2. In the Layout group, click **Daily Task List**, and click **Normal**.

Delete a Task

Once a task has been completed, or should a task fall out of the scope of your responsibility, you can simply delete the task.

There are several ways to delete a task.

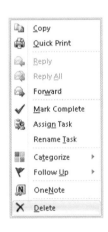

1. Right-click the task in the Outlook Tasks view, and click **Delete** on the context menu.
2. Double-click the task in the To-Do bar or in any Task list to open the Task window and click **Delete** in the Task tab's Actions group.
3. Click the selected task in any list, and press **CTRL+D**.

Rename a Task

As projects progress, it may be necessary to rename a task. You can do this at any time.

1. In Outlook Tasks view, in any list view (or in the Daily Task list in Calendar), click the selected task.
2. Press **F2**. The insertion point is placed at the end of the current name.
3. Press **BACKSPACE** to delete the old name, and type the new name.
4. Press **ENTER**.

NOTE

Be careful *not* to delete tasks that you still need, even if they are completed. Completed tasks provide a record of what has been accomplished, so make sure you no longer need the task before you delete it.

QUICKSTEPS

LINKING A TASK TO A CONTACT

There may be occasions when you want to link a task to one of your contacts. Before you can do this, it is necessary to set contacts to appear in your Outlook Tasks view.

1. In the Outlook Tasks view, double-click the item for which you want to add contacts.

2. Click **File** and click **Options**. In the Outlook Options dialog box that appears, click **Contacts**.

3. In the Linking section, click the **Show Contacts Links To The Current Item** check box. Click **OK** to close the Outlook Options dialog box.

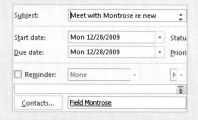

4. At the bottom of the Task window, click **Contacts** to display your Contacts list.

5. Double-click the name of the contact you want linked with this task. The name appears in the Contacts box in your task.

6. From the Task tab Actions group, click **Save & Close**.

Create Status Reports

Outlook allows you to create a status report for a task, which, in reality, is an e-mail message summarizing the status of your task. You can then send the e-mail to anyone who needs the status information. You can also print a copy for your records.

1. In the Outlook Tasks view, double-click the task on which you want to report. The Task window will open.

2. In the Task tab Manage Task group, click **Send Status Report**. An e-mail message will open, as seen in Figure 6-9.

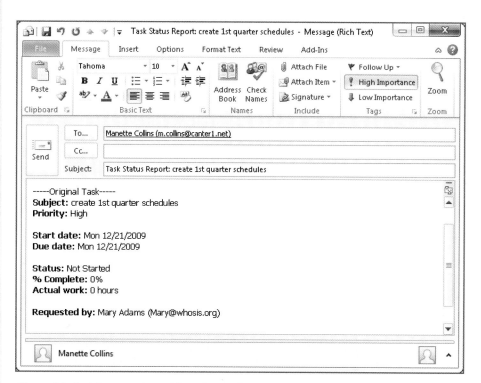

Figure 6-9: *A status report provides a fast and easy way to e-mail progress information on a task.*

3. Click **To** and find and select the e-mail address or the name of the person to whom you are sending the report. If it isn't in your Address Book, type it in the To field.

4. Click **Cc** if you want to send a carbon copy. Find and select the name or e-mail address in the Address Book, or type it in the Cc field.

5. Click **Bcc** and follow the procedure in step 4 for a blind carbon copy. The e-mail subject line is already filled in with "Task Status Report" and the name of your task.

6. Click in the message body, and type any additional comments or notes.

7. Click **Send**.

Work with Follow-up Flags

When you add a flag to any item in Outlook 2010, it is a visual reminder that you need to do something with that item. There are several default settings for the follow-up flags in Outlook 2010. Each is based on a date. Table 6-1 explains how the dates work. You can, however, customize the dates for any flag, and you do not need to set a reminder.

When you add a flag to any item, it is shown in the To-Do bar, the Task list in Calendar, and all Task lists in Tasks.

FLAG	START DATE	DUE DATE	REMINDER SETTING
Today	Today's date.	Today's date.	The reminder will prompt you one hour before the end of your current workday.
Tomorrow	Tomorrow's date.	Tomorrow's date.	You will be reminded at the start of your next workday.
This Week	Today plus two days, but no later than the last workday of this week.	The last workday of this week.	You are sent a reminder at the start time of today's date plus two days.
Next Week	The first workday of the next work week.	The last workday of the next work week.	You are sent a reminder at the start time of the first workday next week.
No Date	No date is set.	No date is set.	You are reminded today.
Custom	You may choose a start date.	You choose a due date.	You are reminded on the due date you set.

Table 6-1: **Default Settings for Follow-up Flags**

Add a Flag to an Existing Task

A flag draws your attention to a task. It is a signal that you need to follow up on this item. If you did not mark a task for follow-up when you created it, you can add the flag at any time.

1. In Outlook, click **Tasks** on the Outlook View to show your Task list.

2. Double-click the task with which you want to work to open the Task window.

3. In the Task tab Tags group, click **Follow Up**.

4. Click your selection from the menu.

5. If you want to include a reminder with this task, click **Follow Up** and then click **Add Reminder**. The Custom dialog box appears.

6. Click the **Flag To** down arrow, and choose an option.

7. The Start Date and Due Date fields are filled in with information from the existing task. Click the **Reminder** down arrow, and choose the date and time at which you want to be reminded.

8. Click **OK** to save your changes and close the Custom dialog box.

9. In the Task tab Actions group, click **Save & Close**.

10. You can also right-click the flag field on any task to set a follow-up date or add a reminder.

Set a Quick Click Flag

You can attach a Quick Click flag to any Outlook item. This flag, which is set to today's date by default, allows you to flag a task, contact, e-mail message, or other item with only one mouse click.

To add a Quick Click flag to a task:

1. In any Task list, right-click in the **Flag** column.

2. Click **Set Quick Click** on the context menu. The Set Quick Click dialog box will appear.

3. Click the **Flag** down arrow to select the settings for the Quick Click flag.

4. Choose the flag from the drop-down list that will appear upon being clicked.

5. Click **OK** to close the dialog box.

Work with the To-Do Bar

The To-Do bar has four parts, three of which can be hidden. The Task list remains displayed at all times.

Set the To-Do Bar to Show Only Tasks

Because, by default, all flagged items in Outlook are shown on the To-Do bar, there may be times when that is too much information. To turn off all items except your tasks:

1. Right-click in the top portion of the To-Do bar (immediately beneath the ribbon).
2. In the resulting context menu, clear the **Date Navigator** check box to hide the Date Navigator.
3. Reopen the To-Do Bar context menu, and clear the **Appointments** check box to hide your appointments.
4. To show either item again, reverse this procedure.

CHANGE THE SIZE OF THE TO-DO BAR

The To-Do bar can be resized using your mouse.

1. Position your mouse pointer at the left edge of the To-Do bar.
2. When the pointer changes to parallel lines with arrows, hold down the mouse button, and drag the To-do Bar to the width you want.

   —Or—

   Click the **Minimize** button at the top-left area of the To-Do bar to minimize it.

TOGGLE THE TO-DO BAR DISPLAY

By default, Outlook 2010 displays the To-Do bar in every view. However, you can choose to display it, minimize it, or turn it off in the current view. When you next start Outlook, the To-Do bar will still be turned off in the current view you were using when you last used Outlook.

1. To cycle through the To-Do bar display, press **ALT+F2**.
2. Use **ALT+F1** to cycle through the Outlook View options.

Chapter 7

Using a Journal and Making Notes

Microsoft Outlook contains two important features that help you stay organized and that can help you manage various pieces of information. These features—Journal and Notes—are designed to help you manage information that you need to record, keep, and use in a variety of ways. In this chapter you'll learn how to use both the Journal and Notes features. You'll see how to work with journal entries, print your journal entries, and even share them. You'll also see how to organize your notes, print them, and use them with other Outlook features.

Explore the Journal

The Outlook Journal is a great way to track and record different kinds of information. Designed for business use, the Journal can help you keep track of associated Office documents, e-mails to a certain contact, phone calls that you make, and other information. In other words, the Journal can help you keep track of your workflow so that you'll know what has been done. In this section you'll explore the Journal, set it up, work with journal entries, and print and share your journal.

Locate the Journal Icon

By default, the Journal is not one of the Outlook views in the Navigation pane or in the button bar at the bottom. You can, of course, access the Journal from the Mail view Home tab by clicking **New Items**, clicking **More Items**, and finally clicking **Journal Entry**; or by pressing CTRL+8. You can also change the Navigation pane to include the Journal in its list of views.

1. Click **Configure Buttons** on the right of the button bar, and select **Navigation Pane Options**.

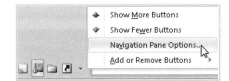

2. On the Navigation Pane Options dialog box, click **Journal.**

3. Click **Move Up** to display the Journal as an Outlook view or in the button bar.

4. Click **OK**.

Explore the Journal

Although the Journal is not immediately visible on the Outlook navigation bar, it is a standard Outlook feature. Once you have found it and positioned it on your Outlook views pane or button bar, you can easily access it from any view and explore its basic structure. (See "Locate the Journal Icon.") As you can see in Figure 7-1, the Journal looks and works much like Tasks, Calendar, and other Outlook features.

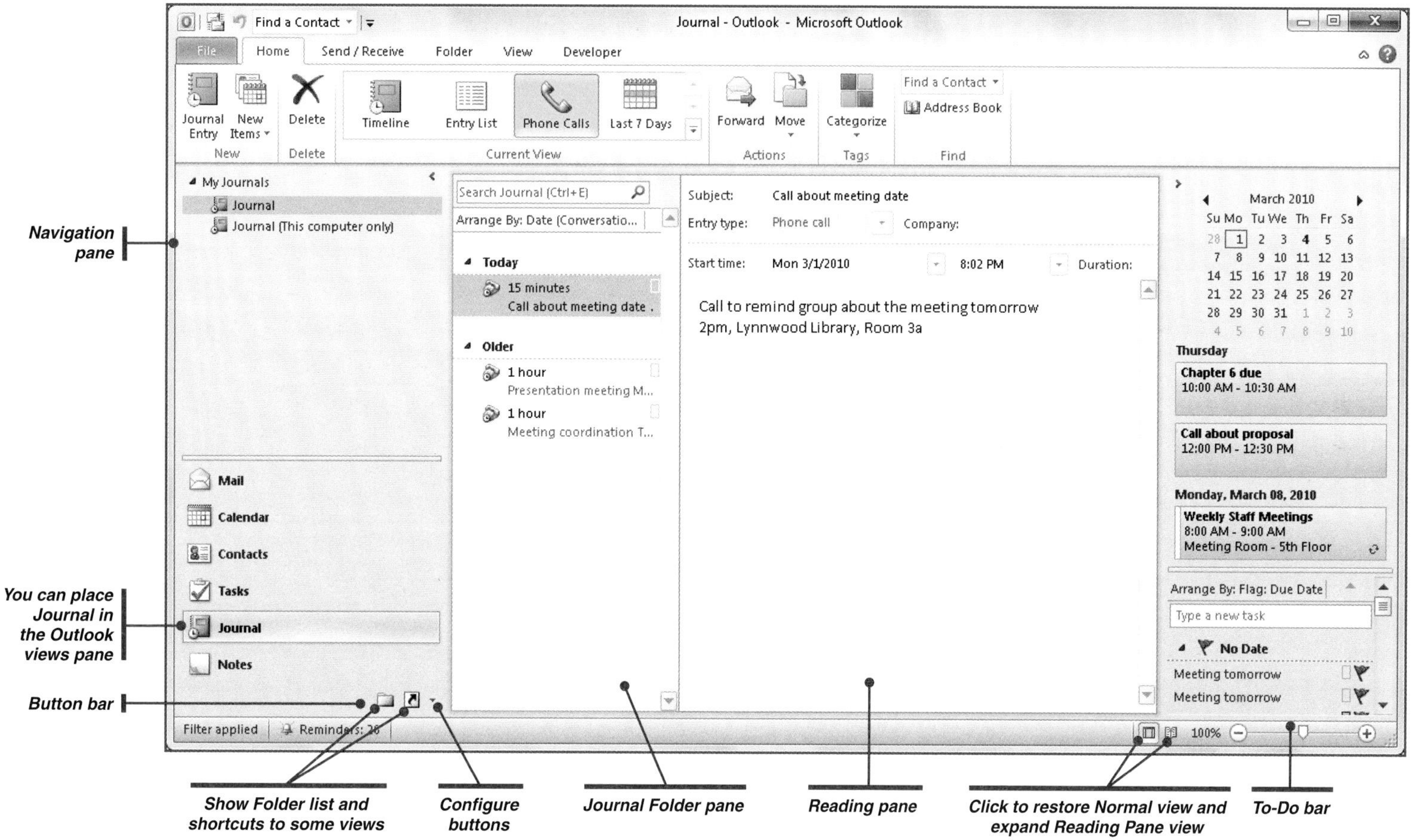

Navigation pane

You can place Journal in the Outlook views pane

Button bar

Show Folder list and shortcuts to some views

Configure buttons

Journal Folder pane

Reading pane

Click to restore Normal view and expand Reading Pane view

To-Do bar

Figure 7-1: Journal entries are a way to collect and organize comments you have on phone calls, e-mails, meetings, and more.

Click **Journal** in the button bar (see "Locate the Journal Icon" to see how to place Journal in the Outlook views or button bar). In Outlook's Journal view, you will see the following features:

● The **Navigation pane**, on the left, shows the structure of Outlook folders. Within it is the Outlook views showing the Outlook windows you can access, such as Mail and Journal.

● The **Journal folder**, in the middle, by default gives you a listing of any existing journal entries.

QUICKSTEPS

SETTING UP THE JOURNAL

If this is the first time you have used the Journal, you'll need to make a decision about how you will use it.

1. If it isn't already displayed, click **Journal** in the button bar.

2. A dialog box appears telling you that the Journal can track Office documents, as well as e-mail sent to contacts. However, the Activities tab on the contact's Properties dialog box is the easiest way to track e-mail. So, the question is whether you want to turn the Journal on for this purpose. Click **Yes** if you want to do this. You can turn it off later if you change your mind.

Microsoft Outlook

⚠ The Journal can automatically track Microsoft Office documents and e-mail messages associated with a contact, but the Activities page in a Contact also tracks e-mail messages, and it does not require the Journal.
Do you want to turn the Journal on?

☐ Do not show this message again

[Yes] [No]

3. In the Journal Options dialog box that appears, shown in Figure 7-2, select the contacts you want Journal to track and what items you want to track for those contacts. Notice that you can also track other Microsoft Office documents. Click **OK** when you're done.

You can make changes to these options at any time by clicking **File** and then clicking **Options**. In the Outlook Options dialog box, click **Notes And Journal**. Then click **Journal Options**. You'll see the dialog box in Figure 7-2.

- The **Reading pane** displays the contents of the selected journal entry.

- The **To-Do Bar**, on the right, displays current task and calendar entries.

- The **Journal** option in the Outlook views allows you to open your Journal folder.

- The **Button bar** contains folders that are initially not shown in the Outlook views, such as Journal and Notes. It also contains the Configure button for reordering the Outlook views.

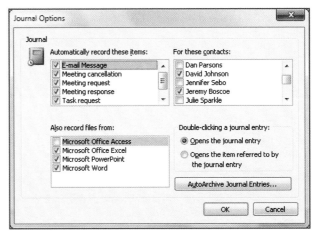

Figure 7-2: **You can select the items that you want the Journal to track, including contact e-mail data.**

Add a Journal Entry

With the Journal open, you can quickly and easily add journal entries as you need them.

1. On the Home tab, click **Journal Entry** in the New group.

2. In the Journal Entry window, type a descriptive name for the journal entry in the Subject text box, as shown in Figure 7-3.

3. Click the **Entry Type** drop-down menu, and choose the type of entry you are creating.

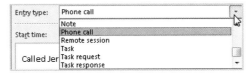

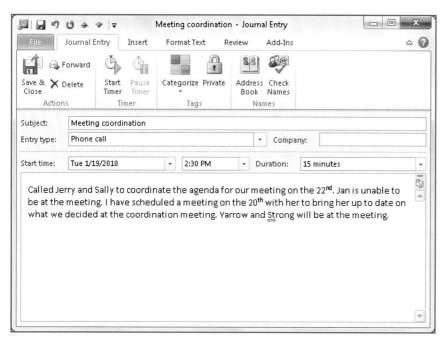

Figure 7-3: *Creating a journal entry allows you to track the time you spend on important activities.*

4. Use the drop-down menus to select the start date and time. You can also use the drop-down menu to choose the duration of the event, if desired.

5. Click in the large text box, and type the journal entry you want to make.

6. If you want to time the entry, such as in the case of a telephone call or meeting, click **Start Timer** in the Journal Entry tab Timer group. The results of the timer appear in the Duration field in even-minute increments. Click **Pause Timer** to stop the timer. You can add time to the existing time in the Duration field by clicking **Start Timer** again; reset the timer by clicking the **Duration** down arrow and clicking **0 Minutes**.

7. Click **Save & Close**. The new journal entry appears in your journal.

Change a Journal Entry

Journal entries, like most anything else you might record in Outlook, may need to be changed. To do that:

1. In your journal, right-click the entry you want to change, and click **Open Journal Entry.**

–Or–

Double-click the journal entry that you want to change.

2. The Journal Entry window shown in Figure 7-3 opens. Make any desired changes to the item.

3. Click **Save & Close**.

Delete a Journal Entry

You can easily and permanently remove journal entries from the journal. You can do this by simply deleting the entry item. To delete a journal entry, choose from these options:

- Right-click the entry in the journal, and click **Delete**.

  –Or–

- Select the entry in the journal, and on the Home tab Delete group, click **Delete**.

  –Or–

- Select the entry in the journal, and press **DELETE**.

Move a Journal Entry in the Timeline

The time and date values placed on journal entries might change. For example, the phone call you were going to make at 10:00 A.M. might have been moved to 4:00 P.M., and meeting times and dates are certainly subject to change, along with most other journal items. You cannot directly drag items within the journal itself, but you can easily change the start date and time for an entry, thus moving it on the timeline.

1. In your journal, right-click the entry you want to edit, and click **Open Journal Entry**.

   –Or–

   Double-click the entry.

2. In the Journal Entry window, change the start date, time, and duration as needed.

3. Click **Save & Close**. The entry item will be updated on the timeline.

Attach Contacts to Journal Entries

You can attach a contact to a journal entry as you are creating a new entry, or you can decide to attach a contact later.

1. For an existing entry, double-click the entry in the journal. If you are creating a new entry, click **Journal Entry** in the Home tab New group. In either case, the Journal Entry window will open.

TIP

It is always a good idea to pause and think carefully before you delete a journal entry. Old journal entries make good records, so make sure you truly no longer need the item before you delete it.

NOTE

Moving a journal entry does not change the start time of the item, document, or contact for that item.

QUICKSTEPS

VIEWING JOURNAL ENTRIES

As with most items in Outlook, you have several different views that you can use with your journal entries.

1. If the journal is not already open, click **Journal** on the button bar.

2. In the Home tab Current View group, choose one of the following view options:

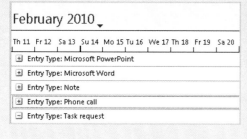

- **Timeline** Shows journal entries on the timeline according to the type of entry (phone call, meeting, e-mail, etc.). This is the default view.

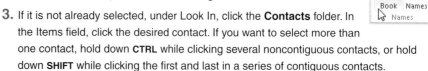

- **Entry List** Removes the timeline and shows you a simple list view.

- **Phone Calls** Lists only phone calls.

- **Last Seven Days** Shows you a list of the journal entries for the last seven days.

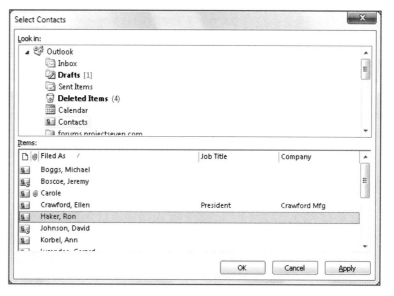

Figure 7-4: *Choose the contact(s) you want to associate with the journal entry.*

2. In the Journal Entry tab Names group, click **Address Book**. The Select Contacts window opens, as shown in Figure 7-4.

3. If it is not already selected, under Look In, click the **Contacts** folder. In the Items field, click the desired contact. If you want to select more than one contact, hold down **CTRL** while clicking several noncontiguous contacts, or hold down **SHIFT** while clicking the first and last in a series of contiguous contacts.

4. Click **OK** and then click **Save & Close**.

Assign a Category to a Journal Entry

You can assign categories to a journal entry. This feature makes it easier for you to keep track of the specific nature of the journal entries.

1. For an existing entry, double-click the entry in the journal. If you are creating a new entry, click the **New** button on the toolbar. In either case, the Journal Entry window will open.

2. In the Journal Entry tab Tags group, click **Categorize**. The drop-down list of categories will appear.

   –Or–

   For an existing journal entry, right-click the entry in the journal, and click **Categorize** to open a similar drop-down list.

3. Click the desired category you want to assign. If the category is one of the initial color categories, the Rename Category dialog box will appear. Type the name of the category, change the color, assign a shortcut key, and click **Yes**. If you have already made the color a specific category, it will be immediately applied to the entry.

4. If you do not see a category in the drop-down list that accurately identifies your task, click **All Categories** to open the Color Categories dialog box. Click **New** to open the Add New Category dialog box. Type the name of the category, change the color, assign a shortcut key, and click **OK**. Your new category will appear in your category list with a check mark. Click **OK** again, and the new category will be attached to the journal entry.

5. Click **Save & Close**.

6. To see the journal entries grouped by category, click the **View** tab, and click **Categories** in the Arrangement group. An example is shown in Figure 7-5.

Print Journal Entries

You can easily print journal entries.

1. To print a memo-style copy of the journal entry, simply right-click the journal entry in the journal, and click **Quick Print**. The journal entry is sent to your default printer. What prints will depend on the current view you are in. For instance, if you are in the Entry List view, a list of all journal entries will print; if you are in the Timeline view, a memo-style printout of the entries in the selected group will print.

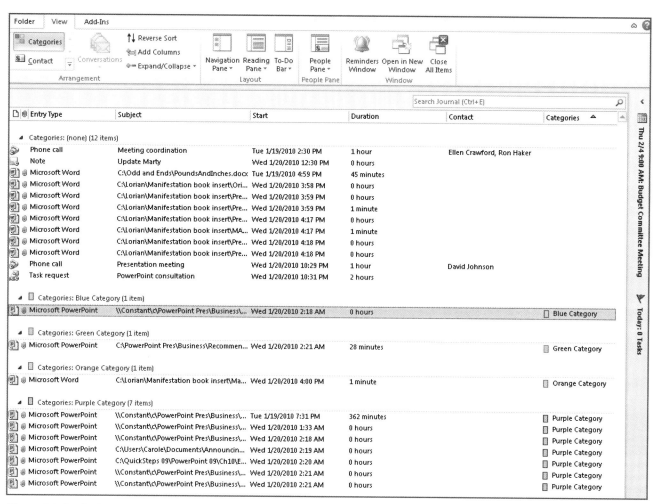

Figure 7-5: **Assigning categories to journal entries allows you to group entries and more easily find them.**

2. For additional printing options, select the entry in the journal, click **File**, and click **Print**.

3. In the Print view, choose the print options you would like, as shown in Figure 7-6. Notice the check box that also allows you to print attached files.

4. Make your selections and click **OK** to start printing.

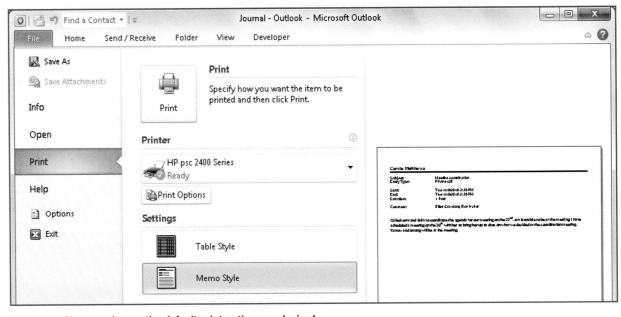

Figure 7-6: *You can change the default print options as desired.*

Make Notes

If you are like most of us, notes are a way of life. Your desk might be littered with scraps of paper where you can scribble important things quickly. Of course, finding the note you need is another story. The great news is that you can keep all of the notes you want and simply let Outlook take care of them. Instead of scribbled notes on paper, you can use the Notes feature in Outlook to collect and organize them all. In this section, you'll learn how to create, manage, and work with your notes.

Find the Notes Folder

The Notes feature is not automatically shown in the Outlook views; by default, it is in the button bar. If you want it to be in the Outlook views, you must place it there.

1. In the button bar, click the **Configure** button, and select **Navigation Pane Options**.

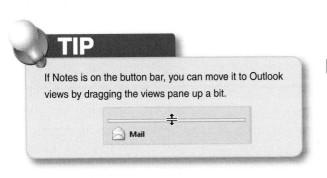

TIP

If Notes is on the button bar, you can move it to Outlook views by dragging the views pane up a bit.

2. In the Navigation Pane Options, select **Notes** (which should have a check mark already in the check box), and click **Move Up** to display Notes in the Outlook views.

–Or–

If you want the Notes icon to remain in the button bar, simply click it to display the Notes view, displayed in Figure 7-7.

Create Notes in Another Outlook View

You can create notes in another Outlook view or in its own view. When you create a note in another Outlook view, it appears as a small note on the screen. You simply fill in the text and click somewhere else to deselect the note. It is safely filed in your Notes folder where you can reference it later. It is also displayed on your desktop where you can drag it where you want it, as shown in Figure 7-8.

1. From another Outlook view, such as Mail, Calendar, Tasks, or Contacts, click the **Home** tab.

2. In the New group, click **New Items**, click **More Items**, and then click **Note**. A small note will spring up in your window.

3. Fill in the note, and either click outside it or click **Close**. The note will disappear. However, it will be stored in your Notes folder.

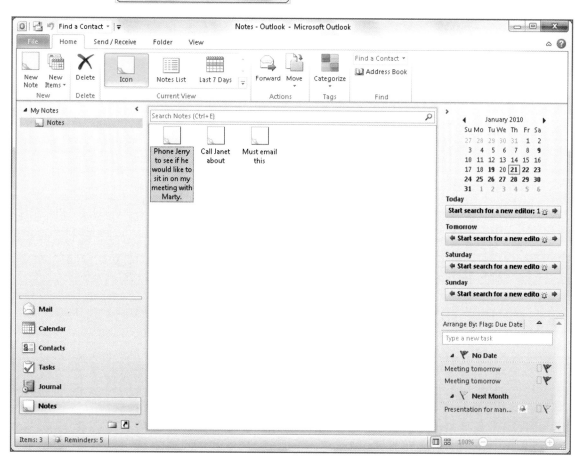

Figure 7-7: *Use the Notes view to manage all the notes you would create on paper or in another Outlook view.*

Figure 7-8: *Keeping notes in Outlook keeps them from getting lost and helps you organize them.*

Add Notes in the Notes View

You can quickly and easily create a note whenever you need to. To add a note to your Notes folder:

1. Click **Notes** in either the Outlook view or the button bar. The Notes view is displayed.

2. Click **New Note** in the Home tab New group. A note appears. Type the information you want directly on the note.

3. When you're done, click the **Close** button on the note. The note now appears in your Notes folder.

You can also right-click anywhere within the Notes folder (provided you are not right-clicking an actual note), and click **New Note** to add a note to the folder.

Change the Note Icon Size

In the View tab, you can change the icon size of the notes from large icons to small icons, and even to a simple list. You can easily switch between these icon views as desired.

1. Click the **View** tab.

2. Click the view you want in the Arrangement group.

3. If your notes are scattered in the folder view, click **Line Up Icons** to arrange them neatly.

TIP

Notice that there is no Save or Save As option for the notes. Once you click the Close button, your changes are automatically saved. Also, there isn't an Undo feature. To undo a change, you must retype the original material.

Notes are designed to be short remarks or comments, so don't worry about complete sentences or other grammatical issues. However, you can type just about as much text as you want, if necessary. You can easily drag the note's corner handle and expand the size of the note as needed.

UICKSTEPS

SETTING UP NOTES

You can make some quick and easy changes to the way notes look.

1. Click **Notes** in the Outlook view or button bar.

2. Click **File** and then click **Options**.

3. In the Outlook Options view, click **Notes And Journal**.

4. Under Note Options, click the **Default Color** drop-down arrow, and click a color for your notes. The default is yellow.

5. Click the **Default Size** drop-down arrow, and click the note size you want. The default size is medium.

6. Click the **Font** button to select a different font. In the Font window that opens (see Figure 7-9), you can choose the font, font style, size, and any effects you might want to use. Make your selections and click **OK**.

7. Click **OK** to close the Outlook Options dialog box.

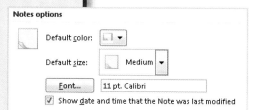

Delete a Note

Notes are designed to be pieces of information that help you stay organized. As such, you'll probably need to update, change, and delete old notes fairly often. To delete a note:

● Right-click the note in the Notes folder, and click **Delete**.

   –Or–

● Select the note and press the **DELETE** button on the keyboard.

   –Or–

● Select the note, click the **Home** tab, and in the Delete group, click **Delete**.

Categorize Notes

As with other Outlook items, you can attach categories to your notes. When you use a category view (which you'll explore later in this chapter), you can easily

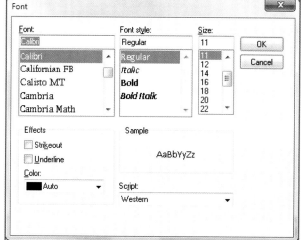

*Figure 7-9: **Select a font that is easy for you to read.***

QUICKSTEPS

USING NOTES IN OTHER OUTLOOK AREAS

You can drag notes to other areas of Microsoft Outlook, where they will change accordingly.

- To automatically create an e-mail message using a note, drag the desired note to **Mail** in Outlook views, as shown in Figure 7-10.

- To send a note to your calendar, drag the note to **Calendar** on Outlook views. The note is converted to a calendar item, which you can configure as needed, as shown in Figure 7-11.

- Repeat this same process to turn a note into a task or a contact.

When you drag a note to Mail, Calendar, Tasks, or Contacts, the information is taken from the note to generate the desired item. However, your original note remains in your Notes folder; it is not moved or deleted.

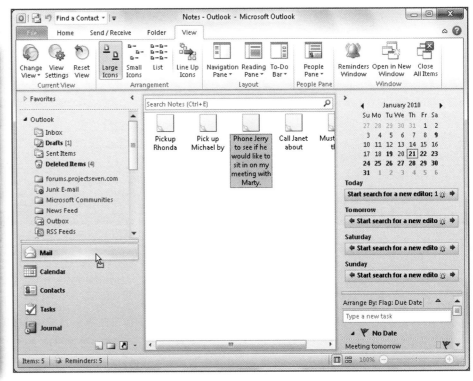

Figure 7-10: *You can drag the note to any Outlook view.*

keep business notes separate from personal notes, and so on. To categorize a note:

1. In the Notes folder, right-click the note and click **Categorize**. The Categories drop-down menu appears.

2. Click the desired category you want to assign. If the category is one of the initial color categories, the Rename Category dialog box will appear. Type the name of the category, change the color, and assign a shortcut key. Click **Yes**. If you have already made the color a specific category, it will be immediately applied to the entry.

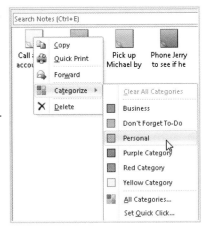

Figure 7-11: *Drag your note to the Calendar icon to turn it into a calendar item.*

NOTE

You can assign more than one category to a note. If this is not what you want, right-click the note, click **Categorize**, and click **All Categories**. Click the check boxes for the categories you want attached to the note, and click **OK**.

3. If you do not see a category in the drop-down list that accurately identifies your task, click **All Categories** to open the Color Categories dialog box. Click **New** to open the Add New Category dialog box. Type the name of the category, change the color, assign a shortcut key, and click **OK**. Your new category will appear in your category list with a check mark. Click **OK** again, and the new category will be attached to the note.

Organize Notes by Category/Color

By default, your notes are all the same color, depending on the color you originally chose in the Outlook Options dialog box. However, if you categorize your notes to better organize them, you can assign the categories any color you choose, thereby color-coding your notes. You might choose to color-code all of your personal notes with one color, all sales notes with another, and all finance notes with a third. Or, you might assign a certain color to urgent notes and another color to those that are not as pressing. No matter what your technique for assigning colors, you can easily use the Categorize feature to change a note's color at any time. With your notes color-coded, it is easy to see the category each note is in, as shown in Figure 7-12. This is simply a by-product of categorization.

To view the notes by color:

1. Click **Notes List** in the Current View group of the Home tab.

2. Click the **Arrange By** field at the top of the list of notes, and click **Categories**. The list will be rearranged by category and hence, by color. (If your Note view Outlook window is wide enough, you will not see Arrange By and can just click the Categories field.)

Forward a Note

The notes you create in Outlook can be attached easily to e-mail and sent to other Outlook users. This feature enables you to easily share information with someone over e-mail without having to retype the information in the e-mail or having to cut and paste the information. To forward a note:

1. In the Notes folder, right-click the note and click **Forward**.

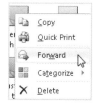

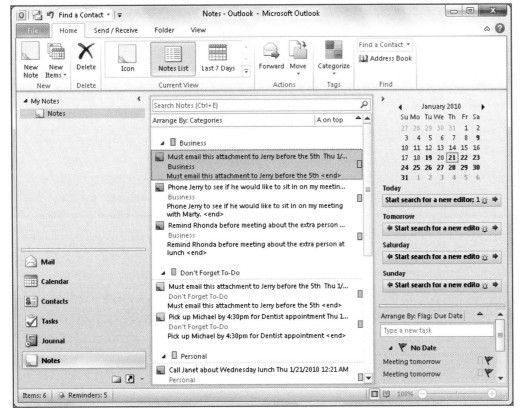

Figure 7-12: *Color-coding gives you a quick way to visually identify related notes.*

2. A new e-mail message appears with the note included as an attachment, as you can see in Figure 7-13. Enter the recipient's e-mail address, and type your message.

3. Click **Send**.

View Notes

The Notes views (available from either the Home tab Current View group or the View tab Current View group Change View command) gives you three options for viewing your notes in the Notes folder:

- **Icons**   This default view shows your notes as icons, as seen in various illustrations in this section.

- **Notes List**   Displays your notes as a list of items, as seen in Figure 7-12.

- **Last 7 Days**   Displays the last seven days of notes as a list.

CUSTOMIZE THE CURRENT VIEW

You can customize the current view by working with advanced Notes settings.

1. In the View tab Current View group, click **Change View** and select the view you want.

2. In the Current View group, click **View Settings**. The Advanced View Settings – Notes List dialog box will appear.

3. Click the desired area button to make any changes that you want in the Advanced View Settings dialog box, shown in Figure 7-14. The function of each button is as follows:

- **Columns** allows you set the number of columns and fields you want displayed in them.

- **Group By** provides the means to group the items in the view.

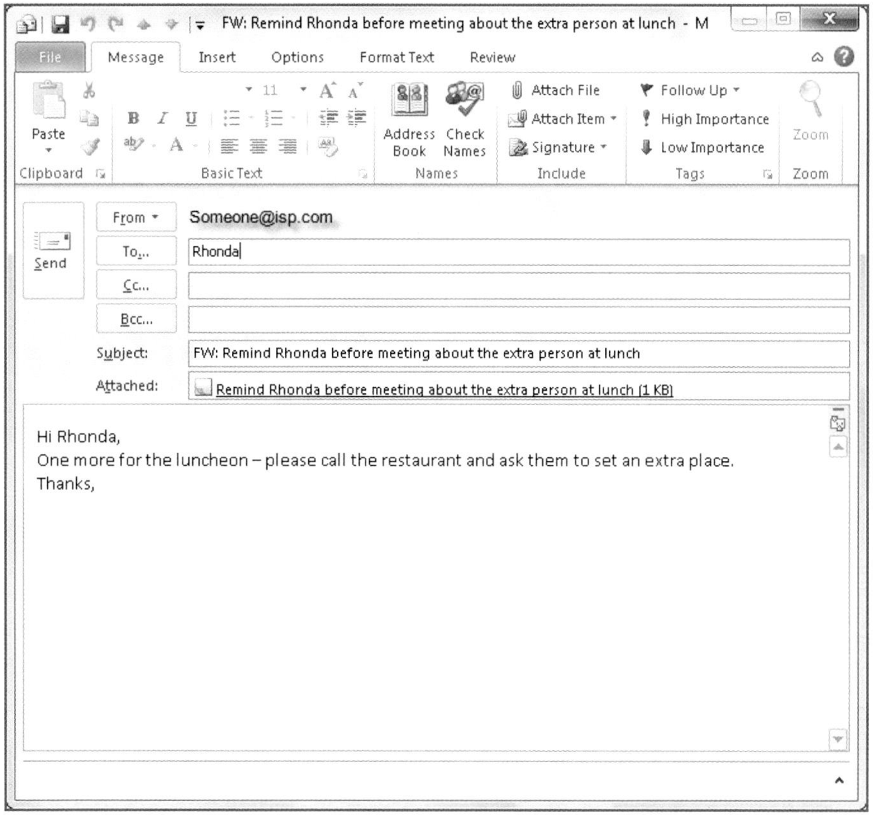

Figure 7-13: *A note can be added automatically to an e-mail message as an attachment.*

- **Sort** provides the means to sort the items in the view.

- **Filter** allows you to select certain items to be displayed and exclude others.

- **Other Settings** provides the means to select the fonts and other display settings.

- **Conditional Formatting** allows you to select rules for formatting unread items, unread group headers, and overdue items.

- **Format Columns** allows you to select the format, label, width, and alignment of each column.

- **Reset Current View** returns all the settings to the original default setting.

4. When you're done making your changes, click **OK**.

USE THE READING PANE

The Reading pane works with most Outlook features, including Notes. The Reading pane allows you to switch easily between scanning notes and reading

Figure 7-14: *You can change the display options by clicking an option button.*

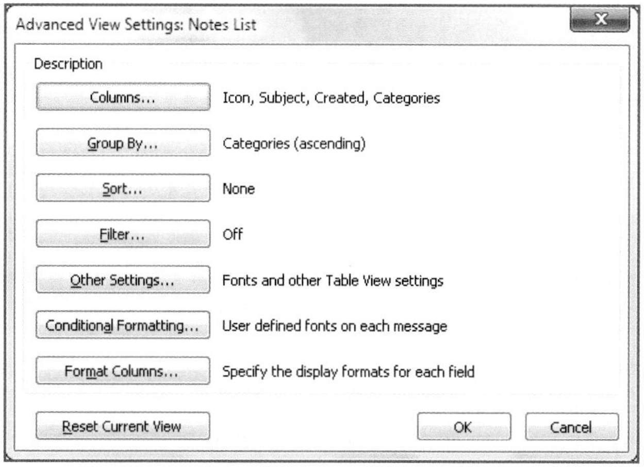

You can print multiple notes at the same time. In the Notes folder, hold down the **CTRL** key on your keyboard, and click the notes you want to print. If your notes are a contiguous list, hold down the **SHIFT** key, and click the first and last note in the list. This creates a "multiple selection" of notes, which you can then print together in either of the two ways described in "Print Notes."

the full content of a note without having to open it. To use the Reading pane with Notes:

1. Click the **View** tab, and in the Layout group, click **Reading Pane**. Then click **Right** to view the notes in a pane to the right of the Note List; click **Bottom** to view notes below the Note List; click **Off** to restore the original view.

2. Click a note in order to view its text in the Reading pane to the right or below.

An alternative view using the Reading pane minimizes the Navigation pane and the To-Do bar and uses the extra space to display the notes. You use the entire window to view the notes. To do this click the **Reading Pane** icon 🔲 in the status bar.

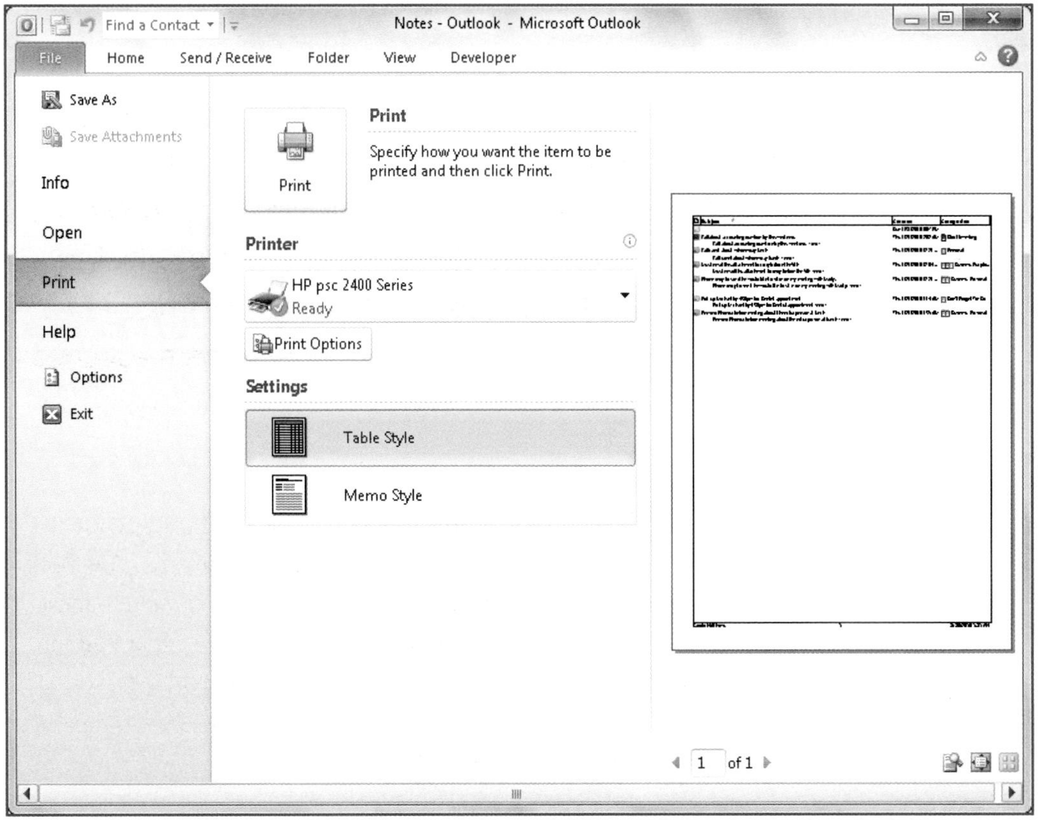

Print Notes

You can easily print your notes, when desired. To print a memo-style copy of the note entry, simply right-click the note, and click **Quick Print**. The note is sent to your default printer. What is printed depends on the current view. For instance, if the Icon view is displayed, you'll get a memo-style printout; if Notes List, a list printout.

1. For additional printing options, select the note you want to print in the Notes folder, click **File**, and then click **Print**.

2. In Print view (see Figure 7-15), choose the print options you would like, such as the Printer default, Print Options for the number of copies, the drop down lists beneath Settings, and so forth.

3. Make your selections and click **Print** to start printing.

*Figure 7-15: **You can print notes in either table or memo style.***

Chapter 8
Managing Files and Folders

As you send and receive e-mail and work with your Outlook data, you'll need to organize and work with data files. Microsoft Outlook makes data management easy. In this chapter you'll see how to work with folders and manipulate files in Outlook. You'll also see how to make Outlook secure by setting security options and encrypting private messages.

Work with Folders

Outlook manages data by storing information in folders, specifically, your personal folders. When you use e-mail, you see folders such as Inbox, Outbox, Deleted Items, Sent Items, and so forth. However, you are not limited to these basic folders. You can create and work with additional folders so that you can easily store e-mail messages and files in an organizational system that works best for you. In this section you'll see how to create different kinds of folders, share them, and work with them in a variety of ways.

8

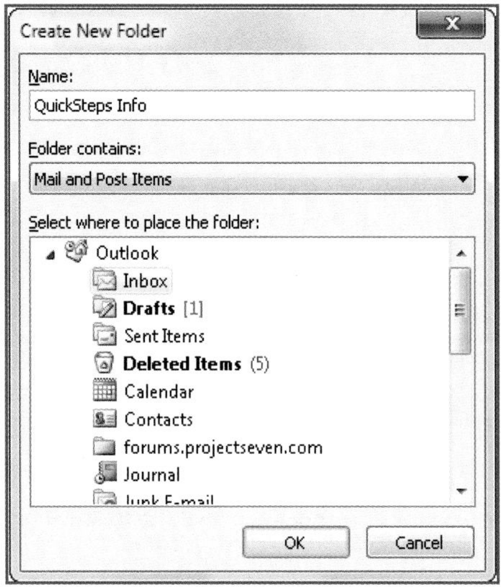

Figure 8-1: *A new Outlook folder can contain only a specific kind of information.*

Create a Normal Folder

Outlook creates a basic set of folders when you create a new account so that you can store e-mail messages and files for that account. You may wish to also create folders based on work and family correspondence, or you can create any structure that is helpful and meaningful to you. To create a normal folder:

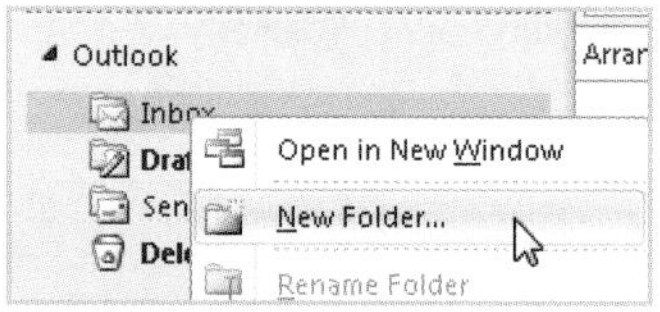

1. Right-click your **Inbox** folder and, on the context menu, click **New Folder**.

2. In the Create New Folder dialog box, shown in Figure 8-1, enter a name for the folder. Click the **Folder Contains** drop-down menu, and choose the type of items you will store in the folder, such as Mail And Post Items. Finally, select the location where you want to store the folder, such as a subfolder within your Inbox.

3. When you're done, click **OK**. The folder will appear in the place where you chose to store it.

Create a Search Folder

Search folders are a helpful feature of Outlook. Using search folders, you can store messages and easily search them for certain types of content, for example, or based on the sender or another attribute. In short, search folders enable you not only to store large numbers of messages, but also to sort easily through and find certain kinds of messages.

Search folders aren't really folders at all. They are virtual folders that search other Outlook folders and give you a report of the messages and information you are looking for, rather than being just a collection of messages that are in one place at one time. This feature allows you to find any message that you want and show it in the search folder, although the original message isn't actually moved there. To create a search folder:

1. Click the **Folder** tab, and in the New group, click **New Search Folder**.

2. In the New Search Folder dialog box, shown in Figure 8-2, choose one of the following options:

Figure 8-2: *Search folders allow you to search Outlook folders for a wide variety of criteria and to create your own folders.*

UICKSTEPS

COPYING AND MOVING FOLDERS

You can easily copy and move folders around as needed.

COPY A FOLDER

1. Right-click the folder in your personal folders hierarchy that you want to copy.

2. Click **Copy Folder**.

3. In the Copy Folder window, shown in Figure 8-3, choose the location where you want to copy the folder.

4. Click **OK**. The folder and its contents are copied to the desired location.

5. Find and right-click the new folder, and click **Rename**. The folder name will be selected and ready for you to type the name you want for the folder. Then press ENTER.

MOVE A FOLDER

You can move the folders you create within your personal folders, but you cannot move the system-created folders such as Inbox, Outbox, and Sent Items.

Continued . . .

- **Reading Mail:**

  - **Unread Mail**   Any mail you have not read in any folder.

  - **Mail Flagged For Follow-Up**   Any mail that is flagged for follow-up in any folder.

  - **Mail Either Unread Or Flagged For Follow-Up**   Unread mail or mail that has been flagged for follow-up in any folder.

  - **Important Mail**   Mail that has been sent with high importance.

- **Mail From People And Lists:**

  - **Mail From And To Specific People**   Mail from and to specific people in any folder.

  - **Mail From Specific People**   Mail from specific people in any folder.

  - **Mail Sent Directly To Me**   Mail that was sent directly to you (rather than by means of a distribution list or as a Cc or Bcc).

  - **Mail Sent To Public Groups**   Mail that was sent to a distribution list.

- **Organizing Mail:**

  - **Categorized Mail**   Mail that has been identified with a category.

  - **Large Mail**   Messages above a specific file size.

  - **Old Mail**   Mail older than a specific date.

  - **Mail With Attachments**   Mail that has an attachment.

  - **Mail With Specific Words**   Mail that contains specific words.

- **Custom:**

  - **Create A Custom Search Folder**   Allows you to create a custom folder that searches for the parameters you specify.

3. Once you have selected the kind of search folder you want, click **OK**. The type of mail you searched for will appear in the Subject pane.

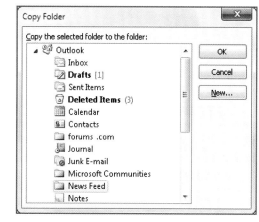

Figure 8-3: **Select a folder location where you want to place the copied folder.**

COPYING AND MOVING FOLDERS

(Continued)

1. In the Navigation pane, right-click the folder you want to move.

2. Click **Move Folder**.

3. In the Move Folder window, choose the location where you want to move the folder, and click **OK**. The folder and its contents are moved to the desired location.

You also copy and move folders using the mouse. You can move the folders you have created by dragging them. You can copy any folder by right-dragging it to a new location and clicking **Copy** from the context menu that appears.

Rename Folders

Folder names should be easily recognizable. To that end, you can change the name of a folder you have created at any time. You cannot change the name of the system folders, such as Inbox and Sent Items in your primary account. In that case, the Rename command will be grayed out (unavailable).

1. Right-click the folder in the Navigation pane, and click **Rename Folder**. The folder name is selected, and your cursor appears in the folder name box.

2. Type a new name for the folder, and press **ENTER**.

Delete Folders

You can delete the folders you have created, but not the system folders in your primary account (the Delete command will be unavailable to you). The folder contents are moved to the Deleted Items folder.

1. In the Navigation pane, right-click the folder you want, and click **Delete Folder**.

2. Click **Yes** in response to the warning message that appears.

Set Folder Properties

Like all folders in Windows, Outlook folders have some basic properties that you can configure as needed. The tabs described here are available with most, but not all, Outlook folders.

1. Right-click the desired folder, and click **Properties**. You have the following options:

   • On the **General** tab, shown in Figure 8-4, you see the name of the folder and its general properties. You can enter a description and choose to show the number of total items in the folder or the number of unread items in the folder. You can click **Folder Size** to find out how much disk space your folder is taking up.

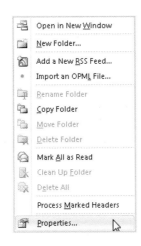

Figure 8-4: *You can get basic information about your folder on the General tab.*

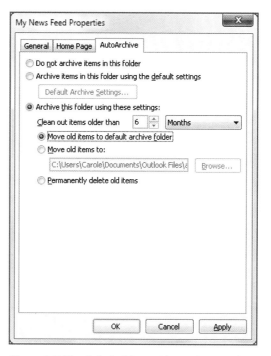

Figure 8-5: *The AutoArchive settings give you the flexibility to automatically archive folder items in a way that works best for you.*

- The **Home Page** tab allows you to configure a default home page for the folder, if your folders are Web-enabled (which is common for folders found on a company intranet).

- On the **AutoArchive** tab, shown in Figure 8-5, you can choose the method of archiving you want to use with this folder. The default will vary, depending on the folder selected. However, you can choose to automatically have the folder archived based on Outlook's default settings, or you can configure your own archive settings for the folder, as I have done in Figure 8-5.

2. Click **OK** when you are done making any desired changes.

Manipulate Files

Just as you can work with individual folders in Outlook, you can also work with individual files and groups of files that are stored in those folders. In this section, you'll see how to manipulate files and work with them by copying, renaming, sharing, deleting, grouping, and sorting files. You'll also see how to import and export files in Outlook.

Delete Files

You can delete individual files from within Outlook as needed. Let's say you have a folder that contains several older e-mail messages. You do not want to delete the entire folder, but you do want to delete all the unneeded messages from the folder. In this case, you can individually select the messages that you want to delete. Deleted messages are moved to your Deleted Items folder.

1. In the Navigation pane, select the folder that contains the file you want to delete.
2. In the Folder pane, click the file and on the Home tab Delete group, click **Delete**. You can also right-click the file and click **Delete**.

Group Files

You can have Outlook automatically group files for you as a part of Outlook's standard grouping arrangement, or you can manually group items. For example, you might want all e-mail from a specific person grouped into one folder, or you might want e-mail that contains attachments to be grouped into one folder. The choice is yours, but you can easily group items in almost any way that you need.

CREATE A CUSTOM GROUPING

1. Click the **View** tab, click the **More** button at the bottom of the scroll bar in the Arrangement group, and click **View Settings**.
2. In the Advanced View Settings dialog box, click **Group By**.
3. In the Group By dialog box, if it is selected, clear the **Automatically Group According To Arrangement** check box. Then select the desired check boxes, and use the drop-down menus to determine how you want to group items within Outlook, as shown in Figure 8-6.
4. Click **OK** twice when you're done.

UICKSTEPS

VIEWING FILES

You can easily select the files within your Outlook folders and then view the file contents in several ways.

1. Select the folder in the Folder List, and then select the file in the Folder pane. You can then see the file's contents in the Reading pane.
2. Double-click the file. This opens the file in a separate window so that you can view it.

8

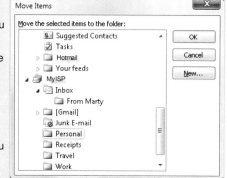

QUICKSTEPS

COPYING AND MOVING FILES

You can easily copy and move files between Outlook folders in basically the same manner as with standard Windows files.

COPYING FILES

1. Select the folder that contains the file you want to move so that the files are displayed in the Folder pane.

2. In the Folder pane, right-drag the file that you want to copy to the folder you want. When you release the mouse, click **Copy** on the context menu.

To copy and paste a file, or cut and paste a file (to move it rather than copy it), first select a file. Then press **CTRL+C** to copy the file, or press **CTRL+X** to cut the file, and then paste it by pressing **CTRL+V**.

MOVING FILES

1. Select the folder that contains the file you want to move so that the files are displayed in the Folder pane.

2. In the Folder pane, right-click the file you want to move, and, on the context menu that appears, click **Move**. A submenu appear.

3. Click the name of the folder, or if the folder you want is not listed, click **Other Folder**. The Move Items dialog box will appear.

4. In the Move Items window, choose the Outlook folder where you want to move the file.

Figure 8-6: **You can group files by up to four items, such as attachments and categories.**

UNGROUP ITEMS

Should you need to ungroup items at any time, you can easily do so.

1. Click the **View** tab, click the **More** button in the Arrangement group, and click **View Settings**.

2. In the Advanced View Settings dialog box, click **Group By**.

3. In the Group By dialog box, for each group setting, click the **Group Items By** drop-down menu, click **None**, and click **OK** twice.

Sort Files

Outlook has the capability to sort files that you receive in your Inbox. This feature can automatically help you manage your e-mail, and is particularly helpful if you typically receive a large volume of e-mail.

1. Click the **View** tab, click **More** in the Arrangement group, and click **View Settings.**

2. In the Advanced View Settings dialog box, click **Sort**.

Figure 8-7: **You can sort files in any folder by up to four levels of criteria.**

The options you see in the Sort dialog box allow you to have up to four levels of sorting. For example, in Figure 8-7, the two-level sorting of files are sorted first by the flag color and then by the conversation of e-mail correspondence. This sorting feature can be helpful in locating items.

3. In the Sort dialog box, shown in Figure 8-7, do the following:

- Click the **Sort Items By** down arrow, and click a sort item, such as **Attachment**, **Contacts**, **Cc**, and so on.

- Choose more sort criteria in the additional drop-down list boxes as needed.

4. Click **OK** when you are done, and click **OK** again on the Advanced View Settings dialog box. Your items in the current view are now sorted as you specified.

Import and Export Files

You can import and explore Outlook files from a variety of sources and in a variety of formats.

IMPORT FILES

1. Click **File**, click **Open**, and then click **Import**.

2. In the Import And Export Wizard, choose what you would like to import, as shown in Figure 8-8. Make your selection and click **Next**. You have the following options:

- **Import A VCARD File (.vcf)** allows you to import an Outlook vCard that you have received to your Contacts folder.

- **Import An iCalendar Or vCalendar File (.vcs)** imports information from an iCalendar or vCalendar file directly into your calendar.

- **Import From Another Program Or File** allows you to import items from other e-mail programs, such as ACT!, Lotus Organizer, and so forth. You can also import text and database files, as well as personal folders (.pst) from another Outlook program.

- **Import Internet Mail Account Settings** allows you to import settings from Outlook Express or Eudora e-mail programs.

- **Import Internet Mail And Addresses** allows you to import Internet mail and e-mail addresses directly from Outlook Express or Eudora e-mail programs.

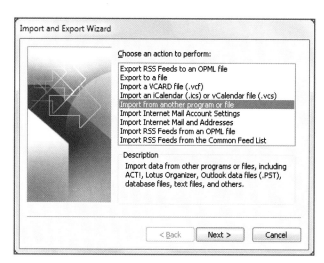

Figure 8-8: *You can import a number of different kinds of files, including those created by Outlook Express, Eudora, ACT!, and Lotus Organizer.*

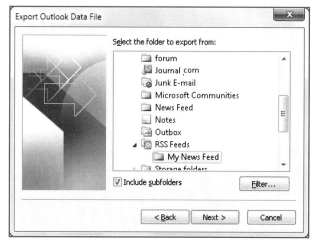

Figure 8-9: *You can choose to export both individual folders and a folder with all of its subfolders.*

- **Import RSS Feeds From An OPML File** or **The Common Feed List** allows you to bring syndicated information to which you subscribe and receive through RSS (Real Simple Syndication) into Outlook.

3. Complete the steps as instructed by the wizard to import the desired files.

EXPORT FILES

Just as you can import files, you can also export files so that they can be used with other programs, or as a way to back up your Outlook files.

1. Click **File**, click **Open**, and click **Import.**

2. In the Import And Export Wizard, click **Export To A File**. Click **Next**.

3. Choose the kind of file you want to export to. You can choose Outlook Data File (.pst), which allows your files to be imported by other Outlook programs, or you can choose file types for other programs. See the other e-mail program for details about the kinds of files it will import so that you make the best decision depending on what you want to do. Click **Next**.

4. Select the folder within Outlook that you want to export, as shown in Figure 8-9. If you choose a parent folder, it will include the subfolders beneath it.

5. If you are exporting to a personal folder file (.pst) and want to filter out some of the messages that you are exporting, click **Filter**, which opens the Filter window. Here, you can search for particular words in specified fields in order to filter out certain messages. For example, you can filter out messages that have certain subjects in the Subject line, messages sent directly to you, and so on. Click the **More Choices** and **Advanced** tabs for additional filtering options, and then click **OK** when you're done.

6. Click **Next**. Choose an export location and file name for the file. Choose how you want to replace previously exported items and duplicate items, and click **Finish**.

7. The Create Outlook Data File dialog box appears so that you can choose to password-protect the exported file so that no one can open it without your password.

8. Make your selections and click **OK**. The files are exported. This process may take some time, depending on the number of files that must be exported.

Make Outlook Secure

Outlook 2010 has a set of security options that you can configure to keep your e-mail, Calendar, Journal, and other Outlook items secure. In this section, you'll see how to set the security options, how to encrypt messages, and how to protect your computer against viruses that may be transmitted through e-mail.

Set Security and Privacy Options

Outlook 2010 shares with the rest of the Microsoft Office 2010 family of programs the *Trust Center*, where you can set a variety of security and privacy options. The Trust Center allows you to set options that affect your privacy; determine if and how you want to secure your e-mail; and how you want to handle attachments, downloads, and macros. We'll explore securing your e-mail in the next section, and then look at virus protection from macros in the upcoming QuickSteps. This section explores the other settings in the Trust Center.

NOTE

It is important to point out that the security provided by Outlook and Microsoft Office is just one level of security against threats from the Internet. You probably also want to enable the Windows Personal Firewall (see the companion book *Microsoft Windows 7 QuickSteps* for further information on the Windows Firewall and other security measures at that level). You may also wish to purchase additional security software or hardware for maximum protection (from companies such as McAfee, Symantec, Zone Alarm, and WatchGuard) for a third level of protection.

To open and explore the Trust Center:

1. Click the **File** tab, and then click **Options**. The Outlook Options dialog box will appear.

2. Click **Trust Center**. In the Trust Center view, click the **Trust Center Settings** button to open the Trust Center dialog box, shown in Figure 8-10.

3. Click **Trusted Publishers** in the left column. A list of trusted software publishers will appear. The list will likely be empty. You add a publisher to the list when you install software or a macro by clicking **Trust All Documents From This Publisher** in the Security Alert dialog box that appears. In the Trust Center page, you can remove a publisher from the list and view a publisher's credentials by selecting a publisher in the list and clicking the relevant button at the bottom of the page.

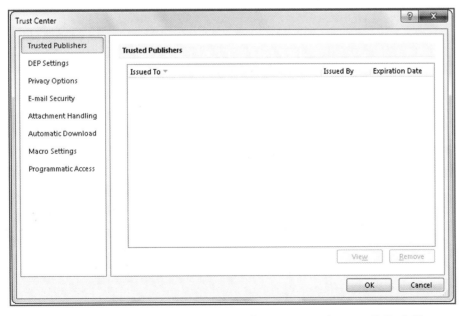

Figure 8-10: **The Trust Center is where you set options to ensure that your Outlook files are protected.**

Privacy Options

☑ Connect to Office.com for updated content when I'm connected to the Internet. ⓘ
☑ Download a file periodically that helps determine system problems ⓘ
☑ Sign up for the Customer Experience Improvement Program ⓘ
☑ Automatically detect installed Office applications to improve Office.com search results. ⓘ
☑ Allow the Research task pane to check for and install new services

Read our privacy statement

Research & Reference

Translation Options...

Research Options...

NOTE

The Research Options button on the Privacy Options page allows you to select the reference sources that will be searched when you choose to do a search.

4. Click **DEP Settings**, which is set by default, to enable the Data Execution Prevention mode. This helps prevent malicious code that might be embedded in data. Clear the check mark to enable data execution to take place.

5. Click **Privacy Options** in the left column of the Trust Center. Select which of the Microsoft programs you want to sign up for, all requiring varying degrees of disclosure on your part. For example, if you sign up for the Customer Experience Improvement Program, you will be expected to divulge some information about what you do with Microsoft Office.

6. Click **E-mail Security** to set encryption, digital IDs, and other security measures. See "Secure E-mail" next for a fuller explanation.

7. Click **Attachment Handling** to add properties to attachments, turn off and on the ability to preview attachments, or specify which preview tools are enabled. Click **Attachment And Document Previewers** to select the applications being used to preview files.

8. Click **Automatic Downloads** and determine how you want to handle the downloading of pictures in e-mail.

9. Click **Macro Security** to see how to protect against viruses. See the "Protecting Against Viruses" QuickSteps later in this chapter to find out how to use this feature in the Trust Center.

10. Click **Programmatic Access** to enable Microsoft security to work in conjunction with your antivirus software to determine the level of warning you will be given when a program is trying to access your Address Book or send messages in your name.

11. Click **OK** to close the Trust Center.

Secure E-mail

You can secure your e-mail by encrypting it so that no one else can read it, and you can add a digital signature to your mail so that the recipient knows you sent it and no one has changed it. Encryption is the process of making an e-mail message unreadable to anyone who is not authorized to view it. Encryption takes a plain-text e-mail message and scrambles it so that it is unreadable. Your recipient must have a private key that matches a public key you used to write the message in order to decrypt and read the message. You can do this in a few different ways:

- **Send a digitally signed message** to the recipient. The recipient can then add your e-mail name to his or her Contacts list, which imports your certificate with a private key.
- **Attach your certificate** (.cer) file to a message you send to the recipient. The recipient can then import the .cer file and add it your contact card. The certificate can be used to exchange keys.
- **Create a contact with your .cer file**, and then send the contact card to the recipient.

No matter which way you choose to go, the recipient must have your .cer file in his or her Outlook program so Outlook can use that to exchange keys to decrypt any encrypted messages you send.

GET A DIGITAL SIGNATURE

A digital signature identifies you, proves the message and its attachments were not changed, and includes a certificate and public key. To get one:

1. Click the **File** tab, and click **Options**. On the Outlook Options dialog box, click **Trust Center**.
2. Click **Trust Center Settings**. In the Trust Center dialog box, click **E-Mail Security**.
3. Under Digital IDs (Certificates), click **Get A Digital ID**. A Microsoft Web site is displayed with suggestions for sources of digital IDs that, for a fee, will validate your identity and issue you a digital ID.
4. Click the source you want, and follow the directions for getting the digital ID. When you are ready, click **OK** twice to close the Trust Center and Outlook Options dialog boxes.

ADD A DIGITAL SIGNATURE TO E-MAIL

To assign a digital signature to an individual message:

1. In a message's Options tab More Options group, click the **Dialog Box Launcher** in the lower-right corner.
2. In the Properties dialog box that appears, click **Security Settings**.
3. Click the **Add Digital Signature To This Message** check box.
4. Click **OK** and click **Close** to return to your message.

Digital IDs (Certificates)

Digital IDs or Certificates are documents t

Import/Export...   Get a Digital ID...

Security Properties

☐ Encrypt message contents and attachments
☑ Add digital signature to this message
　☑ Send this message as clear text signed
　☐ Request S/MIME receipt for this message

To add a digital signature to all your messages:

1. Click **File** and click **Options**. In the Outlook Options dialog box, click **Trust Center**.

2. Click **Trust Center Settings**, and in the Trust Center dialog box on the left, click **E-mail Security**.

3. In the Trust Center dialog box, under **Encrypted E-mail**, click the **Add Digital Signature To Outgoing Messages** check box.

Figure 8-11: **You can encrypt an individual message through the Security Properties dialog box.**

4. Click **OK** twice.

ENCRYPT AN INDIVIDUAL MESSAGE

You can choose to encrypt an individual message as needed. You do need a valid digital ID before you can do this.

1. Create a new e-mail message addressed to the desired recipient.

2. In the Options tab More Options group, click the **Dialog Box Launcher** in the lower-right corner.

3. In the Properties dialog box that appears, click **Security Settings**. The Security Properties dialog box appears, shown in Figure 8-11.

4. Click the **Encrypt Message Contents And Attachments** check box.

5. Click **OK** and click **Close** to return to your message.

6. Click **Send**. The message will be encrypted and sent.

NOTE

If you attempt to encrypt and send a message and you do not have a certificate, you will receive a "Invalid Certificate" message that Outlook cannot send the message for that reason. In that case, click **Change Security Settings** on the bottom of the dialog box, and clear the **Encrypt Message Contents And Attachments** check box.

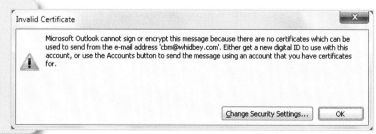

PROTECTING AGAINST VIRUSES

Computer viruses are a major headache in the computing world, and e-mail and Internet usage are major pathways for your computer to become infected. Outlook provides *minimal* protection against viruses. It is not equipped to scan your e-mail and remove viruses, so when Outlook tells you that it can help with virus protection, it really does mean that it "helps" only.

Outlook provides virus protection through macro security options. Different files, especially Microsoft Word files, can contain *macros*, which are little programs, and viruses can be implanted in macros. This is a common way for viruses to be spread. Outlook's macro security simply disables macros that are not from secure or trusted sources, thus reducing the likelihood of getting a macro virus. By default, Outlook disables macros that are unsigned and warns you about signed macros. You can change those settings if you wish.

1. Click **File** and click **Options**. In the Outlook Options dialog box that appears, click **Trust Center**, and then click **Trust Center Settings**.

2. In the Trust Center dialog box, click **Macro Settings** in the left column.

3. Under **Macro Settings**, on the right, click one of the four options for handling macros. The second option is the default.

   The second or third options for macro protection give you the best protection. You can still use macros, but in either case, you are warned before you use them; in the second case, they are not allowed if they are not signed.

4. Click **OK** twice to close the Trust Center and Outlook Options dialog boxes.

ENCRYPT ALL OUTGOING E-MAIL

You can also choose to encrypt all outgoing mail, which saves you from having to configure each e-mail message with encryption. However, keep in mind that this setting will encrypt every e-mail that you send and that everybody who receives your e-mail will need to have a key to open it.

1. Click **File**, click **Options**, and in the Outlook Options dialog box, click **Trust Center.**

2. In the Trust Center view, click **Trust Center Settings**, and then click **E-Mail Security**.

3. In the Trust Center dialog box, under **Encrypted E-mail**, click the **Encrypt Contents And Attachments For Outgoing Messages** check box, as shown in Figure 8-12.

4. Click **OK** twice to close the Trust Center and Outlook Options dialog boxes.

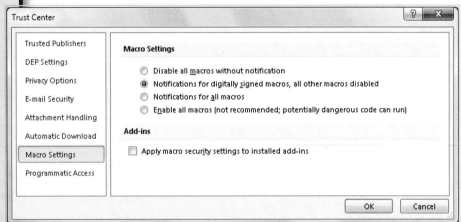

Manage Add-ins

Add-ins are pieces of program code that add functionality to another program. The add-ins are placed on the list when they are installed. You can see which add-ins are currently on the list, activate, or add or remove them.

1. Click **File** and click **Options**. In the Outlook Options dialog box that appears, click **Add-Ins**. A list of installed add-ins will appear, as shown in Figure 8-13.

CAUTION

Keep in mind that Outlook only helps reduce the *likelihood* of a macro virus; it is not a full antivirus program. You should install and use antivirus software on your computer. Visit www.mcafee.com or www.symantec .com to learn more about antivirus programs.

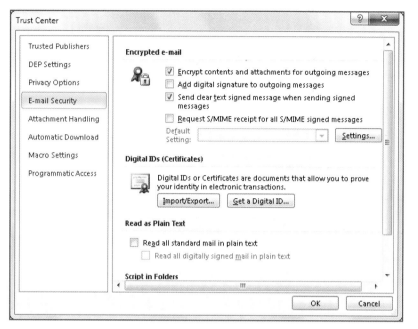

*Figure 8-12: **It is unlikely that you will want to encrypt and/or digitally sign all your mail, but you may want to encrypt individual messages in the e-mail message window.***

2. Click an add-in name to see the information on it below the list: name, publisher, compatibility information, location on your disk, and a description.

3. To manage add-ins, click **Go** at the bottom of the page. The COM Add-Ins dialog box appears, where you can make an add-in active or inactive by selecting or clearing the check box, respectively, or add and remove an add-in with the buttons on the right.

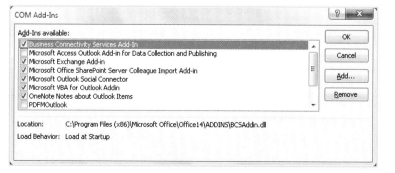

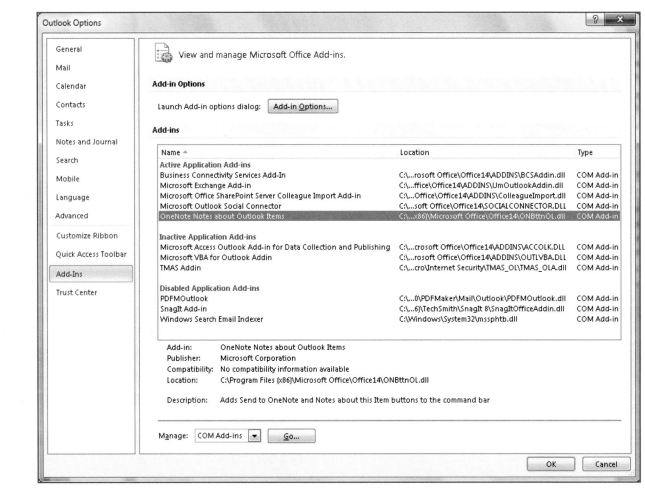

*Figure 8-13: **Most add-ins are from trusted publishers like Microsoft and Adobe, but it is a good idea to keep an eye on them just in case.***

Chapter 9
Using Forms, Labels, and Mail Merge

You've seen that Outlook is a lot more than a mail program. In this chapter we'll expand on that and you'll see how to modify existing forms and create custom forms, how to create and use templates in many Outlook views, and how to set up Outlook to perform a mail merge, as well as how to print both labels and envelopes.

Use Forms

Much of Outlook is built around forms: message forms, appointment forms, contact forms, and many others. *Forms* provide the means to collect information. Forms are built around *fields*, which are individual pieces of information collected by the form, such as the addressee and subject in the e-mail message form shown in Figure 9-1.

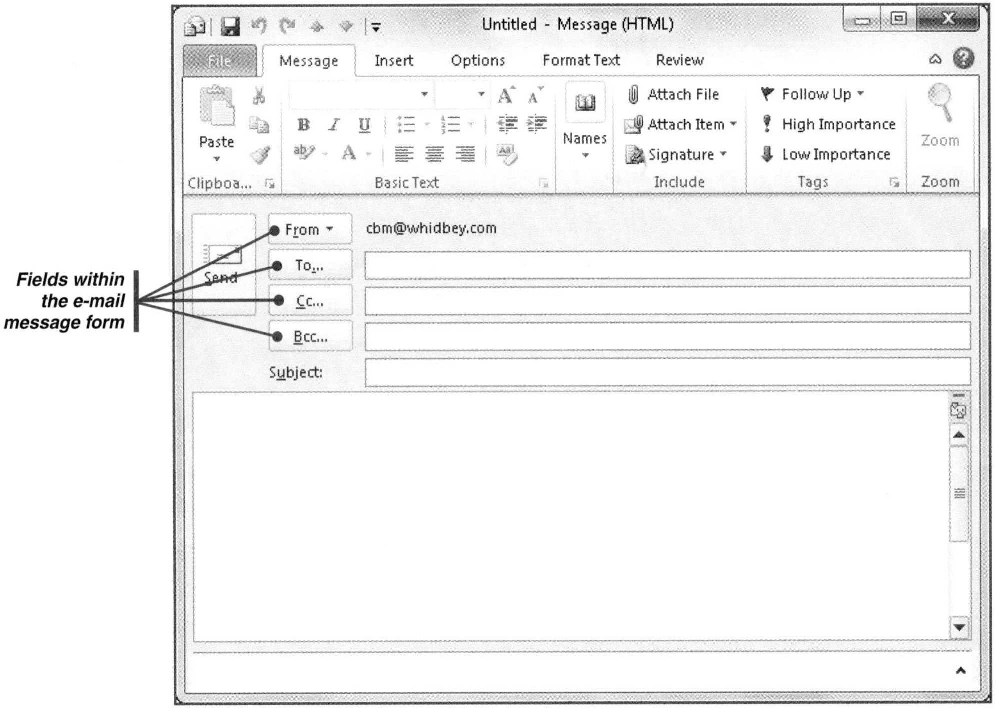

Fields within
the e-mail
message form

Figure 9-1: *Most of what is done in Outlook is done with forms.*

Explore Outlook Forms in the Developer Tab

In earlier chapters you saw how to use various forms from within each of the views. You can also see all the forms together. But first you need to display the Developer tab.

1. Click **File** and click **Options**. In the Outlook Options dialog box, click **Customize Ribbon**.

2. In the right tabs list, under Main Tabs, click **Developer** to select it. Click **OK**. The Developer tab will appear on the ribbon. Now you can find the forms.

3. Click the **Developer** tab, and in the Custom Forms group, click **Choose Form**. The Choose Form dialog box appears, as shown in Figure 9-2.

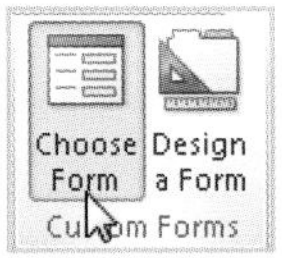

4. Click **Look In** to see the forms available in each folder. Click one of the forms, and click **Advanced**. You'll see a description of the form, who created it, and the message class, which is used in programming for Outlook.

5. Open a form by clicking it and then clicking **Open**.

   –Or–

   Double-click the form.

6. Click **Close** ━━ to close the form.

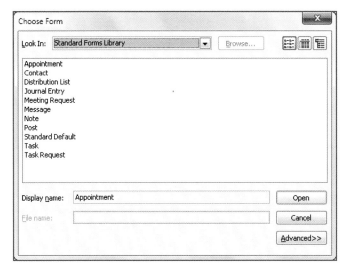

Figure 9-2: *In the Standard Forms Library folder, you will find 11 standard forms that can be modified.*

Modify a Standard Form

You can modify any of the standard forms and then use the revised form in the same way you did as before it was modified.

1. Click the **Developer** tab, and in the Custom Forms group, click **Design A Form**.

2. Click the **Look In** drop-down list, and click the folder that holds the form you want to modify. This feature is particularly useful for the message form, which is used in several different folders.

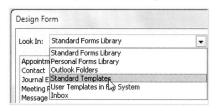

3. Click the form you want to modify, and click **Open**. The form will open in Design mode and, if you can add fields to the form, the Field Chooser dialog box will appear beside it (see Figure 9-3).

Add pages   **Design-related tools**   **Add predefined fields**

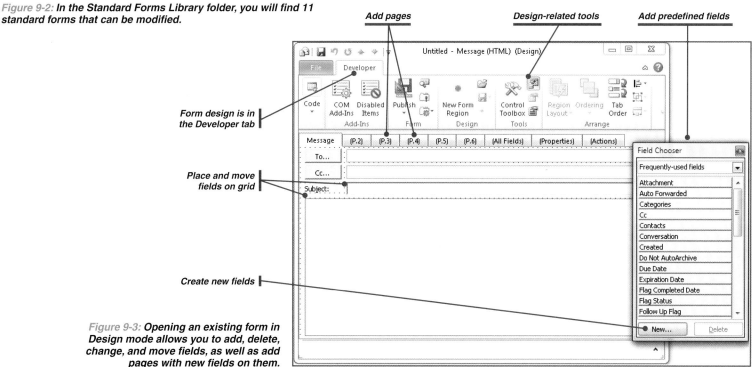

Form design is in the Developer tab

Place and move fields on grid

Create new fields

Figure 9-3: *Opening an existing form in Design mode allows you to add, delete, change, and move fields, as well as add pages with new fields on them.*

4. In the Developer tab Form group, click the **Page** down arrow, and choose between changing the form as the sender will see it (click **Edit Compose Page**) or as the recipient will see it (click **Edit Read Page**).

5. Choose from among the following changes that can be made on the form:

● Click a field whose size you want to change. A shaded border with *sizing handles* (small black or white squares) appears around the field. Drag one of the sizing handles to change the size of the field.

● Click a field you want to delete, and press **DELETE**.

● Click the field categories drop-down list at the top of the Field Chooser dialog box (Frequently Used Fields is selected by default), click a category, and drag a predefined field to the place on the form where you want it.

● To insert a new field in the form, click **New** in the Field Chooser dialog box. In the New Column dialog box that appears, enter a name, select a type and format, and click **OK**. Drag the new field to the place on the form where you want it.

● Click the **Developer** tab, and click **Publish** in the Form group. Click **Publish Form As** from the menu. Accepting the default, Personal Forms Library, type the Form Name, type the Display Name, and click **Publish**. (If you want the two names to be the same, type the Display Name first and the Form Name will be duplicated.) The form will appear in the Personal Forms Library under the Display Name.

6. If you are not ready to publish the form, save it by selecting the File tab and clicking Save As. Select the folder in which you want to save the form. Enter the file name for the form, click Save, and close the form.

Create a Custom Form

Creating a custom form is the same as modifying a form, because Outlook does not allow you to start with a blank form. You can create a form easily, however, by starting with an existing form, deleting all the fields you don't want— possibly all of them—and adding the fields you want. Also, there are a number of additional tools on the Developer ribbon you can use to customize a form, including the Form Design toolbar.

TIP

See both "Modify a Standard Form" and "Create a Custom Form" for the full range of modifications you can make to a form.

USE THE DEVELOPER TAB

The Developer tab and ribbon in the Form Design window allow you to perform the following functions:

- Program small scripts and macros to automate a form.
- Publish the form to a server so that you or anyone else with access can use it.
- View Visual Basic script code you have added to the form.
- Display or rename a page.
- Create a new form region or rename a current one.
- Choose to edit the page as the sender or the reader will see it.
- Open and close the Field Chooser and the Control toolbox.
- Open the Properties dialog boxes for a field.
- Position and align fields.

To perform these functions, the Developer tab has a number of unique options, as shown in Figure 9-4.

The more important options on the Developer tab are as follows:

- Form group:
  - **Publish** allows you to prepare your form for formal testing and use. You publish the form to a personal library or folder, which then can be referred to in the Choose Form dialog box.
  - **View Code** allows you to add and change Visual Basic code associated with a control on the form.

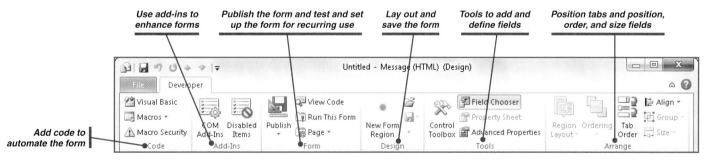

Figure 9-4: The Developer tab provides a number of form design tools.

- **Run This Form** allows you to test your form's appearance and action.

- **Page** allows you to select the Display This Page and Rename Page options with which you can display add-on pages (in addition to the ones displayed in the tabs beneath the ribbon named P.2 through P.6) and rename them from "Message" (or whatever name the standard tab is) and "P.x" to your choice. If your ending form contains one new page, you would activate the page to use it in the final form. When the new form is opened, it will contain only the pages you have included in the modified form. This is also where you choose whether you want to edit the compose page or the read page.

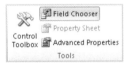

- Design group:

  - **New Form Region** allows you to create a form region, which provides for the inclusion of Web pages and ActiveX controls on a form. Each region is a separate page connected to a form.

  - **Open Form Region**, **Save Region**, and **Close Form Region** opens, saves, and closes a form region.

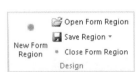

- Tools group:

  - **Control Toolbox** contains tools you can use to build a form, as described in "Use the Control Toolbox" later in this chapter.

  - **Field Chooser** opens and closes the Field Chooser dialog box.

  - **Property Sheet** and **Advanced Properties** allow you to enter detailed specifications, including the name, position, font, color, initial value, and any validation rules you want to establish for a field.

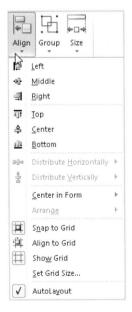

- Arrange group:

  - **Region Layout** allows you to specify that a layout will automatically resize itself when the form is resized, or you can manually resize a  layout to a fixed form size that you set. You can select a control for your region here.

  - **Ordering** displays a menu that allows you to move a selected field toward the reader ("front") or away from the reader ("back").

  - **Tab Order** allows you to specify the order in which the user will progress from one field to the next. See "Change the Tab Order" later in this chapter.

  - **Align** opens a menu that helps you align multiple fields when they are selected together. This includes options for aligning each of the four sides and centering, as well as options to turn on and use the Snap To Grid, which is a "magnetic" property that causes fields to automatically align with the grid intersections.

- **Group** and **Ungroup** allow you to combine two or more fields and then move and place them without disturbing the layout within the group.

- **Size** allows you to make two or more selected objects the same size in width, height, or both and to fit objects within a given space or the grid.

POSITION AND ALIGN TWO FIELDS

To align two fields, first use the Properties dialog box and then the alignment tools on the Developer ribbon. The following steps serve as an example:

1. Click the **Developer** tab, and in the Custom Forms group, click **Design A Form**. Double-click the existing form that will be the foundation of a new form.

2. Delete any existing fields you do not need. Drag two new fields from the Field Chooser dialog box to the new form, and purposely make them unaligned and of different sizes.

3. Click the field that will remain in its current position, and make sure its left edge is where you want it. In the Developer tab Tools group, click the **Property Sheet** icon to open the Properties dialog box, as shown in Figure 9-5.

4. Click the **Layout** tab, note the four position numbers, and close the dialog box. You could simply use those coordinates to align and size the fields, but there is an easier way. Close the Properties dialog box.

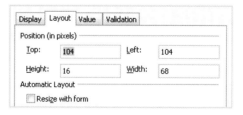

5. Click the field that will remain in its current position, and make sure its left edge is where you want it. It is important that the field that will stay constant be selected first.

6. Hold down **SHIFT** while clicking the second field. Note that the first field has white selection handles, while the second field has black selection handles.

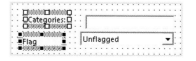

TIP

It works best if the label and content fields are sized and aligned separately. It is also helpful to align fields that are all in a vertical column or all in a horizontal row. Finally, if you are having problems sizing and aligning three or more fields, do them two at a time, with one of the two the way you want all the fields.

Figure 9-5: You can align and similarly size two fields by making all but one of their coordinates the same.

7. In the Developer tab Arrange group, click the **Align** drop-down arrow, and click **Left**. In the same group, click the **Size** drop-down arrow, click **Make Same Size**, and click **Both**. Note that the field with the black handles was the one that moved in both instances.

8. Repeat steps 5–7 with the two field labels, and then with each of the labels and their fields. The result should be four perfectly sized aligned fields, like this:

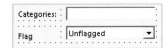

USE THE DESIGN TABS

When you use the Design A Form feature and select a form to use, you'll see that beneath the ribbon in the content area, the Form Design window has a number of new tabs, depending on the type of form. For example, the message form contains eight new tabs in addition to the single Message tab on the standard form. Of the eight new tabs, five are additional blank pages for the form. The three other tabs specify additional aspects of the form.

- **All Fields** allows you to define new fields (by clicking **New** at the bottom of the window) and specify the initial or default value of a field.

- **Properties** allows you to specify the form's categories, version, form number, icons, contact, and description.

- **Actions** contains the user actions that are implemented for the form, such as reply and forward.

Use the Control Toolbox

The Control toolbox is used to add new fields and labels to a form. The Control toolbox is opened with the Control Toolbox button in the Developer tab Tools group, and it contains 15 tools, as shown in Figure 9-6. For example, you can use the Control toolbox to create a combo box and a label.

1. Click the **Developer** tab, and in the Custom Forms group, click **Design A Form**. Double-click an existing form that will be the foundation of a new form.

2. Delete any existing fields you do not need, and otherwise make room, such as moving fields, to add a new label and combo box. In the Developer tab Tools group, click **Control Toolbox**. (If the window is not maximized, you will only see the icon in the Tools group.)

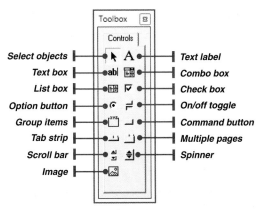

Select objects — Text label
Text box — Combo box
List box — Check box
Option button — On/off toggle
Group items — Command button
Tab strip — Multiple pages
Scroll bar — Spinner
Image

Figure 9-6: Controls and features are added to a new form from the Control toolbox.

3. Click the **Label** ("Text Label" in Figure 9-6) tool. Then, on your form, place the label by clicking to the left of where you want the combo box to be. (Be sure that the label is not placed on another field or you won't be able to type in it.)

4. With the label selected, click the label again until the text box border has slanted lines and the insertion point is available. Then, if there is existing text in the label, drag across the existing text to select it, and type the label you want.

5. In the Control toolbox, click the **Combo Box** tool, and drag a combo box from the right edge of the label to make a box about two inches long and a quarter of an inch wide.

6. Right-click in the new combo box, and click **Properties** from the context menu to open the Properties dialog box. In the Display tab, type the name you want in the Name text box.

7. Click the **Value** tab, and click the **New** button to create a new field in the Outlook field list. In the New Column dialog box, type the field name in the Name text box, indicate what kind of field it is in the Type field, and choose the format you want in the Format drop-down list.

8. Click **OK** to close the New Field dialog box. In the Properties dialog box, on the Value tab, click in the **Possible Values** text box, and type the values that are to be displayed in the drop-down list, separated by semicolons.

9. Click the **Set The Initial Value Of This Field To** check box, click in the text box, and type the value from the drop-down list that you want to be the default. If you have numbers in the default value, place quotation marks around the value. When you are done, your dialog box should look something like that shown in Figure 9-7.

10. Click **OK** to close the Properties dialog box. To see how your new combo box works, in the Developer tab Form group, click **Run This Form**. You should see the default value in the combo box, and if you open the box, you should see the alternatives that you entered. This is what ours looked like.

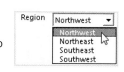

11. Click the **Close** button to close the sample form that was opened and return to the Design view. With the new combo box still selected, hold down **CTRL** and click the field's label. In the Developer tab Arrange group, click the **Group** down arrow, and click **Group** to group the label and the combo box together.

12. Click **File**, click **Save As**, locate the folder in which you want to save the form, type a name for the form, and click **Save**.

Create a new database field

Enter values to be displayed in the drop-down list, separated by semicolons

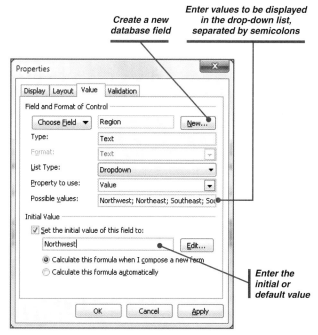

Enter the initial or default value

*Figure 9-7: **The Properties dialog box allows you to set the defaults and values for a field.***

Change the Tab Order

The tab order of a form is the order in which you go from field to field as you are filling out the form by pressing **TAB**. How this works is important, because the tab order should follow, as much as possible, how users would logically move through the form if they were to click each field. With the Form Design window open:

1. In a new form's Developer tab Arrange group, click **Tab Order** to open the Tab Order dialog box.

2. In the Tab Order dialog box, the fields in a form are listed in the order in which they will be selected as you go through the form. You can change the order by moving fields up and down the list.

3. Click a field you want to change, and move it by clicking **Move Down** or **Move Up**.

4. Click **OK** to close the Tab Order dialog box.

Use Separate Compose and Read Layouts

Outlook allows you to have a form for the person who initially fills it out be different from the form for the person who reads it. When you create a form, you can choose to have the *compose layout*—the form the way you fill it out—be different from the *read layout*—the form the way it will be read. You can initiate this feature in the Form Design window in the Developer tab Form group on the Page menu by making sure that **Separate Read Layout** is selected. When this is selected, you will have two options enabled that allow you to switch between the compose layout, and the read layout. (These are also referred to as the compose page or read page.)

The easiest way to see the difference between a compose page and a read page is by using the standard Outlook e-mail message form. The way you first see the form in Design view is as the compose page, as shown in Figure 9-8. In the Developer tab Form group, click **Page** and then click **Edit Read Page**, and you will see a number of changes, as shown in Figure 9-9.

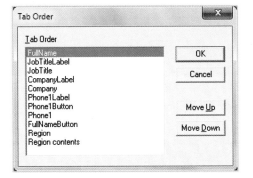

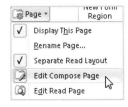

NOTE

Separate read and compose layouts allow you to tailor a form to a specific audience and to add features that are important to either the person filling out the form or the person reading it, but not to both.

9

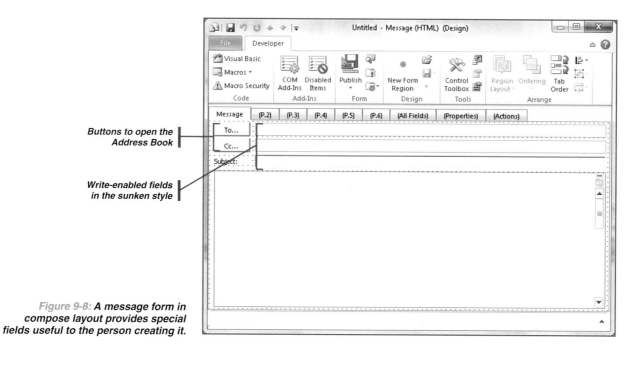

Buttons to open the
Address Book

Write-enabled fields
in the sunken style

Figure 9-8: *A message form in
compose layout provides special
fields useful to the person creating it.*

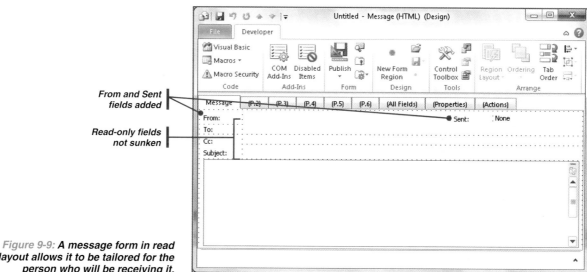

From and Sent
fields added

Read-only fields
not sunken

Figure 9-9: *A message form in read
layout allows it to be tailored for the
person who will be receiving it.*

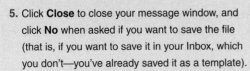
Publish a Form

When you are ready for people to start using a form, you need to *publish* it. Publishing a form puts it into a different state than just saving it. When you save a form and then reopen and use it, you are using the original and only copy of the form—it can only be used once. If you publish the form and then open and use it, you are using a copy and not the original—it can be reused multiple times. Every time you use a published form, you are using a copy of the form. To publish a form that is open in the Form Design window:

1. In the new form's Developer tab Form group, click **Publish** and then click **Publish Form**.

2. Click the folder you want to use (Personal Forms Library is recommended), type the name of the form in the Display Name box (it is automatically repeated in the Form Name box, but you can change it), and click **Publish**, as shown in Figure 9-10.

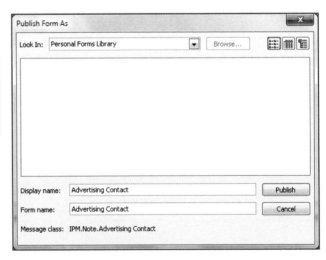

*Figure 9-10: **Publishing a form allows it to be used over and over.***

CREATING AND USING A TEMPLATE

(Continued)

USE A TEMPLATE

1. In the Home tab New group, click the **New Items** down arrow in the toolbar, click **More Items**, and then click **Choose Form**. The Choose Form dialog box appears.

2. In the Look In drop-down list, click **User Templates In File System**. The template you just created should be displayed.

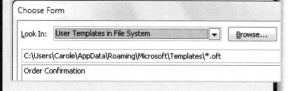

3. Double-click your template name, and it opens as a new message window, with the subject line and body filled in according to the template. All you need to do is fill in the To information and click **Send**, as you can see in Figure 9-11. Of course, you can modify or add to the text.

TIP

Any of the built-in Outlook forms you see in the Developer tab Custom Forms group can be customized by you and then saved under a new template name. Select the form you want to customize by clicking **Choose Form**.

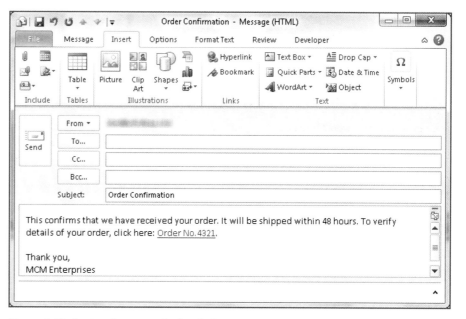

Figure 9-11: *Custom forms can be handy for such things as order confirmations.*

3. If you are asked if you want to save the form definition with the form, click **Yes**. (It's very important to save the form definition information with the message if you're going to send it to someone who doesn't have the form.)

4. When you are done, close your Form Design window, clicking **Yes** when asked if you want to save your changes.

Use a Custom Form

Using a custom form is easy.

1. In one of the Outlook views, such as Mail window, click the **New Items** down arrow in the New group. On the menu, click **More Items**, and then click **Choose Forms**, and the Choose Form dialog box appears. Click the **Look In** down arrow, click **Personal Forms Library**, and you will see the display name of your custom form.

2. Double-click your form and it will open, ready to be filled in, as you can see in Figure 9-12.

UICKSTEPS

SELECTING CONTACTS

You can select contacts to use in a mail merge in four ways: manually, using Outlook's Mail Merge feature; using Outlook's filters; or using Word's Mail Merge feature. The first three are discussed here. The fourth is discussed in "Prepare a Mail Merge Document in Word" later in this chapter.

SELECT CONTACTS MANUALLY

To add contacts to a mail merge folder:

1. In the Navigation pane, click **Contacts** in the Outlook views pane. The contacts will be displayed in the Folder pane.

2. Right-drag contacts from your main Contacts folder to your new mail merge folder, and click **Copy**.

   –Or–

   Select several contacts, either by holding down **CTRL** while clicking the contacts you want or by holding down **SHIFT** while clicking the first and last members of a contiguous range of contacts. These can then be dragged to the new folder or used directly in Outlook's Mail Merge feature.

USE OUTLOOK'S MAIL MERGE FEATURE

This technique is often used when you are ready to do the mail merge in "real time." You have the contacts and the letter or document you are going to send them, and

Continued . . .

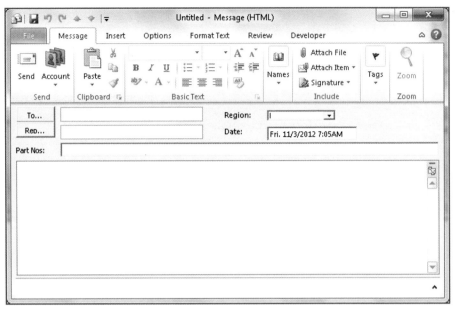

Figure 9-12: *Templates can speed up the handling of a large volume of e-mail.*

Perform a Mail Merge

Performing a mail merge allows you to merge a form letter with your Outlook contacts, thereby sending each contact a unique letter addressed just to him or her. This can be done with all contacts in a folder or just a subset of them. This section discusses sending form letters to a subset of your contacts, although the steps for sending form letters to all of your contacts are much the same—and simpler.

There are three steps to performing a mail merge using the Contacts list in Outlook with a Microsoft Word document. First, within Outlook, you prepare the contacts you wish to use in the mail merge, and then you export them in a form that Word can use with its Mail Merge feature. Second, in Word, you create the document that will be used to perform the mail merge. Finally, you perform the mail merge itself in Word.

QUICKSTEPS

SELECTING CONTACTS (Continued)

you are ready to move right into the actual merge. In this approach, you link your contacts (either in the Contacts folder or your own folder of selected contacts) to a previously prepared Word document containing the mail merge text.

1. In the Navigation pane, click **Contacts** in Outlook views so that the contacts are displayed in the Folders pane.

2. In the Home tab Actions group, click **Mail Merge**. The Mail Merge Contacts dialog box appears, as shown in Figure 9-14.

3. Either click **All Contacts In Current View**, which can be filtered (see "Use Outlook Filtering") or click **Only Selected Contacts** when contacts have been manually selected (see "Select Contacts Manually").

4. Click either **New Document** or **Existing Document**, which you can then identify.

5. Click **Permanent File** and browse to or type the file name you wish to use. This will be the file for saving the selected contacts.

Continued . . .

Prepare Contacts

If you are only going to perform a mail merge on some of your contacts, it is a good idea to first create a new folder to hold the contacts you wish to include in the mail merge. Then, in Word, you select that folder as your data source. To create a new folder and export it:

1. In the Navigation pane, click **Contacts** in the Outlook views pane.

2. Right-click the **Contacts** folder, and choose **New Folder**. The Create New Folder dialog box appears.

3. Type the name for the new folder, and make sure that **Contact Items** is selected under Folder Contains and that **Contacts** is highlighted under Select Where To Place The Folder, as shown in Figure 9-13.

4. Click **OK**. Your new folder appears below the Contacts folders at the top of the Folder List.

Figure 9-13: **Creating a special folder for a mail merge allows you to easily send mail to the same people in the future.**

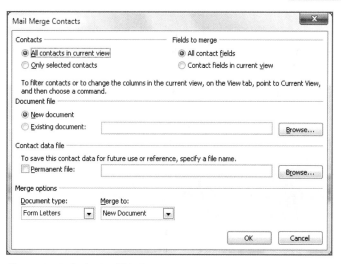

Figure 9-14: **Outlook will help you set up your contacts for a mail merge and then will open Word to access the document and do the merge.**

QUICKSTEPS

SELECTING CONTACTS *(Continued)*

6. Select the merge options, such as form letters, labels, or envelopes to a new document, printer, or e-mail that are correct for you, and then click **OK**.

Outlook will prepare your contact data, open Microsoft Word, and create a new mail merge document linked to your contact data and ready for you to type the message contents. See "Prepare a Mail Merge Document in Word."

USE OUTLOOK FILTERING

Outlook's filtering capability allows you to select the contacts you want to use in a mail merge. The filtered contacts are placed in a file within a new folder you create specifically for the mail merge.

1. With the Contacts list still open, click the **View** tab, and in the current group, click **View Settings**.

2. Click **Filter** in the Advanced View Settings dialog box. In the Filter dialog box, type the criteria to select only the contacts you want, and then click **OK** twice. The list of filtered contacts will appear in the Contacts pane.

3. Click a name in the Contacts list and press **CTRL+A** for Select All. Right-drag the contacts to the new folder you created, and click **Copy** in the context menu to keep the contacts also in the Contacts folder.

4. Click your new folder in the Folder List to see the selected contacts, as shown in Figure 9-15. This folder can now be used to merge contacts into a Word document.

Prepare a Mail Merge Document in Word

You can approach a mail merge from Outlook and then use Microsoft Word just to produce a document, or you can start from Word and just use Outlook to supply the contacts. Since this book is on Outlook, we will use the first approach and assume you have used Outlook's Mail Merge feature (see the "Selecting Contacts" QuickSteps) to prepare your contacts and then opened Word to create a new mail merge document. You should, therefore, have Word open on your screen to type the document and place field names where you want the Outlook contact information.

1. Type the body of a new letter, or paste an existing one that you will be sending to your selected contacts. Leave blank the areas that will contain the recipient's name and address.

2. When the body of the letter is the way you want it, return to the top of the page. In the Mailings tab Write & Insert Fields group, click **Address Block**. The Insert Address Block dialog box appears.

3. Review the default settings. In most cases, they work well. Click **Match Fields**. Make sure the field on the right matches the required information on the left. Click **OK** twice when ready.

4. Under the address block that just appeared, leave a blank line or two. Then, in the Mailings tab Write & Insert Fields group, click **Greeting Line**. The Insert Greeting Line dialog box appears. Select the options that are correct for you, and click **OK**.

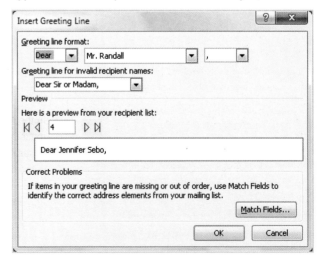

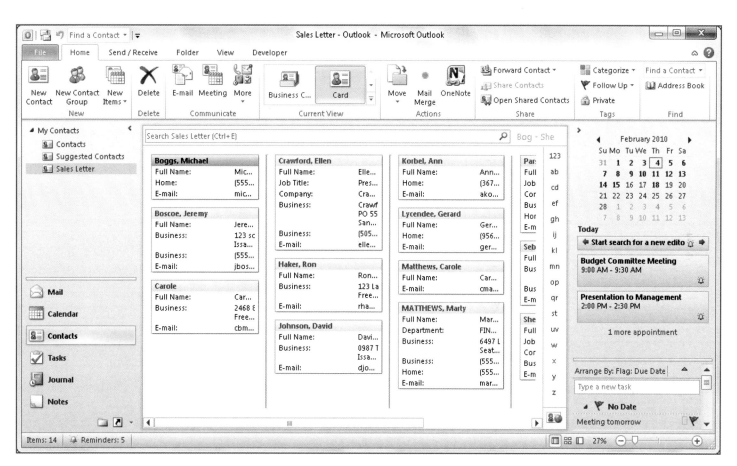

Figure 9-15: *Use one of several options within Outlook to select contacts for use in a mail merge.*

5. In the Mailings tab Start Mail Merge group, click **Edit Recipient List**. Here you can make a final selection of your recipients, as shown in Figure 9-16. Use the check boxes on the left to select individuals; click a column heading to sort the list on that column; click the down arrow in a column heading to select a particular entry in the column, including "blanks" and "nonblanks"; click the data source in the lower-left area; and then click **Edit** to change an individual record. When you have the recipients the way you want them, click **OK**.

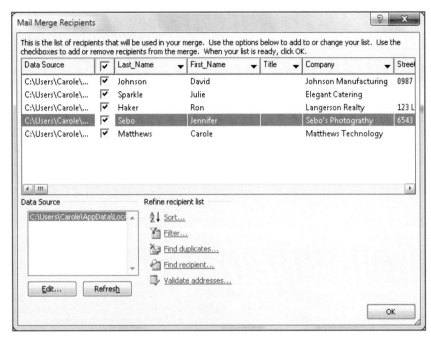

Mail Merge Recipients

This is the list of recipients that will be used in your merge. Use the options below to add to or change your list. Use the checkboxes to add or remove recipients from the merge. When your list is ready, click OK.

Data Source	☑	Last_Name ▾	First_Name ▾	Title ▾	Company ▾	Street
C:\Users\Carole\...	☑	Johnson	David		Johnson Manufacturing	0987
C:\Users\Carole\...	☑	Sparkle	Julie		Elegant Catering	
C:\Users\Carole\...	☑	Haker	Ron		Langerson Realty	123 L
C:\Users\Carole\...	☑	Sebo	Jennifer		Sebo's Photograthy	6543
C:\Users\Carole\...	☑	Matthews	Carole		Matthews Technology	

Data Source

C:\Users\Carole\AppData\Loca

Edit...   Refresh

Refine recipient list

A↓ Sort...
Filter...
Find duplicates...
Find recipient...
Validate addresses...

OK

*Figure 9-16: **Word provides a means of filtering, sorting, and selecting contacts in the Mail Merge Recipients dialog box.***

Checking and Reporting Errors

● Simulate the merge and report errors in a new document.

○ Complete the merge, pausing to report each error as it occurs.

○ Complete the merge without pausing. Report errors in a new document.

OK   Cancel

6. In the Mailings tab Preview Results group, click **Preview Results** to display your contacts merged with the letter (if your Word window is narrow and there is a down arrow under Preview Results, you'll need to click **Preview Results** a second time in the drop-down options). Use the arrows at the top of the Preview Results group to cycle through your letters. An example is shown in Figure 9-17.

7. When the document is as you want it, click **Save** on the Quick Access toolbar.

Perform a Mail Merge

When you perform a mail merge, you can print letters, mailing labels, or envelopes, or you can send e-mail messages to Outlook contacts. Once you have the document and contacts the way you want them, run tests—first of the data and then of the merge—to see if any fields are missing in the data and if the merge is picking up the right fields. When you are satisfied with the results, print the actual letters, labels, or envelopes, or send the e-mail.

1. In Word's Mailings tab Preview Results group, click **Auto Check For Errors** to see if there are any needed fields missing. In the Checking And Reporting Errors dialog box, click **Simulate The Merge And Report Errors In A New Document**, and click **OK**. You will receive either a message of errors in the data or a message that there are no errors.

2. When you have fixed any errors, in the Mailings tab Finish group, click **Finish & Merge**, click **Edit Individual Documents**, accept the default selection (**ALL**) to merge all records, and click **OK**. A new document will be created containing all of the letters you want created. Use the scroll bar in the Word window to scroll down and look at the succession of letters you have created.

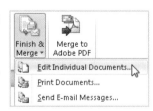

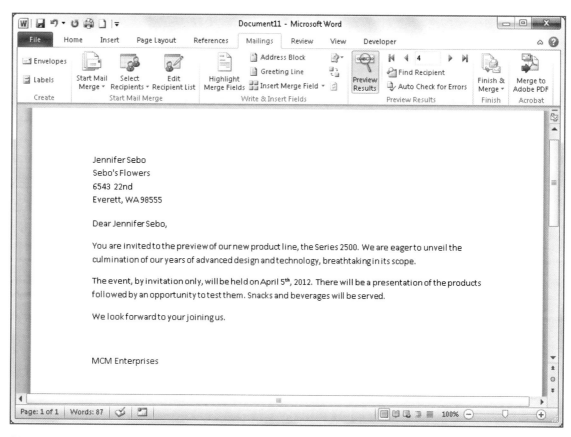

Figure 9-17: **A well-done mail merge letter is impossible to tell from an individually typed letter.**

3. When you are ready to print your merged letters, click **File** and then click **Print**. You'll see a letter in the Preview pane. In the Print view, you can click the **Next Page** and **Previous Page** arrows at the bottom of the Preview pane. When you're ready, click **Print**.

–Or–

In place of creating the individual merged documents in step 2, in the Mailings tab Finish group, click **Finish & Merge** and then click **Print Documents**, or click **Send E-mail** Messages.

4. If you wish, save your new merged document, and once more save the original mail merge document.

Print Labels

Printing labels is done the same way as the mail merge. First, you prepare your data file in Outlook (which you've already done while preparing for the mail merge). Then switch to Word, create a blank document, and perform a mail merge.

1. If you haven't already prepared a contacts file for the mail merge, follow the steps described in "Prepare Contacts" and in the "Selecting Contacts" QuickSteps earlier in this chapter to get a data file for the names and addresses.

2. In Word, open a new, blank document. Then, in the Mailings tab Start Mail Merge group, click the **Start Mail Merge** down arrow, and click **Labels**. The Label Options dialog box appears.

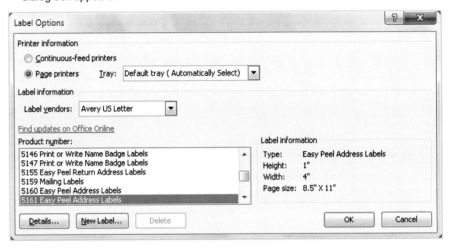

3. Select the label vendor and product number you want to use (Avery 5160 or its equivalent is a common 30-per-sheet address label), and click **OK**. The label outlines will appear as divisions in the rulers and, if paragraph marks are displayed, on the Word document page.

4. In the Mailings tab Start Mail Merge group, click **Select Recipients** and click **Select From Outlook Contacts**. Double-click the Contacts folder you want to use, make any needed selections or changes in the Mail Merge Recipients dialog box (shown earlier in Figure 9-16), and click **OK**. Your Word page will be filled with label fields, mostly <<Next Record>>.

5. Click in the upper-left corner label (the first label on the sheet—the insertion point may already be there). Then, in the Mailings tab Write & Insert Fields group, click

Address Block. Make any needed changes to the address block, check for any unmatched fields, and click **OK**.

6. In the Mailings tab Write & Insert Fields group, click the **Update Labels** icon
   ⌨ Update Labels . The address block will be added to all labels.

7. In the Mailings tab Preview Results group, click **Preview Results** (if your Word window is narrow and there is a down arrow under Preview Results, you'll need to click **Preview Results** a second time in the drop-down options), and you will see the labels populated with your contact list, as you can see in Figure 9-18.

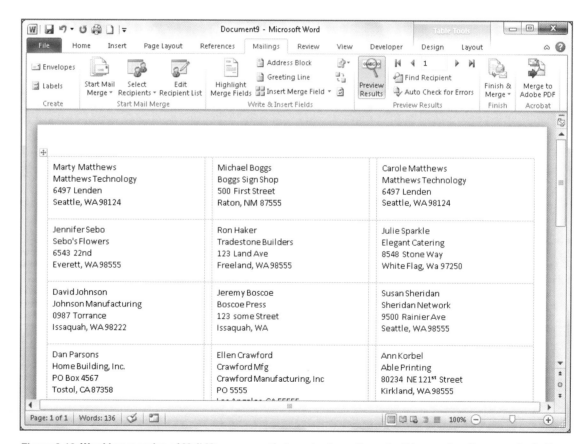

Figure 9-18: **Word has a series of Mail Merge pages that can lead you through all types of mail merges, including letters, labels, and envelopes.**

8. Scroll through the preview document. After making sure your blank labels are correctly loaded in your printer, in the Mailings tab Finish group, click **Finish & Merge** and then click **Print Documents**. If you want to save your merged labels document for later use, click **Save** in the Quick Access toolbar, enter a name, select a folder, and click **Save**.

Print Envelopes

You may want to print names and addresses directly onto envelopes. As with the mail merge and printing labels, printing envelopes first requires that you create a contacts data file. This is described earlier in "Prepare Contacts" and in the "Selecting Contacts" QuickSteps. After that, you can create a mail merge envelope document in Word.

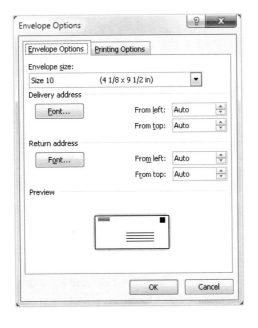

1. In Word, open a new, blank document. In the Mailings tab Start Mail Merge group, click the **Start Mail Merge** down arrow, and click **Envelopes**. The Envelope Options dialog box will appear.

2. Make any needed changes, and click **OK**. An envelope-shaped document will be displayed.

3. In the Mailings tab Start Mail Merge group, click **Select Recipients** and click **Select From Outlook Contacts**. Double-click the Contacts folder you want to use, make any needed selections or changes in the Mail Merge Recipients dialog box (shown earlier in Figure 9-16), and click **OK**.

4. With the insertion point in the addressee area in the middle of the envelope, click **Address Block** in the Mailings tab Write & Insert Fields group. Make any needed changes to the address block, check for any unmatched fields, and click **OK**.

5. Click in the upper-left corner of the envelope displayed in Word, and type the return address if the envelopes aren't preprinted.

6. In the Mailings tab Preview Results group, click **Preview Results** (if your Word window is narrow and there is a down arrow under Preview Results, you'll need to click **Preview Results** a second time in the drop-down options), and you will see your first address appear on the envelope, as shown in Figure 9-19.

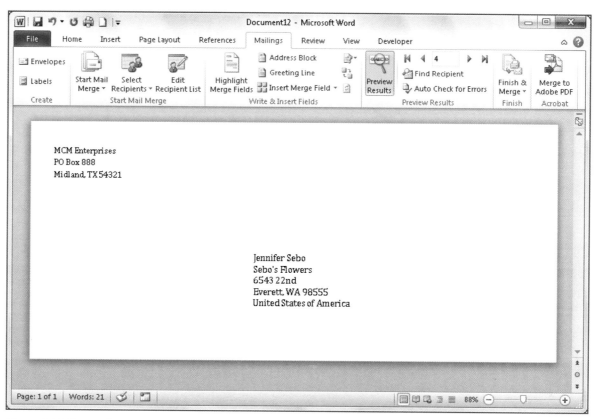

Figure 9-19: *Generating mail merge envelopes is almost the same as creating labels.*

7. After making sure your envelopes are loaded correctly in your printer, in the Mailings tab Finish group, click **Finish & Merge** and then click **Print Documents**. If you want to save the merged envelope document for later use, click **Save** in the Quick Access toolbar, type a name, select a folder, and click **Save**.

Chapter 10

Using Outlook in Other Ways

Being a part of Microsoft Office and the Microsoft family brings a number of features and capabilities to Outlook that extend what it can do and how it functions. In this chapter you'll see some of those features and capabilities, including using Outlook with instant messaging and with a potpourri of extensions. These supplementary applications, such as Office Clipboard and business cards, help integrate Outlook with fellow members of the Office suite or, in the case of using Outlook as a Web browser, with the Windows product line.

Use Instant Messaging with Outlook

If you're addicted to instant messaging, you'll be glad to know that Outlook can launch you right into a conversation. If you've never used instant messaging, now's the time to try it, because Outlook 2010 has instant messaging built into it.

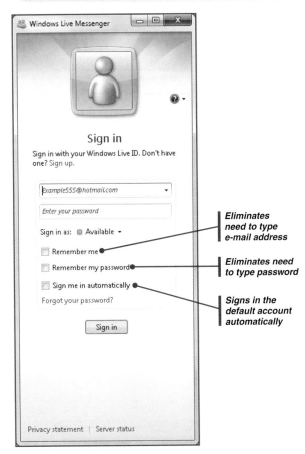

Figure 10-1: Other persons using the same computer can use their Passport accounts to sign on to instant messaging.

You just might get hooked on this quick and easy tool for making plans, solving problems, or catching up. You can do it with one person or with several at a time. If you have a Microsoft Passport or MSN Hotmail account, you're ready to go. If not, get one and come back when you're ready.

Set Up Instant Messaging

Get some IM-savvy friends to send you the e-mail addresses they use for in IM. If an address is different from the person's regular e-mail address, enter it the IM Address field in your Contacts list. Send yours to your friends, too, of course. Once you have done that, you can proceed to enter the world of IM-ing.

FIND WINDOWS LIVE MESSENGER

Windows Vista and Windows 7 install Windows Live Messenger by default. In this case, it automatically will be displayed when you turn on your computer. In this book we assume Windows Live Messenger is already on your computer. However, if it doesn't appear when you first turn on your computer, you can easily find and activate it.

1. If you have previously installed Windows Live Messenger and it didn't automatically start when you started Windows, click **Start**, click **All Programs**, scroll down and click **Windows Live**, and click **Windows Live Messenger**. The Windows Live Messenger window will open, as shown in Figure 10-1.

2. Assuming you have already signed up for a Windows Live or Hotmail ID, enter your e-mail address (ID) and password.

3. Indicate whether you want your computer to remember your ID and password and whether you should be signed in automatically to this account.

4. Click **Sign In** to complete the action.

5. A Welcome To Windows Live Messenger message appears, informing you about connecting with others, as seen in Figure 10-2. Click **Do It Now** on the Thanks For Choosing Windows Live Messenger window, or click **Add A Contact** from the Welcome To Windows Live Messenger dialog box beneath to immediately add contacts from Facebook, MySpace, or your e-mail Address Book; or click **Close** to do it later.

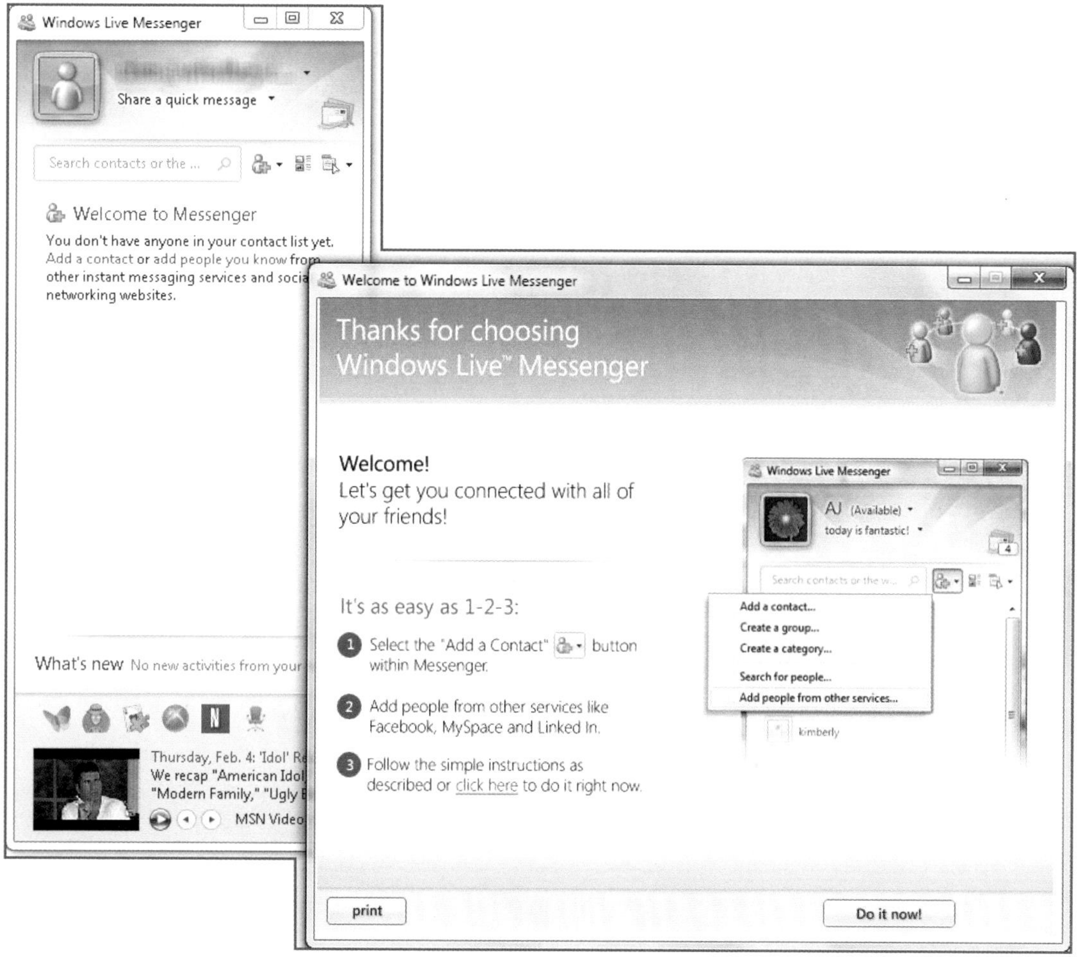

Figure 10-2: *Windows Live Messenger offers access to Web sites such as Facebook and MySpace, video, audio, games, telephone service, and text messaging.*

ACTIVATE INSTANT MESSAGING IN OUTLOOK

You can also access instant messaging from within Outlook without affecting your ability to do so from Windows Live Messenger. Using IM from Outlook allows you to easily access Outlook's features at the same time. Start by activating IM in Outlook.

1. Click **File**, click **Options**, and click **Contacts**.

NOTE

If you want to create a new ID but seem stuck with the one you have set up sometime in the distant past, click the ID field down arrow, and select **Sign Out From Here**. Then in the Sign In window, click **Sign In With A Different Windows Live ID**. Then type your desired e-mail address and password to add a new IM identity.

A Smart Tag is a small button that appears in Microsoft Office products to allow you to perform some function related to a piece of information next to the button. In this case, when you point to a person's name in an e-mail field, a green Windows Messaging button will appear if that person has been entered as an IM contact and is available. The button will be red if the contact is busy; it will be clear (or it may look yellow) if the contact is away. Clicking the button opens a menu of various options, including replying with an instant message.

■ Marty Matthews

2. Under Online Status And Photographs, click the **Display Online Status Next To Name** check box, if it is not already selected, and click **OK**.

This allows you to see who is online at the moment through a Smart Tag (a colored square) next to an e-mail sender's name in the Reading pane. This tells you that you can then use the Outlook messaging feature to send a message.

CREATE A NEW IM CONTACT

1. Click **Add A Contact** on the right of the text box in the Windows Live Messenger window. Click **Add A Contact** from the menu. The Enter The Person's Information dialog box appears, as you can see in Figure 10-3.

2. Type the contact's instant messaging address (usually the same as his or her e-mail address, but not always), a mobile phone number for text messaging, and a category. Click **Next**.

3. In the next dialog box, you can type your message or invitation to your contact (this is optional) and ask them to add you to their Windows Live Messenger Contacts list.

4. Click **Send Invitation**.

RESPOND TO AN OUTLOOK INVITATION

You may receive an invitation via e-mail to communicate by IM. Adding a new contact is easy.

1. Click the e-mail invitation in the Message pane to select it.

2. In the Home tab Respond group, click the **IM** down arrow, and click **Reply With IM**.

Figure 10-3: Your IM contacts have to be added manually, since there is not a way to transfer them from Outlook.

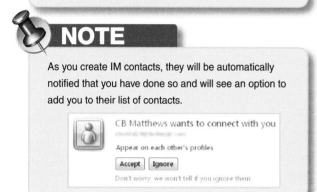
3. In the IM dialog box, click **Add To Contact List**. The contact will be automatically added to your IM list of contacts.

Respond to an Instant Message and Chat

You can respond to an e-mail with an instant message, if the person is online. Once they get your message, the two of you can carry on a real-time chat. See if the person is online by pointing to his or her name in any of these locations:

- New message window
- Reading pane return address
- Opened message

1. Point to a Smart Tag for someone who is online, and a menu opens.

2. Click **Send An Instant Message To**. An IM window will open.

3. Start typing a greeting or message in the lower pane. When you press **ENTER**, it will be sent. You can see it in the upper pane along with any replies that come back from your contact, as seen in Figure 10-4. You can tell that someone is responding to you by the icon above the text box.

4. You can change fonts for your text, add emoticons, and more by clicking the icons at the bottom of the window.

5. When you're finished, click **Close**.

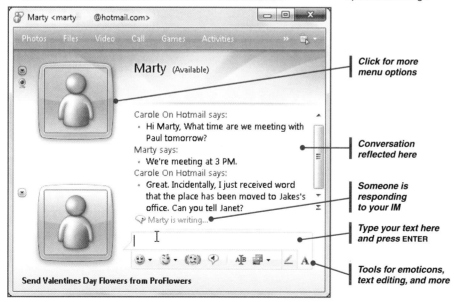

Click for more menu options

Conversation reflected here

Someone is responding to your IM

Type your text here and press ENTER

Tools for emoticons, text editing, and more

Figure 10-4: You can initiate a real-time conversation with another person online.

You can decide how your name appears to other people—you may not want your real e-mail address showing in your IM window. In the Windows Live Messenger window, click the down arrow to the right of your ID, click **Options**, and in the Options dialog box, enter your choice for a name in the top text box. Click **OK** to close.

By default, Windows Live Messenger does not display its menus. You can display them temporarily or permanently by clicking the **Show Menu** icon on the far right of the Contact Search text box. The menu will be displayed. Select the **Show The Menu Bar** check box. The menu bar will appear at the top of the Windows Live Messenger window.

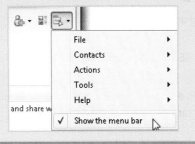

MAKE IT A PARTY

Several people can talk at a time when you are using IM, provided that you have already set them up as IM contacts. Get a conversation going with one other person, and then:

1. Click **Invite** in the toolbar to add another person to the conversation (if you haven't set up another person as an IM contact, the Invite menu option will not appear on the toolbar). The dialog box lets you see which of your IM contacts are currently online.

2. Select the person and click **OK**.
3. Continue conversing as before.

STATE YOUR AVAILABILITY

1. Click the down arrow to the left of your display name, and select a status.

Implement RSS Feeds

RSS, or *Really Simple Syndication*, allows you to receive and store in one place information from a number of sources on an on-going basis. The information can be from any source on the Web that has implemented RSS and to which you have subscribed, often for free, but sometimes at a cost. Normally, the information is from sites that frequently update their content, such as news organizations like CNN, MSN, and CNET, or active blogs (personal Web logs

or online journals) from both individuals and companies. The information frequently consists of short summary text headings in the form of a link that you can click to download and read the full article; but increasingly, the RSS feed includes larger blocks of text, pictures, and even multimedia content, which are called *podcasts*.

The primary reason for RSS feeds is that they allow you to collect information from a number of sources without having to visit many different sites. You subscribe to the feed, and it is automatically downloaded for you by the program handling the RSS feed. You might do this because of a particular interest you have, or a desire to stay informed, or because it supports your work.

You can receive RSS feeds from many sources using a number of different programs, including Internet Explorer, the Windows Sidebar in Windows Vista, and the Windows Gadgets in Windows 7. Outlook allows you to subscribe, receive, read, organize, store, and delete RSS content. The process is similar to how e-mail is handled.

- Locate and subscribe to an RSS feed.
- Outlook creates a folder for that feed under the RSS Feeds folder in the Navigation pane.
- Outlook periodically goes out to the RSS publisher's server and downloads any new or updated articles.
- On your own schedule, you can open the folder, read the new content, move it to new folders, or delete it. You can also forward it to someone else and flag it.

Locate and Subscribe to RSS Feeds

You can locate RSS feeds by having the Internet address, or URL, sent to you in an e-mail message, see it in an article or publication, or find an RSS link in a Web site. Also, you can do searches on Google or MSN, or look at lists of RSS feeds by clicking the **RSS Feeds** folder in Outlook or at www.search4rss.com and www.syndic8.com. On Web pages, RSS feeds usually are identified with an icon.

TIP

You can share RSS feeds and content with others by sending or receiving the RSS Internet address, or URL, in an e-mail message and by exporting and transferring RSS content using .opml files.

SUBSCRIBE

Figure 10-5: *When you add an RSS feed to Outlook, you can determine how you want feeds handled.*

SUBSCRIBE TO AN RSS FEED FROM A WEB SITE

Internet Explorer 8 and Outlook 2010 work together to capture and use RSS feeds. The feeds can be added in either program and, once captured, can be accessed in either program.

1. In Internet Explorer, open the Web site in which you want to capture an RSS feed.

2. When you see an RSS feed icon 📶 or **RSS**, click the icon. A page displaying examples of what that RSS feed offers will be displayed and possibly offer a menu of subscription options. One option that works particularly well with Outlook is NewsGator Outlook Edition.

3. Click **Subscribe** or follow whatever directions are given for access to the RSS feed. The RSS feed will appear in an RSS folder. If you don't see an option to easily transfer your feed into Outlook, copy the URL of the page and paste it into the Outlook RSS folder, as described in "Use an RSS Feed in an E-mail."

4. If you copy and paste the URL, a dialog box will ask if you want to add this to Outlook. Before you continue, click **Advanced** to set certain options, as shown in Figure 10-5.

5. Consider changing the folder to automatically downloading enclosures, downloading the full article, and using the publisher's recommended update frequency; and make the needed changes. Under most circumstances, the default settings shown in Figure 10-5 are recommended.

6. When you are ready, click **OK** and click **Yes**. You'll see the new RSS feed folder added to your RSS Feeds folder.

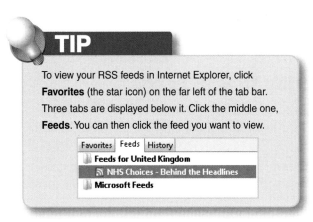

TIP

To view your RSS feeds in Internet Explorer, click **Favorites** (the star icon) on the far left of the tab bar. Three tabs are displayed below it. Click the middle one, **Feeds**. You can then click the feed you want to view.

USE AN RSS LINK IN AN E-MAIL

If someone sends you a link with the URL for an RSS feed, such as the one in Figure 10-6, you can add it to Outlook's RSS folders.

1. In Outlook, with the Inbox open, click the message with the RSS link, drag across the link to select it, and press **CTRL+C** to copy the link to the Clipboard.

2. In the Navigation pane, right click the **RSS Feeds** folder, and click **Add An RSS Feed**. The New RSS Feed dialog box appears.

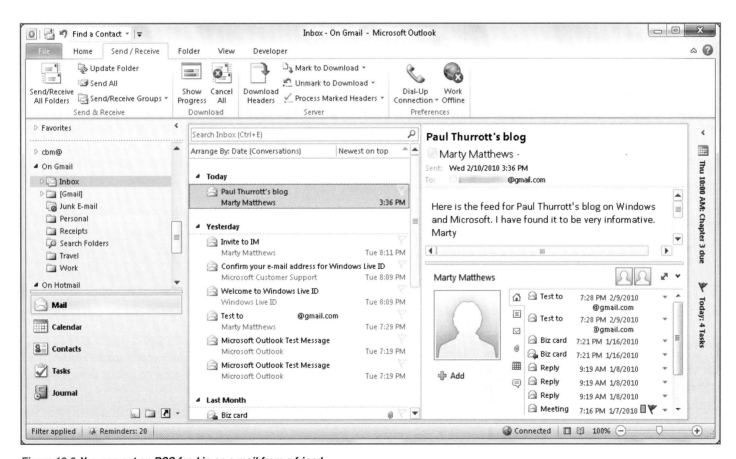

Figure 10-6: You can get an RSS feed in an e-mail from a friend.

New RSS Feed

Enter the location of the RSS Feed you want to add to Outlook:

http://community.winsupersite.com/blogs/paul/rss.aspx

Example: http://www.example.com/feed/main.xml

[Add] [Cancel]

NOTE

In case you want to check the settings for current RSS feeds or to change or remove them, you can also display the RSS Feed Options dialog box by double-clicking an RSS entry in the Account Settings dialog box. To do this, click **File**, in the Info option, click **Account Settings**, and click **Account Settings** on the menu. The RSS Feed Options dialog box appears. Click the **RSS Feeds** tab, and double-click the specific RSS feed you want to change.

CAUTION

RSS feeds can potentially download a lot of information that can both clog your Internet connection and take up a lot of room on your hard disk. Start out by downloading as little as possible and look at the impact caused before choosing to download attachments or full articles.

3. Click in the text box, press **CTRL+V** to paste the link into the dialog box, and click **Add**. A dialog box appears confirming that you want to add the feed to Outlook.

4. Click **Yes** to add it, or click **Advanced** to set some conditions described in the previous section. If you click Advanced, you'll see the RSS Feed Options dialog box, as shown in Figure 10-5. When you click Yes, the new RSS feed folder is added to your RSS Feeds folder.

Read and Work with RSS Articles

Reading and working with RSS articles is exactly like reading and working with e-mail messages.

SELECT AND VIEW RSS ARTICLES

1. In Outlook, click **Mail** from the Outlook View.

2. In the Navigation pane under Personal Folders or your top-level primary folder, scroll down until you see RSS Feeds. Then click the white triangle opposite RSS Feeds to open the folder.

3. Click the RSS feed folder you want to view, and it will open and display its articles in the Folder pane.

4. Click the article that you want to read.

5. If the Reading pane isn't already open, click the **View** menu, click **Reading Pane**, and click **Right**, unless you want it on the bottom. The RSS article will appear in the Reading pane for you to read, as shown in Figure 10-7.

OPEN THE RSS WINDOW

You can open a window containing special tools that you can use to download content, share the feed with others, categorize it, or flag it with a follow-up flag. Figure 10-8 shows an example of the ribbon tools you'll find.

1. Double-click the RSS article in the Folder pane to open the article in its own window (see Figure 10-8).

2. In the RSS Article tab Forward/RSS/Tags groups, click one of these options:

   - **Forward** the article to someone else you know would be interested in it using e-mail.

   - **Download Content** to download attachments and the full article.

   - **Share This Feed** to e-mail the RSS feed to someone else.

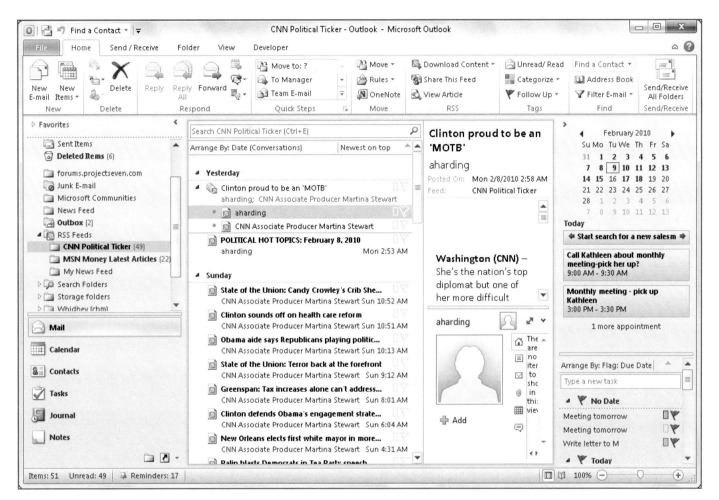

Figure 10-7: RSS feed articles look, behave, and are treated just like e-mail messages.

- **View Article** to view the article in a browser.
- **Mark Unread** to keep the article bold so you won't forget about it.
- **Categorize** to assign a color code to it so you can organize it better (see the "Organizing RSS Articles" QuickSteps).
- **Follow-Up** to assign a flag or send yourself a reminder (see "Flag and Forward RSS Articles").

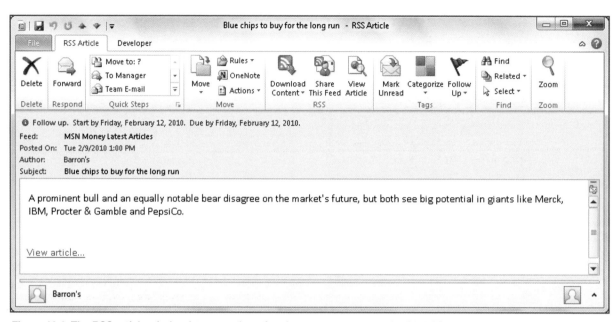

Figure 10-8: The RSS article window has a number of tools you can use to work with RSS articles.

FLAG AND FORWARD RSS ARTICLES

You can either flag the RSS article for further handling or immediately forward it on to someone else.

To forward or flag the RSS article:

- Click the RSS article in the Folder pane that you want to forward. In the Home tab Respond group, click **Forward**. An e-mail message window will open. Address the message and click **Send**.

- Click the RSS article in the Folder pane. In the Home tab Tags group, click **Follow Up** and click a flag signifying when you want to return to the RSS item. You may also click **Add Reminder** to set a date on which you want to be reminded.

DELETE RSS ARTICLES

1. Click the RSS article in the Folder pane that you want to delete.

2. Click **Delete** on the Home tab Delete group.

   –Or–

   Press **DELETE**.

ORGANIZING RSS ARTICLES

By default, RSS articles are placed in the originating feed folder. That may work for some RSS feeds, but for others, you may want to separate the articles into categories or some other segregation. This is especially true for general news feeds, where it is almost required that you provide some organization for the articles you keep. Do this by first adding folders, and then by moving the articles to the folders.

CREATE ADDITIONAL FOLDERS

Set up the folder structure you need to organize a particular RSS feed.

1. Right-click the folder for the feed, and click **New Folder**. The Create New Folder dialog box appears.

2. Type the name of the new folder, click the parent folder that will contain the new folder (as shown in Figure 10-9), and click **OK**.

3. Repeat steps 1 and 2 as needed to create the folder structure you want.

MOVE ARTICLES TO FOLDERS

Once you have the folder structure in place, you then have to get the articles into the folders.

1. To display and identify the articles that you want to move into another folder, click the folder containing the RSS feeds. The Folder pane displays the potential articles to be moved.

2. Drag an article from the Folder pane to the desired folder in the Folder List in the Navigation pane.

3. Repeat step 2 as needed to move the articles you want segregated.

Figure 10-9: By setting up a folder structure and separating out your RSS feed articles, you'll be better able to find what you want in the future.

Transfer RSS Feeds

As you build up a collection of RSS feeds, you may want to share those feeds with others. You can do that for a single feed or for a group of feeds.

SEND AN RSS FEED

To send an RSS feed to another person:

1. Right-click an article from the RSS feed you want to send, and click **Share This Feed**. An e-mail message will open with the RSS feed attached.

   –Or–

   Double-click an article from the RSS feed you want to send to open the article in its own window. In the RSS Article tab RSS group, click **Share This Feed**.

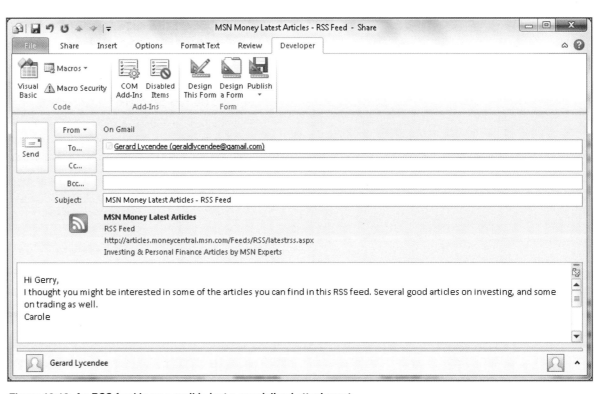

Figure 10-10: An RSS feed in an e-mail is just a specialized attachment.

2. Address the e-mail message, add any comments you want (as shown in Figure 10-10), and click **Send**.

3. Upon receiving an RSS feed in an e-mail, the recipient opens the message and clicks **Add This RSS Feed** on the left of the Share tab to have the RSS feed added to the list of feeds in Outlook.

SEND SEVERAL RSS FEEDS

If you want to send several RSS feeds in a single transaction, the best approach is to export feeds to an .opml file, e-mail that file or copy it to a shared folder or removable media (CD, DVD, or flash memory stick), and then have the recipient import the file to his or her Outlook program.

1. In Outlook, click the **File** tab, click **Open**, and click **Import**. The Import And Export Wizard starts.

NOTE

You can import and export RSS feeds as .opml files. Exporting your RSS feeds to an .opml file is an efficient way to back up your RSS feeds, should you want to save them for future reference. Refer to Chapter 8 for information on exporting and importing files.

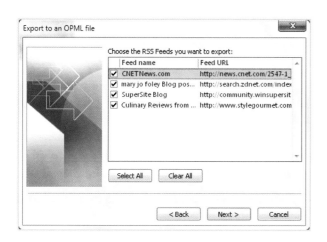

2. Click **Export RSS Feeds To An OPML File**, and click **Next**. A list of your RSS feeds appears. By default, all your RSS feeds are selected to be exported.

3. Click the feeds you do not want to export to deselect them, and click **Next**.

4. Click **Browse** and locate the folder to store the file in. Type the file name for the exported file, click **Save**, and then click **Next**.

5. To move the exported file to a shared folder or removable drive, open Windows Explorer, locate the folder where the file is stored (by default, this is the Documents or My Documents folder), and drag the file to the folder or drive.

6. To send the file as an attachment in an e-mail message, in Outlook, with Mail selected, click **New**; type an address, subject, and message; drag the file to the message; and click **Send**.

Cancel an RSS Feed

If you are not getting what you want from an RSS feed and want to discontinue receiving its articles, you can either cancel the feed and keep the articles, or cancel the feed and delete the articles.

CANCEL A FEED AND KEEP ARTICLES

1. In Outlook Mail, click the **File** tab Info view, click **Account Settings**, and click **Account Settings** again. The Account Settings dialog box appears.

2. Click the **RSS Feeds** tab.

3. Click the name of the feed you want to remove, click **Remove**, and click **Yes** when asked to confirm the removal. The folder for the feed and the articles will remain in Outlook, but no more articles will be downloaded.

4. Repeat step 2 to remove several feeds, or use **SHIFT** or **CTRL** to select several feeds, and then click **Remove**. Click **Close** to close the Account Settings dialog box.

DELETE RSS ARTICLES OR THE RSS FOLDER

You can delete just the RSS articles in the RSS Feeds folder, or you can delete the whole folder. When you delete just the articles, you can keep them up to date by downloading the current issues. When you delete both the articles and the folder, you cannot download current issues any longer.

- To delete just the RSS articles, right-click the RSS folder containing the articles you want to delete. On the context menu, click **Delete All**. When asked to confirm the action, click **Yes**. This will delete the articles but retain the folder. To bring in new articles, click **Download Content** in the Home tab RSS group.

- To delete the RSS folder and all of the articles, right-click the RSS folder, and click **Delete Folder**. When you are asked to confirm, click **Yes**. This will delete the folder and all the articles. You will have to subscribe again to this RSS feed to be able to download articles from it again.

Use Other Extensions of Outlook

Looking across the Office and Microsoft family of products, you can see that many add features to Outlook. Among those discussed here are the Office Clipboard, using Word as an e-mail editor, and using handwriting in Outlook.

Use the Office Clipboard

The Microsoft Office Clipboard connects all the programs in the Office suite, letting you copy items from various programs and paste them into others. That means you can lift a paragraph and a picture out of Word, a slide out of a PowerPoint presentation, or a graph from Excel. Then you can select from the Clipboard the items that best serve your needs and paste them into an Outlook message.

1. Start a Microsoft Office 2010 program other than Outlook, and either create or open a document with that program, such as:

   - An Excel workbook

   - A Word document

   - A PowerPoint presentation or slide

   - An Access database

   - A Publisher publication

2. In the program, select the items or text you want to copy, and in the Home tab Clipboard group, click **Copy** or press **CTRL+C**.

3. In the Home tab Clipboard group, click the **Clipboard Dialog Box Launcher**. You'll see the item you copied. An example is shown in Figure 10-11.

Empty Clipboard

Paste every item in sequence

Copied items

Choose display options for Office Clipboard

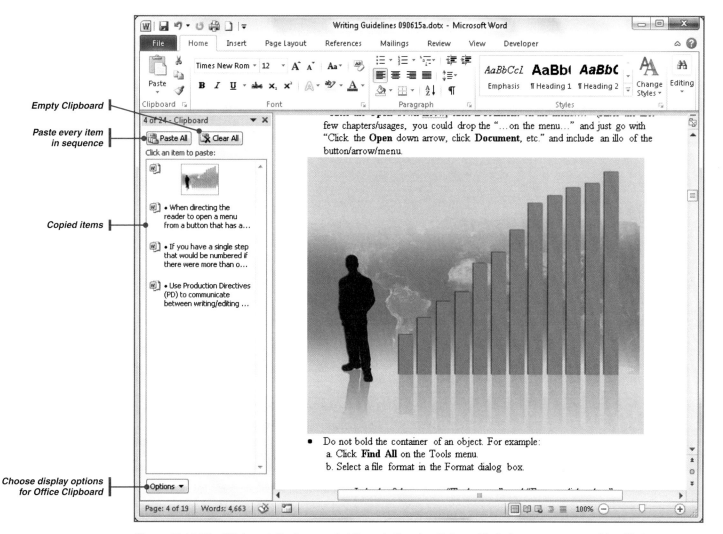

Figure 10-11: The Clipboard displays copied items in thumbnail size, with their source program identified.

4. Start or display Outlook, and in the Outlook Mail view New group, click **New E-mail** to create a new message.

5. Click in the message body, and in the Message tab Clipboard group, click the **Dialog Box Launcher**. The Clipboard task pane opens next to the message.

6. Click the desired item on the Clipboard. This "pastes" the item into the message where the cursor was located, as shown in Figure 10-12.

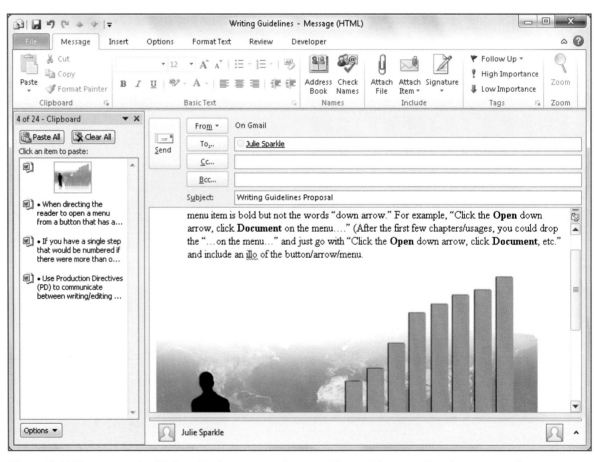

Figure 10-12: You can use the Clipboard task pane to paste several items at the same time, but you can also copy or cut and paste a single item between Office (and many other) programs by simply using CTRL+C, CTRL+X, and CTRL+V, respectively.

10

USING MICROSOFT WORD FEATURES

Outlook 2010 uses Microsoft Office Word 2010 to create and edit e-mail messages. This gives you access to many special features in Word. See Chapter 3 for information on basic e-mail editing. Several of the more useful features in Word that you can use are AutoCorrect, AutoFormat, and the Table menu.

USE AUTOCORRECT

AutoCorrect, which automatically corrects many common typing and spelling errors, is turned on from the Outlook window.

1. Click the **File** tab, click **Options**, and click **Mail.** In the Mail view in the Compose Messages section, click **Editor Options.** The Editor Options dialog box appears.

2. Click the **Proofing** tab, and then click **AutoCorrect Options.** The AutoCorrect In Email dialog box appears, as shown in Figure 10-13.

AutoCorrect Options...

3. Click **Show AutoCorrect Options Buttons**, if it isn't already selected and if you want to be able to right-click a potentially misspelled word or grammatical error, see potential corrections, and select other options.

4. Set the other options for correction conventions as you see fit.

5. If it isn't already selected and you want to use it, click **Replace Text As You Type** to use that feature.

Continued . . .

CLEAR ITEMS FROM THE CLIPBOARD

Although the Clipboard holds up to 24 items, you might want to discard some items as you go.

● Right-click an item on the Clipboard that you want to remove, and click **Delete**.

–Or–

Click the item, click the down arrow on the item, and click **Delete**.

● To remove all items from the Clipboard, click **Clear All**.

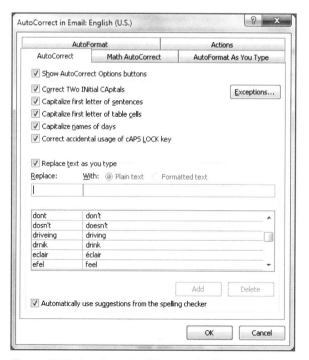

*Figure 10-13: **AutoCorrect will automatically make changes to your text as you type.***

6. Scroll through the list of common typographical errors, select any you do not want, and click **Delete**.

7. Type your common personal typos and their corrections in the Replace and With text boxes, and click **Add**.

USE AUTOFORMAT

In the AutoCorrect dialog box, click the other tabs to see additional popular options, such as:

- **AutoFormat** automatically applies formatting, such as typographical quotation marks, superscripted ordinals (1st), fraction characters (½), and em-dashes (—).

- **Math AutoCorrect** replaces written math symbols with the actual symbol. For example, it replaces "\pi" with "Π," "/int" with "∫," or "/div" with "÷."

- **AutoFormat As You Type** defines styles based on formatting you set, automatically creates bulleted and numbered lists, and turns e-mail addresses and URLs into hyperlinks when you press **SPACEBAR**.

- **Actions** tell Outlook (really Word) to flag certain data types in an e-mail so that you can do something. For example, if you type an e-mail address, you can add it to your Address Book. If you type a date, you can schedule a meeting. You determine the action, and a Smart Tag is assigned to the data type. You click the Smart Tag and choose an action from a menu.

Continued . . .

Create Electronic Business Cards

Electronic business cards encapsulate personal information in a way that can be easily transferred to others, either as an attachment to an e-mail message or as an e-mail signature. Electronic business cards look like their paper equivalent, and you can customize them with photos and logos, as well as text. When you receive someone else's electronic business card, you can save it to a Contacts folder and forward it to others. When you create a new entry in your Contacts folder, you are creating an electronic business card.

CREATE YOUR OWN ELECTRONIC BUSINESS CARD

Start the construction of an electronic business card by choosing a layout and background; follow this by adding a picture, logo, or other graphic element; and finish by adding text fields.

1. Click **Contacts** in the Outlook view bar. In Contacts, in the Home tab New group, click **New Contact**.

2. In the Contact tab Options group, click **Business Card**. The Edit Business Card dialog box will appear.

3. To change the layout, click the **Layout** down arrow, and select a different position, text only, or a background image.

4. To insert an image, click **Change**, locate the folder with the image you want to use, and double-click the image. Adjust the image area and alignment as you see fit.

5. Under Fields, select the first field you want on the card. If this is not the first field in the list, click the up arrow to move it to the top.

6. With the first field selected, type what you want in the Edit text box on the right, and apply any of the formatting attributes above the text box.

7. Repeat steps 5 and 6 for the remaining fields you want on the card. If there is a field in the list that you don't want, click it and click **Remove**. If you want to use a field that is not on the list, click **Add** and click the field name.

8. See Figure 10-14 for an example of a finished card. When you are ready, click **OK** to save the electronic business card, and click **Save & Close** to close the Contact window.

QUICKSTEPS

USING MICROSOFT WORD FEATURES *(Continued)*

Click **OK** to close the AutoCorrect In Email dialog box, and then click **OK** twice to close the Editor Options and Outlook Options dialog boxes.

MAKE A TABLE

Use Word's Table menu to organize information into a grid that will display properly, even for recipients who don't use Word.

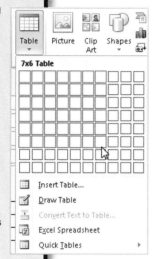

1. Create a new message by clicking **New E-Mail** in the Home tab New group. In the Outlook Message window, click in the Message pane. In the Insert tab Tables group, click **Table**, and in the menu that opens, drag the pointer across the squares to give you the table size you want, and then click.

   —Or—

   In the same Table menu, click **Insert Table**, type or use the spinner to enter the numbers of columns and rows to start with, and click **OK**.

2. Add or delete columns and rows, and format the table using the Table Tools Design and Layout tabs that appear on the ribbon, as shown in Figure 10-15.

NOTE

Placing characters in parentheses (1/4) as you type shields them from AutoFormat, so add the parentheses *after* you type the characters, and press **SPACEBAR** after the closing parentheses to indicate that you want the (1/4) changed to (¼).

Figure 10-14: Outlook provides a comprehensive tool for creating and editing electronic business cards.

SEND AN ELECTRONIC BUSINESS CARD

You can send an electronic business card with an e-mail message.

1. In Outlook Mail view, on the Home tab New group, click **New E-mail** to open a new message form. Type an address, subject, and message as normal.

2. In the Message tab Include group, click **Attach Item**, click **Business Card**, and click the name you want (the list shows the last 10 business cards you inserted). If you don't see the name you want, click **Other Business Cards**, click the name you want, and click **OK**.

3. The card will be added as a .vcf attachment to the e-mail message, as shown in Figure 10-16. When you are ready, click **Send**.

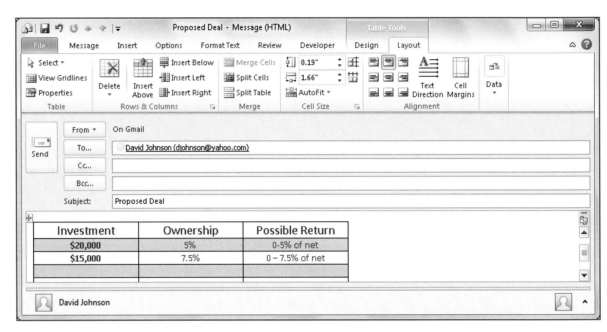

Figure 10-15: *The Outlook Message window has the full power of Microsoft Word formatting available to it.*

INCLUDE AN ELECTRONIC BUSINESS CARD IN YOUR SIGNATURE

You can also add your electronic business card to your e-mail signature and automatically include it in all the e-mail you send. An example is shown in Figure 10-16.

1. In Outlook Mail view, in the Home tab New group, click **New E-mail** to open a new message form. In the Message tab Include group, click **Signature** and then click **Signatures**.

2. In the E-mail Signature tab, click **New**. Type a name for the signature, and click **OK**.

3. Under Edit Signature, click in the text box and add the text, graphics, and possible link you may want in the signature area, and then format it as needed.

4. Position the insertion point where you want the electronic business card positioned, click **Business Card** in the toolbar, click the name of the person on the business card, and click **OK**.

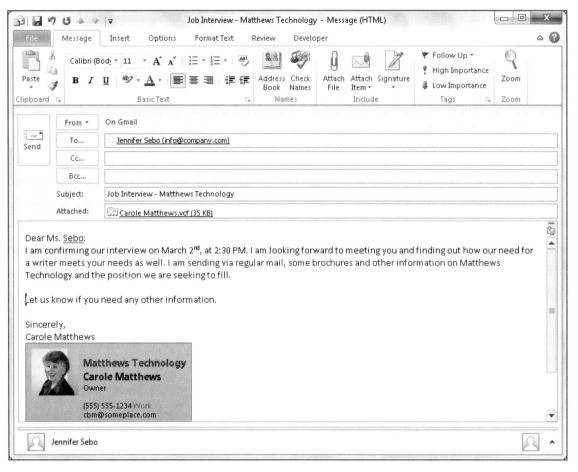

Figure 10-16: Including an electronic business card in an e-mail is a fast way to give the recipient all your contact information.

5. Click the **E-mail Account** down arrow, and select the e-mail account you want the signature to apply to and whether to apply it to either or both new and reply e-mails. Make any other adjustments to the signature, and click **OK**. Close the original message used to edit the signature.

6. In Outlook Mail view, again click **New E-mail** to open another message. If you chose to automatically add your signature to all new messages, you'll see your signature with the business card. Also, your business card .vcf file will be attached.

7. If you chose to not have your signature automatically added to your messages, you can add a signature. In the Message tab Include group, click **Signature** and click the name of your signature. Again, your signature with the business card and the attached .vcf file appears in the message.

RECEIVE AND STORE AN ELECTRONIC BUSINESS CARD

When an e-mail message is received with an electronic business card attached, the recipient will see an image of the card, provided he or she is using Outlook 2010 or is using HTML to view the message in older versions of Outlook. The recipient will also receive an attachment with the card. To store the electronic business card in Contacts:

1. In Outlook Mail view, double-click the message in the Inbox to open the message window.

2. Double-click the attached .vcf file. A new Contact window will open with all the information on the electronic business card placed in the proper fields.

3. Make any needed changes or additions to the Contact form, and click **Save & Close**. Close the message that contained the electronic business card.

deleting
    categories, 44
    color categories, 87
    contacts, 99
    files, 176
    folders, 174
    Journal entries, 158
    lines from messages, 56
    messages, 47
    notes, 165
    paragraphs from messages, 56
    recurring activities, 126
    RSS articles, 222, 225–226
    RSS folder, 225–226
    tasks, 148
    words from messages, 56
Design mode, opening forms in, 189
Design tabs, using with forms, 194
Developer tab
    Arrange group, 192–193
    Design group, 192
    displaying for forms, 188
    Form group, 191
    Tools group, 192
    using with forms, 191–193
Dialog Box Launcher
    described, 7
    location of, 8
dictionary
    adding words to, 67
    editing, 68
digital certificate, acquiring, 66
digital ID, importing and exporting, 66
digital signatures
    adding to e-mail, 182–183
    adding to messages, 66
    getting, 182
domain, defined, 39
driving directions, getting for contacts, 98–99

E

electronic business cards
    creating, 230–231
    creating contacts from, 81
    including contacts as, 85
    including in signature, 232–234
    receiving, 234
    sending, 231
    storing, 234
e-mail. *See also* IM (instant messaging); junk mail; messages
    accessing, 33
    adding contacts to, 84–85
    adding digital signatures to, 182–183
    assigning categories to, 44
    checking for, 34–35
    copying contacts from, 81
    encrypting, 181–182
    including hyperlinks in, 61
    mail merging, 99–102
    message window, 37
    reading, 36
    receiving automatically, 36
    receiving headers manually, 37
    sending to contact groups, 83
    sorting, 45–46
    using RSS links in, 219–220
e-mail accounts
    adding, 28–29
    removing, 34
e-mail attachments. *See also* files
    adding notes as, 169
    including contacts as, 84–85
    opening, 48
    previewing, 49
    saving, 48
    selecting, 49
e-mail data files, locating, 34

e-mail files, importing into Outlook, 4–5
e-mail messages. *See also* messages in folders
    adding Bccs to, 55–56
    adding Ccs to, 55–56
    adding digital signatures to, 66, 183
    adding tasks from, 143
    archiving, 48
    changing search options for, 24–25
    changing time for being read, 41–42
    checking spelling in, 67–68
    completing addresses automatically, 54
    creating, 52
    creating from Contacts window, 79
    delaying delivery of, 72–73
    deleting, 47
    dragging files to, 61
    editing, 56–58
    embedding pictures into, 63–64
    encrypting, 183
    forwarding, 70
    inserting files in, 62
    inserting signatures in, 65–66
    marking as read or unread, 41
    obtaining receipts for, 71–72
    performing instant searches, 22–23
    personalizing for contacts, 99–102
    printing, 48–49
    refining searches of, 23–24
    replying to, 68–69
    scrolling through, 42
    selecting from Address Book, 54
    sending, 72
    timing sending of, 72–73
    turning off Auto-Send, 72
    typing addresses for, 53
    unblocking, 39
    using Flag options with, 42–43
    using Today red flag with, 42
    window for, 53

HTTP (HyperText Transfer Protocol), 33
hyperlinks, including in e-mail, 61

I

IM (instant messaging). *See also* e-mail; messages;
   Windows Live Messenger
      activating in Outlook, 213–214
      changing appearance of name in, 216
      chatting, 215–216
      creating contacts for, 214–215
      explained, 212
      finding Windows Live Messenger, 212–213
      initiating real-time conversations, 215
      responding to, 215–216
      responding to Outlook invitations, 214–215
      seeing who is online, 214–215
      stating availability, 216
Import Summary report, saving, 4
imported messages, locating, 5
Inbox, opening, 35
Inbox arrangements, availability of, 43
Indexing Status, using in searches, 23
Insert File dialog box, displaying, 62
Instant Search feature, using, 22–23
Internet calendars, types of, 121. *See also* calendars
Internet e-mail. *See* e-mail
Internet Explorer, viewing RSS feeds in, 218
invitations
      receiving via e-mail, 214–215
      responding to, 131
ISP (Internet service provider), finding, 34

J

Journal
      features of, 155–156
      setting up, 156
      using Timer feature with, 157

journal entries
      adding, 156–157
      assigning categories to, 159–160
      attaching contacts to, 158–159
      changing, 157
      deleting, 158
      moving in timeline, 158
      printing, 160–162
      viewing, 159
Journal icon, locating, 154
junk mail. *See also* e-mail
      adding addresses to filter lists, 39–40
      choosing protection level for, 39–40
      filtering, 39
      unblocking picture downloads, 41
      updating lists quickly, 40

K

keyboard shortcuts
      assigning to categories, 45
      Calendar, 105
      contact groups, 83
      contacts, 79, 99
      copying and pasting files, 177
      copying to Clipboard, 228
      cutting operations for Clipboard, 228
      deleting files, 176
      exiting Outlook, 5
      Help window, 21
      Journal, 154
      minimizing ribbon, 10
      pasting operations for Clipboard, 228
      resizing ribbon, 52
      scheduling meetings, 129
      selecting all items in folders, 47
      sending and receiving e-mail, 34
      tasks, 140
      Tasks window, 134

L

labels
      adding to forms, 195
      printing, 206–208
letters, printing, 102
lines
      deleting from messages, 56
      inserting in messages, 59
      moving in messages, 56
      replacing in messages, 56
lists, using in messages, 59

M

Macro Security option, setting, 181
mail. *See* e-mail
Mail Merge feature
      creating folder for, 201
      preparing contacts for, 201
      preparing documents in Word, 202–204
      using filtering capability with, 202
mail merge folder, adding contacts to,
      200–201
mail merge, performing, 204–205
Mail view, operations in, 34–35
mail-merged e-mail, creating, 99–102
MAP (Messaging Application Programming
      Interface), 33
Map It utility, using with contacts, 97–99
Maximize button
      described, 7
      location of, 8
meetings
      defined, 105, 121
      scheduling, 129–131
menus, using, 10
merging form letters. *See* mail merge
message format, selecting, 57–58

message formatting
    aligning paragraphs, 59
    Bold effect, 58
    borders, 59
    bulleted lists, 59
    coloring fonts, 59
    fonts, 58
    Italic effect, 58
    lines, 59
    multilevel lists, 59
    numbered lists, 59
    shifting paragraphs, 59
    sizes, 58
    Strikethrough effect, 58
    Underline effect, 58
message priority, setting, 71
message request, receiving, 131
Message window, maximizing, 60
messages. *See also* e-mail; IM
    (instant messaging)
    adding Bccs to, 55–56
    adding Ccs to, 55–56
    adding digital signatures to, 66, 183
    adding tasks from, 143
    archiving, 48
    changing search options for, 24–25
    changing time for being read, 41–42
    checking spelling in, 67–68
    completing addresses automatically, 54
    creating, 52
    creating from Contacts window, 79
    delaying delivery of, 72–73
    deleting, 47
    dragging files to, 61
    editing, 56–58
    embedding pictures into, 63–64
    encrypting, 183
    forwarding, 70

inserting files in, 62
inserting signatures in, 65–66
marking as read or unread, 41
obtaining receipts for, 71–72
performing instant searches, 22–23
personalizing for contacts, 99–102
printing, 48–49
refining searches of, 23–24
replying to, 68–69
scrolling through, 42
selecting from Address Book, 54
sending, 72
timing sending of, 72–73
turning off Auto-Send, 72
typing addresses for, 53
unblocking, 39
using Flag options with, 42–43
using Today red flag with, 42
window for, 53
messages in folders
    adding colored categories to, 44
    arranging, 43
    contract symbols for, 44
    editing categories, 44–45
    expand symbols for, 44
Minimize button
    described, 7
    location of, 8
Minimize Navigation pane
    described, 7
    location of, 8
Minimize ribbon
    described, 7
    location of, 8
Minimize To-Do bar
    described, 7
    location of, 8
Mobile version, accessing, 6

N

Navigation pane
    Button bar in, 11
    described, 7
    Folder list in, 11
    location of, 8
    minimizing, 12
    Outlook views in, 11
    reordering buttons in, 12
Next Week flag, using, 150
No Date flag, using, 150
Note icon, resizing, 164
notes
    adding as e-mail attachments, 169
    adding in Notes view, 163–164
    categorizing, 165–167
    color-coding, 167–168
    composing, 165
    creating in views, 163
    customizing current view, 168–169
    deleting, 165
    dragging in Outlook, 166–167
    forwarding, 167–168
    organizing, 167
    printing, 170
    selecting fonts for, 165
    setting up, 165
    using Reading pane with, 169–170
    viewing, 168–170
    viewing by category, 167
    viewing by color, 167
Notes folder, finding, 162–163
numbered lists, using in messages, 59

O

Office 2010, versions of, 6–7
Office Clipboard
    clearing items from, 229
    using, 226–228

.opml files, sending RSS feeds as, 224
Outlook
    academic edition, 7
    enterprise editions, 7
    exiting, 5
    getting summary of info in, 13–14
    pinning to taskbar, 4
    starting, 2–4
    updating, 30
    upgrading to, 4–5
    window features, 6–8
Outlook Today
    changing, 14
    making default page, 14
    opening, 13
Outlook views
    changing, 10, 137
    changing display of, 12
    creating notes in, 163
    displaying, 11
    selecting, 11

P

paragraphs
    aligning in messages, 59
    deleting from messages, 56
    moving in messages, 56
    replacing in messages, 56
    shifting in messages, 59
parentheses (), using to prevent
    AutoFormat, 231
People pane
    described, 7
    location of, 8
Phone List view, displaying contacts in, 87
pictures
    adding to contacts, 81
    embedding into messages, 63–64

plain text format
    using in messages, 56
    using with contacts, 84
podcast, defined, 217
POP3 (Post Office Protocol 3), 33
preferences
    adding e-mail accounts, 28–29
    setting advanced options, 26–28
    setting General options, 25–26
Print Setup dialog box, options in, 129
printing
    calendars, 127–129
    contact information, 93–96
    envelopes, 208–209
    labels, 206–208
    letters, 102
    messages, 48–49
    notes, 170
privacy options, setting, 180–181
Professional version, availability of, 7

Q

Quick Access toolbar
    adding commands to, 19
    customizing, 19
    described, 6
    features of, 10
    location of, 8
    moving, 20
    rearranging tools on, 20
Quick Click flag, setting, 151
Quick Launch toolbar, starting Outlook from, 3

R

read layout, using with forms, 196–197
Reading pane
    described, 6
    location of, 8

opening, 27
    placing beneath Folder pane, 34
    using with notes, 169–170
Really Simple Syndication (RSS), overview of,
    216–217
receipts, obtaining for messages, 71–72
recipients, replying to, 69
red X, appearance of, 64
reference tools, availability of, 24
reminders, using, 127
reply layout, changing, 69
Reply options using with messages, 68–69
Research Options button, explained, 181
ribbon
    adding commands and tools to, 18
    automatic adjustment of, 9
    in Contacts window, 77–78
    creating tabs and groups on, 17
    creating tasks from, 139–140
    customizing, 16, 18
    described, 6
    features of, 9–10
    location of, 8
    minimizing, 10, 52
    rearranging tabs and groups on, 16–17
    removing commands and tools from, 18
    resetting, 17
    ribbon, 8
    tabs in, 15–16
    tabs on, 6
ribbon groups
    described, 6
    location of, 8
Rich Text Format (RTF), using in messages, 56
RSS (Really Simple Syndication), overview of,
    216–217
RSS articles
    creating folders for, 223
    deleting, 225–226

marking as complete, 146–147
recurring, 141
removing color categories of, 142
renaming, 148–149
showing in To-Do bar, 152
skipping recurring, 141
tracking, 145
viewing, 134, 136–137, 145
viewing in to-do list format, 136
Tasks window
accessing, 134
components of, 135
opening, 143
templates
creating, 198
using, 199
themes
searching online, 61
using, 60
This Week flag, using, 150
Timeline view, using, 137
Timer feature, using with Journal, 157
times, entering in Calendar, 122
Title bar
described, 6
location of, 8
To button, using, 55
Today flag, using, 150

Today red flag, inserting beside messages, 42
To-Do bar
creating tasks in, 142
customizing, 12
described, 7
location of, 8
minimizing, 13
resizing, 152
setting to show tasks, 152
showing completed tasks in, 148
toggling display of, 152
Tomorrow flag, using, 150
Trust Center, opening, 180–181. *See also* security

U

updates, checking for, 30

V

View buttons
described, 7
location of, 8, 11
views
changing, 10, 137
changing display of, 12
creating notes in, 163
displaying, 11
selecting, 11

viruses, protecting against, 184. *See also* antivirus
software
voting options, inserting, 64

W

Web Apps version, accessing, 6
Windows Live Messenger. *See also* IM (instant
messaging)
changing ID in, 213
displaying menus in, 216
finding for IM, 212–213
Word
AutoCorrect feature, 229–230
AutoFormat feature, 230–231
Mail Merge pages in, 207
making tables in, 231
preparing mail merge documents in, 202–204
words
adding to dictionary, 67
deleting from messages, 56
moving in messages, 56
replacing in messages, 56
work week, defining in Calendar, 114–116

Z

Zoom buttons
described, 7
location of, 8